LIFE AMONG
THE INDIANS

Frontispiece.

A Sioux Village on the Upper Missouri. — p. 57.

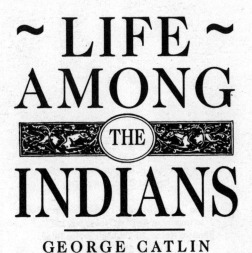

~ LIFE ~
AMONG
THE
INDIANS

GEORGE CATLIN

Life Among the Indians

First published in 1875 by Gall & Inglis,
London & Edinburgh

This edition first published in 1996 by Bracken Books,
an imprint of Random House UK Ltd,
Random House, 20 Vauxhall Bridge Road,
London SW1V 2SA

Reissued by Senate in 1997

ISBN 1 85170 535 X

Printed and bound in Guernsey by
The Guernsey Press Co Ltd

PREFACE.

———◆◇◆———

ON my recent return from a long and toilsome campaign amongst the Indian tribes of South and Central America, as well as those on the Pacific side of the Rocky Mountains in North America, I was requested to prepare a book of facts for youthful readers on the character and condition of the American Indians. I at once embraced the suggestion made to me, and am here entering upon the plan, the results of which will be met and judged of in the following pages.

As the youthful readers of this volume will scarcely have read my work on the North American Indians published some years since, they may reasonably expect me to give some introduction of myself before we start together, which I will here do in a few words, and leave them to learn more of me when I may incidentally appear in scenes and scenery to be described.

The place of my nativity was Wilkesbarre, in the Valley of Wyoming, rendered historically famous by its early and disastrous warfare with the Indians whom the civilized races had driven out of it, and celebrated in lore by the popular poem by Campbell, the " Gertrude of Wyoming."

In my early youth I was influenced by two predominant and inveterate propensities, those for hunting and fishing. My father and mother had great difficulty in turning my attention from these to books. But when at the proper age, I commenced reading the law for a profession, I attended the law school of the celebrated Judges Reeve and Gould, in Connecticut, for two years, and after reading for a couple of years longer, passed my examination, was admitted to the bar, and commenced the practice of the law, which I followed for several years.

During this time, fortunately or unfortunately, another and a stronger passion was getting the advantage of me, that for painting, to which all my love of pleading soon gave way; and after having covered nearly every inch of the lawyers' table (and even encroached upon the judge's bench) with penknife, pen and ink, and pencil sketches of judges, juries, and culprits, I very deliberately resolved to convert my law library into paint-pots and brushes, and to pursue painting as my future, and apparently more agreeable, profession.

I thus took leave of professional friends and my profession, and immediately commenced portrait-painting in the city of Philadelphia; and after a few years, in the midst of success, I again resolved to use my art, and so much of the labours of my future life as might be required, in rescuing the looks and customs of the vanishing races of native man in America from that oblivion to which I plainly saw they were hastening before the approach and certain progress of civilization.

To do this I was obliged to break, with apparent great cruelty, from friends the most dear to me, who could not appreciate the importance of my views, and who all magnified the apprehended dangers before me. With these, and many other obstacles to encounter, I started in 1832 with canvas and colours, and penetrated the vast solitudes from whence I have brought the information to be given in the following pages.

I devoted eight years of my life in visiting about fifty tribes in North America, and brought home a collection of more than six hundred oil paintings (in all cases made from nature) of portraits, landscapes, and Indian customs, and every article of their manufacture, of weapons, costumes, wigwams, etc., altogether forming an extensive museum, which was exh.bited for several years in the Egyptian Hall, in London, and afterwards in the *Salle du Séance*, in the Louvre, in Paris, at the invitation of His Majesty, Louis Philippe, who paid it many visits, with the Queen and the rest of the Royal Family.

Not content with the collection I had thus made and shown to the world, I started again in 1853 for Venezuela, in South America, and subsequently traversed British and Dutch Guiana, the Valley of the Amazon, and other parts of Brazil, the Andes, Peru, Equador, Bolivia, California, to Kamtschatka, the Aleutian Islands, the Pacific Coast to the mouth of the Columbia, across the Rocky Mountains to Santa Fé, by the Rio de Norte to Matamoros in Mexico, to Guatemala, to Yucatan, to Cuba, and back to the starting point.

These last roamings, which have been performed in three successive campaigns, have been in some parts extremely difficult and hazardous, but full of interest, which was sufficient to enable me to overcome all obstacles; and from incidents, and people, and customs, and countries, that I have met with in these and my former campaigns, I shall endeavour, in this little work, to select and describe for the instruction and amusement of the youthful readers, such as will the most forcibly and correctly illustrate native man and his modes on the American continent.

The Author.

CONTENTS.

ILLUSTRATIONS.

LIFE AND ADVENTURES

AMONG THE

AMERICAN INDIANS.

CHAPTER I.

The Name "Indian"—General Character—Indian Civilisation —National Character.

THE native races of man, occupying every part of North and South America at the time of the first discovery of the American continent by Columbus, and still existing over great portions of those regions, have generally been denominated "*Indians*," from that day to the present, from the somewhat curious fact that the American continent, when first discovered, was supposed to be a part of the coast of India, which the Spanish and Portuguese navigators were expecting to find, in steering their vessels to the west, across the Atlantic.

To an appellation so long, though erroneously applied, no exception will be taken in this work, in which these races will be spoken of as *Indians*, or

17

savages, neither of which terms will be intended necessarily to imply the character generally conveyed by the term "*savage*," but literally what the word signifies, *wild* (or wild man), and no more.

These numerous races (at that time consisting of many millions of human beings, divided into some hundreds of tribes, and speaking mostly different languages; whose past history is sunk in oblivion from want of books and records; three-fourths of whmo, at least, have already perished by fire-arms, by dissipation, and pestilences introduced amongst them by civilized people; and the remainder of them from similar causes, with no better prospect than certain extinction in a short time) present to the scientific and the sympathising world, one of the most deeply interesting subjects for contemplation that can possibly come under their consideration; and I feel assured that parents will justify the inculcation of just notions of these simple and abused people, into the minds of their children, as forming a legitimate part of the foundation of their education.

Confident in this belief, my young readers, for whom I have said this book is intended, we will now start together—myself upon my task, and you for your own instruction and amusement; halting but for one impression more, which I deem it important you should start with, and never lose sight of for a moment when you are estimating the character, the thoughts, the actions, the condition, and the wrongs of these poor people to be set forth in this little book,—that they are *children*—like yourselves, in many senses of the word. They are without the knowledge and arts of civilized man ; they are feeble ; they are in the ignorance of nature, but they all acknowledge the Great Spirit. In their relationship with civilized people they are like orphans. Governments who deal with them assume a guardianship over them, always calling them their "red children ;" and they, from their child-like nature, call all government officials in their country, "Fathers ;" and the President of the United States, their "Great Father ;" and whenever they can have the pleasure of shaking the hand of a little white boy, or a little girl (as would be the case if they could take you by the hand), the relationship is always that of "brother and sister."

The civilized races in the present enlightened age are too much in the habit of regarding all people more ignorant than themselves as anomalies (or "oddities," as they have been called), because they do not live, and act, and look like themselves. They are therefore mostly in the habit of treating the character of the American Indians—which, from the distance they are from them, is more or less wrapped in obscurity—as a profound *mystery;* but there, owing to their ignorance of them, they judge decidedly wrong : for, like everything else nearest to nature, they are the most simple and easy of all the human family to be appreciated and dealt with, if the right mode be adopted.

I have said that these people are like children ;

and from what I have seen, I am quite sure that if
you were amongst them you would learn their true
character and their feelings much sooner than your
parents would; for with children they would throw
off the mask and the reserve which their justly-
founded suspicions of white men induce them to
wear in their presence. I believe, therefore, that
instead of the frightful impressions too often made
upon the youthful mind, your early days is the time
when the foundation of a lasting knowledge and just
appreciation of the true character of these simple
people should be formed; and with that view, from
what I have learned in fourteen years of my life
spent in familiarity with them, I will try in this
little work to bring the condition and customs of
these *children* of the forest in a true light before
you.

Distributed over every part, and in every nook
and corner of North, and South, and Central America,
we find these people living in their rude huts, or
"wigwams," at present numbering something like
four millions, though, in all probability, their numbers were nearer twelve or fourteen millions at the
time of the discovery of America by Columbus; and
yet the world is left (and probably will remain) in
profound ignorance of their origin, for want of his-
torical proof to show from whence they came.

It seems to be the popular belief that the two
Americas have been peopled from the Eastern continent by the way of Behring's Strait—of this there
is a *possibility*, but no proof; and I think there is

much and very strong presumptive proof against its probability. The subject has been one of great interest to me for many years past, and of so exciting a nature, that I have recently made a tedious and expensive tour to Eastern Siberia, to the Koriaks and the Kamtschatkas, the Aleutians—equi-distant between the two continents—and the natives on the American coast opposite to them, and from all that I could learn, there has been a mutual intercourse across the strait, sufficiently proved by the resemblances in language and in physiological traits ; but no proof of the *peopling of a continent* either way.

In the progressive character with which the Creator has endowed mankind, as distinguished above the brute creations, the American savages have, in several instances, made the intended uses of their reason, in advancing by themselves to a high state of civilization, but from this they have been thrown back by more than savage invaders—as seen in the histories of Mexico and Peru—and by the hand of Providence, in some way not yet explained, in the more ancient destruction of the ruined cities of Palenque and Uxmal, in Central America.

All history on the subject goes to prove (and without an exception to the contrary) that, when first visited by civilized people, the American Indians have been found friendly and hospitable ; and my own testimony, when I have visited nearly two millions of them, and most of the time unprotected, without having received any personal injury or insult, or loss of my property by theft, should go a great way to corroborate the fact, that, if properly treated, the American Indians are amongst the most honest, and honourable, and hospitable people in the world.

In their primitive and natural state they have always been found living quite independently and happily, though poor ; with an abundance of animals and fish in their country for food, which seems to bound nearly all their earthly wishes. As they know nothing of commerce, and are totally ignorant of the meaning and value of money, they live and act without those dangerous inducements to crime; and stimulated to honesty by rules of honour belonging to their society, they practise honesty without any " dread of the law ;" for there is no punishment amongst them for theft or fraud, except the disgrace that attaches to their character in case they are convicted of such crimes.

If these people, under such circumstances, would guard my life and my property, as they have done, and help me in safety through their country, of which I shall give you many proofs in this little book, you, my young readers, will at once decide with me, that their hearts are good—are like your own ; and that their true character and modes are worth your understanding.

The contemptuous epithets of " the poor, naked, and drunken Indians," are often habitually applied to these people by those who know but little or nothing about them. And these epithets are sometimes correctly applied ; but only so to those classes of Indian society who, to the shame and disgrace of civilized people, have been reduced to these conditions by the iniquitous teachings of white men, who, with the aid of rum and whisky, have introduced dissipation and vices amongst them, which lead directly to poverty, and nakedness, and diseases which end in their destruction.

In their primitive state, these people are all temperate—all "*teetotallers;*" and sufficiently clad for the latitudes they live in; and their poverty, properly speaking, with their other misfortunes, only begins when the treacherous hand of white man's commerce and the jug are extended to them.

To estimate the Indian character properly, it should be constantly borne in mind that these people invariably have, as their first civilized neighbours, the most wicked and unprincipled part of civilized society to deal with; and these white people, using rum, and whisky, and fire-arms, in a country where they are amenable to no law; and amongst a people who have no newspapers to explain their wrongs to the world.

It should also be known that there are two classes of Indian society; the one nearest to civilization, where they have become degraded and impoverished, and their character changed by civilized teaching, and their worst passions inflamed, and jealousies excited by the abuses practised amongst them. This district being the first and most easily reached by the tourist, who fears to go farther, he too often contents himself by what he can there see, the semi-civilized and degraded condition of the savage; and

too often endorses what he sees, as the true definition of the appearance and modes of the American
Indians; thus doing injustice to the character of
the people, and less than justice to those who read
for information.

My labours have generally commenced where that
state of civilization leaves off; and, as I have always
believed, I have been in the greatest safety when in
the primitive state of Indian society. It has been
there, and there chiefly, where my ambition has led
me, and there where I have laboured, as the only
legitimate place to portray the true character of
Indian life.

The American Indians, as a race, a great and
national family, have a national character and appear·
ance very different from the other native races of the
earth. They differ in language, in expression, and
in colour; and in their native simplicity they have
many high, and honourable, and humane traits of
character, which will be illustrated in the following
pages.

There are no people on earth more loving and
kind to their friends and the poor; and yet, like all
savage races, they are correctly denominated cruel:
and what people are not so? There is an excuse for
the cruelty of savages. Cruelty is a necessity in
savage life: and who else has so good an excuse
for it?

Indian society has to be maintained, and personal
rights to be protected, without the aid of laws; and
for those ends each individual is looked upon as the

avenger of his own wrongs; and if he does not punish with cruelty and with certainty there is no security to person or property. In the exercise of this right, he not only uses a privilege, but does what the tribe compel him to do, or be subjected to a disgrace which he cannot outlive; so that cruelty is at the same time a right and a duty—the law of their land.

The Indian's "cruelty and treachery in warfare," we hear much of, but cruelty and treachery in Indian and civilized warfare are much alike.

The Creator has also endowed the North American Indians, everywhere, with a high moral and religious principle, with reason, with humanity, with courage, with ingenuity, and the other intellectual qualities bestowed on the rest of mankind.

They all worship the Great Spirit, and have a belief in a spiritual existence after death. Idolatry is nowhere practised by them, nor cannibalism, though you may read of many instances of both to the contrary.

After these brief suggestions on their general character and condition, which it has taken you but a few minutes to read, you are now prepared to follow me through scenes and events in which I shall endeavour to show you how these interesting people live, how they look, and how they act. I have told you that they are children, that they call themselves such, and that if you were amongst them they would take you by the hand as brothers and sisters; and I believe, therefore, you are now fully prepared in

estimating their character and actions, which I am
to explain to you, to make those allowances which
Nature prompts all kind hearts to extend to the
actions of all those who are oppressed, and are
ignorant and feeble, but who are doing the best they
can under their peculiar circumstances.

CHAPTER II.

Wyoming Massacre — Valley of the Oc-qua-go — The Old
Saw-mill Lick — A Chill, a Shiver, and False Alarm—
John Darrow—Story of the Panther—Deer in the Lick—
A Huge Indian—Red Indian at the Lick—A Run from
the Lick — Johnny O'Neil's "Gipsies"—George's Indians
— The Saddle of Venison — On-o-gong-way's Story—The
Kettle of Gold—My Tomahawk.

THE first Indian I ever saw was in this wise.
I have before told you that I was born in
the beautiful and famed Valley of Wyoming, which is on the Susquehanna River, in the State
of Pennsylvania. Not a long time after the close of
the Revolutionary War in that country, a settlement
was formed in that fertile valley by white people,
while the Indian tribes, who were pushed out, were
contesting the right of the white people to settle
in it. After having practised great cruelty on the
Indian tribes, and been warned from year to year by
the Indians to leave it, it was ascertained one day
that large parties of Indians were gathered on
the mountains, armed and prepared to attack the
white inhabitants.

27

The white men in the valley immediately armed, to the number of five or six hundred, and leaving their wives and children and old men in a rude fort on the bank of the river, advanced towards the head of the valley in search of their enemies.

The Indians, watching the movements of the white men from the mountain tops, descended into the valley, and at a favourable spot, where the soldiers were to pass, lay secreted in ambush on both sides of the road, and in an instant rush, at the sound of the war-whoop, sprang upon the whites with tomahawks and scalping-knives in hand, and destroyed them all, with the exception of a very few, who saved their lives by swimming the river.

Amongst the latter was my grandfather on my mother's side, from whom I have often had the most thrilling descriptions. This onslaught is called in history, the "*Wyoming Massacre.*" Some have called it "*treachery.*" It was *strategy*, not treachery; and strategy is a *merit* in the science of all warfare.

After this victory, the Indians marched down the valley and took possession of the fort containing the women and children, to whom not one of the husbands returned at that time. Amongst the prisoners thus taken in the fort was my grandmother, and also my mother, who was then a child only seven years old.

These several hundreds of prisoners, though in the hands of more than a thousand fierce and savage warriors, were not put to death, but kept as prisoners for several weeks, when a reinforcement of troops arriving over the Pokona mountains for their relief, the Indian warriors left the fort, with the women and children in it, having hunted for them and supplied them with food, and painted their faces red, calling them "sisters and children," and to the honour of the Indian's character, be it for ever known (as attested by every prisoner both men and women), treating them in every sense, with the greatest propriety and kindness.

These brief facts, which happened many years before I was born, with a thousand others which could be narrated, having become startling legends of that region, will account for the marvellous and frightful impressions I had received in my childhood, of Indian massacres and Indian murders, and also for the indelible impression made on my mind and my nerves by the thrilling incident I am about to describe.

Whilst my infant mind was filled with these impressions, my father, for the relief of his health, impaired by the practice of the law, removed some forty miles from the Valley of Wyoming to a romantic valley on the banks of the Susquehanna River, in the State of New York, where he had purchased a beautiful plantation, resolving to turn his attention during the remainder of his life to agricultural pursuits.

This lovely and picturesque little valley, called by its Indian name "*Oc-qua-go*," surrounded by high and precipitous mountains and deep ravines, being nearer to the straggling remnants of the defeated Mohawk and Oneida Indians, who had retreated before the deadly rifles of the avengers of Wyoming's misfortunes, I was in a position to increase rather than to diminish the excitements already raised in my mind relative to the Indians who had barricaded and bravely defended in their retreat, one by one, every defile and mountain pass, and whose paths and other markings were still recent.

The ploughs in my father's fields were at this time daily turning up Indian skulls or Indian beads, and Indian flint arrow-heads, which the labouring men of his farm, as well as those of the neighbourhood, were bringing to me, and with which I was enthusiastically forming a little cabinet or museum; and one day, as the most valued of its acquisitions, one of my father's ploughmen brought from his furrow the head of an Indian pipe-tomahawk, which was covered with rust, the handle of which had rotted away.

At this early age, when probably only nine or ten years old, I had become a pretty successful shot, with a light single-barrelled fowling-piece which my father had designated as especially my own, and with which my slaughter of ducks, quails, pheasants, and squirrels was considered by the neighbouring hunters to be very creditable to me.

But I began now to feel a higher ambition—that of *killing a deer*—for which the rifles of my two elder brothers were the weapons requisite, and which (they being absent, and pursuing their

academical studies in a distant town) I began now
to lay temporary claim to.

In my then recent visits to the "*Old Saw-mill,*"
on the "*Big Creek*"—a famous place, to which my
co-propensity, that of trout-fishing, often called me
—I had observed that the saw-mill lick was
much frequented by deer, and that I soon fixed as the
scene of my future and more exciting operations.

The "old saw-mill" was the shattered remains
of a saw-mill which had been abandoned for many
years, and consisting only of masses of thrown-down
timbers and planks, converted into piles by the force
of the water, under and around which I always had
my greatest success in trout-fishing.

This solitary ruin, about one mile from my father's
back fields, was enveloped in a dark and lonely
wilderness, with an old and deserted road leading to
it, following mostly along the winding banks of the
creek. Near by it, in a deep and dark gorge in the
mountain's side, overshadowed by dark and tall
hemlocks and fir-trees, was the "*lick,*" to which
my aspiring ideas were now leaning. The paths
leading to it down the mountain sides were freshly
trodden, and the mud and water in the lick, still
riley with their recent steps, showed me the frequency with which the deer were paying their visits
to it.

A "lick" (a "deer lick"), in the phrase of the
country, is a salt-spring which the deer visit in warm
weather, to allay their thirst, and to obtain the salt,
which seems necessary for digestion. Most of the

herbivorous animals seem to visit these places as if from necessity, and appear oftentimes under a sort of infatuation in their eagerness for them, in consequence of which they fall an easy prey to wild beasts, as well as to hunters, which lie in wait for them.

Stimulated by the proofs aboved named, and by my recollections, yet fresh, of the recitals of several of the neighbouring hunters of their great success in the old saw-mill lick, I resolved to try my first luck there.

A rifle for this enterprise was absolutely necessary—a weapon which I never had fired, and as yet was not strong enough to raise, unless it was rested upon something for its support.

For this I foresaw a remedy, and I had every confidence in my accuracy of aim. But the greater difficulty of my problem was the positive order of my father that I was not to meddle with the arms of my elder brothers, which were in covers and hanging against the wall. This I solved, however, by a manœuvre, at a late hour of the night, by extracting one of them from the cover, and putting my little fowling-piece in its place, and taking the rifle into the fields, where I concealed it for my next afternoon's contemplated enterprise.

The hour approaching, and finding the rifle loaded, I proceeded, with a light and palpitating heart, through the winding and lonely road, to the old saw-mill lick; creeping along through narrow defiles, between logs and rocks, until, by a fair glance, at the lick, I found there was no game in it at the moment. I then took to a precipitous ledge of rocks in the side of the hill partly enclosing the dark and lonely place where the salt-spring issued, and where the deer were in the habit of coming to lick.

The nook into which I clambered and seated myself was elevated some twenty or thirty feet above the level of the lick, and at the proper distance for a dead shot. I here found myself in a snug and sly little box, which had evidently been constructed and used for a similar purpose on former occasions by the old hunters.

Having taken this position about the middle of the afternoon, with the muzzle of my rifle resting on a little breastwork of rock before me, I remained until near nightfall without other excitement than an occasional tremor from the noise of a bird or a squirrel in the leaves, which I mistook for the footsteps of an approaching deer! The falling of a dry branch, however, which came tumbling down upon the hill side above and behind me, in the midst of this silent and listless anxiety, gave me one or two tremendous shivers, which it took me some time to get over, even after I had discovered what it was; for it brought instantly into my mind the story which I had often heard Darrow relate, of "killing the panther," which, it had not occurred to me until that moment, took place, not long before, at the old saw-mill lick!

John Darrow, a poor man living in the neighbourhood of my father, often worked for him in his fields, but was more fond of hunting, for which his success had gained him a great reputation in that vicinity. He often supplied my father with venison, and as he took a peculiar fancy to me for my hunting propensities, one can easily see how I became attached to this wonderful man, and how I came to take my first lessons in deer-stalking and bear-hunting with him.

Well, Darrow had been in the habit of "watching" a great deal in the old saw-mill lick, and of placing beyond the lick, at the height of the middle of a deer's body a small bit of phosphorescent wood (a rotten wood which often occurs in those wildernesses, and called by the inhabitants "fox-fire," probably from phosphor) and which is always visible in the darkest night, looking like a small ball of fire. Then secreting himself before dark on the ground, on a level with his target, his rifle resting in a couple of crotches and aiming directly at his phosphor light, at any time of the night when he heard the stepping of the deer in the lick, and his light was obscured, to pull trigger was a certain death.

His story of the panther, which I was now revolving in my mind, he had told on arriving at my father's house one morning at an early hour from one of these nocturnal hunts, himself covered from head to foot with blood, and with a huge panther slung upon his back, with a bullet hole between its eyes, ran thus :—" I was watching last night, *Squire* (as he called my father), at the old saw-mill lick, and it getting on to be near midnight, I fell asleep. Seated on the ground, and my back leaning against a beech tree, I was waked by a tremendous blow, like a stroke of lightning—'twas this beast, d'ye see; he sprung upon me, and landed me some ten or twelve feet, and dropped me, and made only one jump farther himself, as I knew by the noise when he stopped. I knew it was a *painter*, though I could see nothing, for it was total darkness. I was badly torn, and felt the blood running in several places. My rifle was left in the crotches, and feeling my way very gradually with my feet, but keeping my eyes set upon the brute, for I knew exactly where he was lying, I at length got hold of the rifle, but it could do me no good in the dark. My knife had slipped out of the scabbard in the struggle, and I had now no hope but from knowing that the cowardly animal will never spring while you look him in the face.

" In this position, with my rifle in both hands, and cocked, I sat, not hearing even a leaf turned by him, until just the break of day (the only thing I wanted —it was but a few hours, but it seemed a long time, I assure you), when I could just begin to discover his outline, and then the wrinkles betwixt his eyes ! Time moved slowly then, I can tell you, *Squire;* and at last I could see the head of ' Old Ben:' there was no time to be lost now, and I let slip ! The beast was about twenty feet from me."

One can easily imagine my juvenile susceptibilities much heightened by such reflections in such a place ; and every leaf that turned behind me calculated more

or less to startle me. My resolve, of course, was
not to trust myself in that gloomy place in the night,
nor to wait much longer for the desired gratification,
which I was then believing I should have to forego
for that day at least.

The woodlark was at that moment taking its
favourite limb in the lofty and evergreen hemlocks
for its nightly rest, and making the wooded temple
of solitude ring and echo with its liquid notes,
whilst all else was still as death, and I was on the
eve of descending from my elevated nook and wending my way home. Just then I heard the distant
sounds of footsteps in the leaves, and shortly after
discovered in the distance a deer (a huge buck !),
timidly and cautiously descending the hill and approaching the lick, stopping often to gaze, and
sometimes looking me, apparently, full in the face,
when I was afraid even to wink, lest he should discover me.

My young blood was too boilable, and my nerves
decidedly too excitable for my business. Successive
chills seemed to rise, I don't recollect where from,
but they shook me, each one of them, until after
actually shaking my head, they seemed to go out at
the top of it.

The deer kept advancing, and my shakes increasing,—at length it entered the pool, and commenced
licking ; and the resolve that the moment had arrived
for my grand achievement, set my teeth actually
chattering. My rifle, cocked, was rested before me
on the surface of the rock, and all things, save my-

self, were perfectly ready; after several useless attempts I got my aim, but before I could pull trigger, from another chill and a shake, I lost it again. I tried again and again, but in vain, and then more prudently resolved to lie still a few moments until I could get my nerves more steady, and at all events, until I could see more clearly the forward sight of my barrel, which, as yet, seemed to be enveloped in a sort of a mist.

Just at this moment also popped into my head another idea that gave me one or two renewed shivers. I had fired my little fowling-piece hundreds of times without harm, but I never had fired a rifle—" It may be overloaded, or so long loaded as to kick, or to explode !—but never mind, I must run those risks." After checking my latter apprehensions for a few moments, and feeling again more calmed, I was getting my aim with tolerable accuracy, when away went another of those frightful chills, like a snake running through me from my feet to the top of my head, because I was just about to pull trigger !

The deer at this time seemed to have got enough of licking, and, stepping out of the lick, disappeared in the thicket. " Oh, what a loss !—what a misfortune ! What a chance is gone ! What a coward, and what a poor fool am I ! But if he had stopped, though, one minute longer, I am sure I could have killed him, for I don't tremble now."

Just at this cool moment the deer came gliding through the bushes and into the lick again, much nearer than before. One little chill began; but by gritting my teeth tight together I succeeded in getting a more steady aim, when—bang! went the crack and the flash of a rifle, a little to the left of me! and the deer, bounding a few rods from the pool on to an elevated bank, and tumbling upon the ground, quite dead, showed me that I was too late!

My head and the breech of my rifle were instantly lowered a little more behind my stone breastwork, and then—oh, horrid! what I never had seen before, nor ever dreamed of seeing in that place—the tall and graceful form of a huge *Indian*, but half bent forward, as he pushed his red and naked shoulders, and drew himself slowly over the logs and through the bushes. Trailing his rifle in his left hand, and drawing a large knife with the other from its sheath in the hollow of his back, he advanced to the carcase of the deer, which had fallen much nearer to me than it was when it was shot.

His rifle he leaned against a tree, and the blade of his bloody knife, which he had drawn across the neck of the deer, he clenched between his teeth, while he suspended the animal by the hind legs from the limb of a tree to let it bleed. "Oh, horrid! horrid! what—*what* a fate is mine! what *am* I to do?"

No length of life could ever erase from my recollection the impression which this singular and unexpected scene made upon my infant mind, or the ease, and composure, and grace with which this

phantom seated himself upon the trunk of a large
and fallen tree, wiping his huge knife upon the
moss and laying it by his side, and drawing from
his pouch his flint, and steel, and spunk, with which
he lit his pipe, and from which it seemed, in a few
moments, as if he were sending up thanks to the
Great Spirit in the blue clouds of smoke that were
curling around him.

Who will ever imagine the thoughts that were
passing through my youthful brain in these exciting
moments? for here was before me, for the first time
in my life, the living figure of a *Red Indian !* "If
he sees me I'm lost; he will scalp me and devour
me, and my dear mother will never know what became of me !"

From the crack of that rifle, however, I had not
another chill, nor a shiver : my feeling now was no
longer the ebullition of childish anxiety, but the
awfully flat and stupid one of dread and fear ; and
every muscle was quiet. Here was "perhaps death
in a moment" before me. My eyeballs, which
seemed elongated as though they were reaching
half-way to him, were too tightly strained to
tremble. An instant thought came to me, when
his naked back and shoulders were turned towards
me—"My rifle is levelled, and I am perfectly cool ;
a bullet would put an end to all my fears." And a
better one followed when he turned gently around,
and moved his piercing black eyes over and about
the ledge where I was sitting, and the blue streams
were curling upwards from his mouth and his nos-

trils ; for I saw then (though a child), in the momentary glance of that face, what *infant* human nature could not fail to see, and none but *human* nature could express.   I saw *humanity*.

His pipe burned out ; the deer, with its fore and hind legs tied together, he slung upon his back, and, taking his rifle in his hand, he silently and quietly disappeared in the dusky forest, which at this time was taking the gloom of approaching night.

My position and reflections were still like lead that could not be removed, until a doubly reasonable time had elapsed for this strange apparition to be entirely out of my way.   He having seemingly, at last view, to have taken the direction of the " old road" by which I had expected to return, my attention was now turned to a different but more difficult route.   By clambering the huge precipice still above me, which I did as soon as perfect safety seemed to authorise it, and by a run of more than a mile through the woods, scarcely daring to look back, I was safely lodged in my father's back fields, but without hat or rifle, and without the least knowledge of the whereabouts in which either of them had been deposited or dropped.   The last of these, however, was recovered on the following day, but the other never came to light.

Such was the adventure, and such the mode of " my first seeing an Indian."

Having *seen* him, the next thing was to *announce* him, which I did without plan or reserve, but solely with youthful impulse ; exclaiming as I approached

Plate I.

Johnny O'Neil's "Gipsies."— *p.* 41.

the vicinity of my father's house, and as pale as a
ghost, "I've seen an Indian! I've seen an Indian!"

No one believed me, as no Indian had been seen
in the neighbourhood for many years. I related the
whole of my adventure, and then they thought "the
boy was mad." I *was* mad—I went to bed mad
and crying; and my poor dear mother came and
knelt by my bed, and at last comforted me a little
by saying, "My dear George, I do believe you—
I believe your story to be true—I believe you have
seen an Indian." I had a restless night, however,
and in the morning, when I awoke, Johnny O'Neil,
a faithful farm-labourer in my father's employment,
was at the door, announcing that, "Jist in the toother
eend of the bag whate-field, where ye sae thit lattle
smohk areesin, has kimmed thae japsies; sae ye
may be lookin' oot for yer toorkies, an' yer suckin'-
pigs, an' yer chahkins, for I tal ye ther'll be nae
gude o' 'em."

Poor Johnny O'Neil! he was not believed either;
for, said my father, "That's almost a bull, Johnny,
for there are no gipsies in this country." "I bag
yer parthen," said Johnny; and my father continued
—"I'll be bound these are George's Indians!" and
putting on his hat, and taking me by the hand, he
and Johnny O'Neil and myself started off for the
farther corner of the "big wheat-field," where we
found my Indian warrior (Paddy's gipsy) (Plate No.
I.) seated on a bear-skin spread upon the ground.
His legs were crossed, his elbows resting on his
knees, and his pipe at his lips; with his wife, and

his little daughter of ten years old, with blankets
wrapped around them, and their necks covered with
beads, reclining by the side of him; and over them
all, to screen them from the sun, a blanket, suspended by the corners from four crotchets fastened
into the ground, and a small fire in front of the
group, with a steak of venison cooking for their
breakfast.

"There's the japsies!" said Johnny O'Neil, as we
were approaching. "There is the Indian, father!"
said I; and my father, who had been familiar with
Indians, and had learned to sing their songs and
speak somewhat of their language in his early life,
said to me, "George, my boy, you were right,—
these are Indians." "Yes," said I, "and that's the
very man I saw."

He was smoking away, and looking us steadily in
the face as we approached; and though I began to
feel something of the alarm I had felt the day before, my father's stepping up to him and taking
him by the hand with a mutual "How—how—
how," and the friendly grip of his soft and delicate
hand, which was extended to me also, soon dissi-
pated all my fears, and turned my alarm to perfect
admiration.

Understanding and speaking a little English, he
easily explained to my father that he was an Oneida,
living near Cayuga Lake, some one hundred and
fifty miles distant, that his name was On-o-gong-
way (a great warrior). He asked us to sit down by
him, when he cleaned out his pipe, and, charging it

afresh with tobacco, lighted, and gave it to my father to smoke, and then handed it to me, which, my father explained, was a pledge of his friendship.

My father then explained to him the story of my adventure the day before at the old saw-mill lick, to every sentence of which I was nodding "yes," and trembling, as the Indian was smoking his pipe, and almost, but not quite, commencing a smile, as he was earnestly looking me in the face.

The story finished, he took me by both hands, and repeated the words, "Good—good—good hunter." He laid his pipe down, and very deliberately climbing over the fence, stepped into the shade of the forest, where he had suspended a small saddle of venison, and brought it, and laying it by my side, exclaimed, as he laid his hand on my head, "Dat you, you half—very good;" meaning that I was a good hunter, and that half of the venison belonged to me.

The saddle of venison, though very small, was no doubt a part of the animal I had seen in the lick, though it had appeared to me the day before, as I had represented it at home, a "*buck* of the most enormous size," and the Indian a *giant*, though on more familiar acquaintance, to my great surprise, he proved to be no larger than an ordinary man.

This generous present added much to my growing admiration, which was increased again as I listened to his narrative, made to my father and myself, of his history and of some of his adventures, as well as the motive which had brought him some hundreds of miles over a country partly of forest and partly inhabited by a desperate set of hunters whose rifles were unerring, and whose deep-rooted hostility to all savages induced them to shoot them down whenever they met them in their hunting grounds.

His father, he said, had been one of the warriors in the battle of Wyoming, and amongst them was afterwards driven by the white soldiers, after many battles and great slaughter, up the shores of the Susquehana to the country where the remnant of his tribe now lived, between the Oneida and Cayuga Lakes.

During this disastrous retreat, he being a boy about my size, his father made him assist in carrying many heavy things which they had plundered from the white people, where they fought a great battle, at the mouth of the Tunkhannock; amongst which, and one of the most valuable, as one of the most difficult to carry, was a *kettle* of *gold*. "What!" said my father, "a kettle of gold!" "Yes, father," said he,—" now listen.

"The white soldiers came through the narrows you see yonder" (pointing to a narrow gorge in the mountains, through which the river passes); "and on those very fields, which then were covered with trees" (pointing to my father's fields, lying beneath and in front of us), "was a great battle, and many were the warriors that fell on both sides; but at that time, father, another army of white men came from the north, and were entering the valley on that side, and the poor Indians had no way but to leave

the river and all their canoes, and to cross these high
mountains behind us, and make their way through
the forests to Cayuga.

"In passing these mountains, my father, they followed the banks of that creek to its head" (pointing
to the creek on which the old saw-mill was built,
and which passed in a serpentine course through
my father's farm to the river). "On the banks of
that creek many things were buried by the Indians,
who were unable to carry them over the mountains;
and amongst them, somewhere near that bridge, my
father, where the road crosses, on the farther bank,
I saw my father and my mother bury the 'kettle of
gold,' with other things, in the ground.

"When my father was old and infirm, I was
obliged to hunt for him, and I could not come; but
since he has gone to the land of his fathers, I have
made the journey a great way, to dig up the 'kettle
of gold.' But I see this day, from where I now sit,
that there is no use in looking for it, and my heart
is very sad.

"My father—we buried the 'kettle of gold' at
the foot of a large pine-tree that stood on the bank;
but I see the trees are all gone, and all now is
covered with green grass; and where shall I go to
look? This, my father, I kept a secret for many
years, but I see there is no use in keeping it a secret
any longer, and this makes my heart sad. I have
come a great way, my father, and my road in going
back I know is beset with many enemies.

"These green fields, my father, which are now so

beautiful to look upon, were once covered with large and beautiful trees, and they were then the hunting grounds of my fathers, and they were many and strong ; but we are now but a very few—we live a great way off, and we are your children."

My father asked him many questions about the "kettle of gold," and in answering these, he extended both arms in the form of a circle, his fingers' ends just touching each other. "There," said he, "it was about thus large, and just as much as I could lift ; and must be of great value."

My father, after a study of a few minutes, turned to me, and said, "George ! run down to the house and ask your mother to give you the ' little brass kettle,' and bring it here as quick as you can." I never, perhaps, had run more nimbly (but on *one occasion*) in my lifetime, than I ran and scaled the fences on this errand.

While this conversation was passing about the "kettle of gold," it had occurred to my father that Buel Rowley, one of his hired men, had ploughed up a small brass kettle a few years before, on the bank of the creek, and at the identical spot designated by the forefinger of the Indian ; and that kettle being brought by me from my mother's culinary collection, was now under the eyes of the child of the forest.

Whilst he was in silence gazing upon it, and turning it over and over, my father described to him the manner and place in which it was found, and that it was made of *brass*, which, to be sure, looked like gold, but was much harder, and of much less value. After a pause of a few minutes, and without the change of a muscle, but drawing a deep sigh, as i. he recognised the long-hidden treasure, and trying his knife two or three times on the upper rim of it, he laid it down, and drawing a deep breath or two through his pipe, said to my father, that he had no doubt but it was the same kettle, but that two things troubled his mind very much—the first was, that the kettle should be so small; and the other, that he found it was not a "kettle of *gold.*" The first error he attributed to his having carried it when he was quite a small boy, as it was then a heavy load for him; and the other, from having learned amongst the white people that a very small piece of gold was worth ten dollars; and having estimated from this standard the probable value of a "kettle of gold," not having as yet learned enough from the white people to know the difference between *gold* and *brass.*

Poor ignorant child of the forest! he had learned from his teachers something of the *value* of gold before he knew what it was; and he had risked his life, and those of his wife and his little daughter, in wending his way for hundreds of miles through the forests infested with hunters whose rifles were levelled upon every Indian they could meet. His long journey had cost him no gold, for he had none to spend; his rifle had supplied him and his family with food, and he had thus far escaped his enemies, and in this wise accomplished his object; but his dangerous steps, which were to be retraced, were

rendered tenfold more dangerous from the vague
reports which had accidentally and unfortunately
got into circulation amongst the hunters and bri-
gands of the forests through which he had to pass,
that he had dug up, and was returning with, a
"kettle of gold."

My father and several of his neighbours paid
frequent visits to his little bivouac; and I spent
nearly all my time there, so completely were all my
fears turned into admiration. My rusty tomahawk
head I brought to him, for which he made me a
handle, and curiously carved it with his knife. The

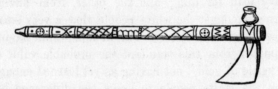

handle was perforated for smoking through, a mystery which no one of the neighbours could solve, as
"there was no gimlet long enough to make such a
hole," little thinking, as he explained the secret to
me, that the handle was made of a young ash, the
pith of which is easily burned away with a heated
wire, or a piece of hard hickory wood.

The handle finished, my friend Johnny O'Neil
laid the head and blade of it on the grindstone
while I turned, until it was everywhere silvery
bright, and its edge as sharp as a knife. This
lighted the eyes of the child of the forest, and he
gave a new gleam to mine, when he filled the bowl

of it with tobacco (or k'nick-k'neck, an Indian substitute for tobacco) and commenced smoking through it.

And yet the great charm and mystery of the tomahawk was still to come—yet to be learned. My young readers must know that the tomahawk (like the scalping-knife, which generally has the Sheffield mark upon it) is a contrivance of civilized invention and construction, too deadly and destructive to have been made by the poor Indian; combining the two essential requisites—of being capable of being used in war as the most efficient and deadly weapon, by throwing or striking with, and, when war is at an end, of being turned into a luxury, for which it is equally valued, the smoke passing through it when charged with tobacco.

The first of these characters of the tomahawk having been illustrated as above stated, to my inexpressible delight, and the tobacco all burned out; my good and confiding friend now arose with the tomahawk in his right hand, and raised my astonishment and admiration still higher, by throwing it at the trunk of a tree some rods distant, and burying its blade in the solid wood, explaining to me the certain fate of an enemy within an equal distance. I had not the power to draw it out; but under his practised hand it seemed to leave the tree like a breath of wind.

He then stepped back again some ten or fifteen steps, with the end of the handle in his hand, when —chick! it seemed to pronounce, as quick as electricity, and was there buried again! This he did more than twenty times, without failing once, to the astonishment of my father and others looking on; the weapon revolving many times in the air, and the blade, no matter what the distance, always entering the tree. Here I was left in one of the several inexplicable mysteries which I have met in Indian life, and never have been able to solve, even to the present day.

My flint arrow-heads I brought to him, which he looked upon with an evident gloom. He made me shafts (which he feathered) to a number of them; and from a young hickory he made me a beautiful bow, and ornamented it with woodpeckers' feathers; and from the skin of the fawn (the "huge buck," which I *would* have killed) he made me a quiver, and, with the arrows in it, slung it on my back. What could more completely have capped the climax of my boyish ambition than this?

The honesty and childlike simplicity of these poor people gained them many friends in the neighbourhood, and yet there were, no doubt, murderous enemies in disguise plotting and prowling around them. My father made them many presents, and my attachment to them laid my mother's pantry under daily and heavy contributions.

My father was under constant apprehensions for their safety, and while he was maturing a plan for sending them home by a different route, and at his own expense, it was discovered one morning that their smoke was missing in the corner of my father's "big wheat-field;" and on the same morning was found hanging in my father's wood-house, which was always open on one side, a fine saddle of venison, with one of the beautiful and well-known eagle quills from the head of On-o-gong-way fastened in it!

Poor, honest, and harmless man! he had left, to meet the chances for his life on his long journey home; and as an unmistakable evidence of his friendship and gratitude, he had left this silent parting gift, and with it, as he could not write his name, his choicest plume, to identify the giver.

"The Indians are gone! the Indians are gone?" was echoed everywhere, and through the neighbourhood, in the morning; and poor Johnny O'Neil, when he looked upon the saddle of venison containing the eagle's quill, exclaimed, "Upon my word, *squire*, thase is nae japsies—an' I'll be shot if thot mon's not a gintleman!"

A few days after the departure of the Indians, two neighbouring boys and myself were practising with my tomahawk, by throwing it at the trunk of a tree; and when thrown by the hand of one of the boys, it glanced from the tree, by which I was standing too closely, when the sharp blade struck me on the left cheek, cutting deep into the cheek-bone, and felling me to the ground, covered with blood; giving me a wound which was several months in healing, and a scar which any one of my youthful readers may always know me by, if they have the opportunity of seeing me.

This was the *first* catastrophe growing out of the
new and singular acquaintance thus recited, but not
the saddest; *that* came to our knowledge a few days
later, and in this lamentable form—that the dead
body of poor *On-o-gong-way* was found, pierced by
two rifle bullets, in Randolph Valley, a dark and
dreary wilderness, some eight or ten miles from my
father's plantation, which it was necessary for him
to cross in order to reach his own country and
friends.

What became of his poor wife and the interesting
and innocent little daughter, no mortal was ever
able (or willing) to say; and the "kettle of gold,"
which my father had confident hopes would have led
to the detection of so foul a murder, notwithstanding
his exertions from year to year, never furnished any
clue to the villainy.

CHAPTER III.

Indian Tribes—Portraits and Costumes—The Sioux—Sioux Village—Interior of Wigwams — Drying Meat — Indian Slavery—Scalp-Day—Skin-builders — Grass-builders—Dirt-builders—Bark-builders—Timber-builders.

IN the foregoing chapter I have shown how I received my earliest impressions of the Indian character ; and skipping over the intervening part of my life, from my boyhood to the age of thirty-three, when, as I have said, I entered the forests to learn more of it, we will now enter upon scenes that I witnessed in those pursuits, from which a more intimate knowledge of these people and their customs may be gleaned.

The great valley of the Mississippi and Missouri, containing nearly one-half of North America, with its vast prairies, and mountains, and lakes, was the first field of my roamings, which occupied some five or six years of my life; during which time I visited many tribes, and some of the finest races of mankind in America or in the world; the principal, and most numerous, and most interesting of these were the *Sioux*—the *Blackfoot*—the *Crows*—the *Mandans*—

53

the *Pawnees—Ojibbeways—Camanchees—Osages*
and *Choctaws;* and in my subsequent travels west
of the Rocky Mountains, a few of the numerous
tribes, the *Flatheads*—the *Apachees*—the *Shoshonees*
—the *Arapahos*, and others; and in South and
Central America, the *Caribbees*—the *Arowaks*—the
Chaymas—the *Gooagives*—the *Macouchis*—the
Guarani—the *Tupi*—the *Botocudos*—the *Connibos*
—the *Chiquitos*—the *Moxos*, and fifty others.

A connected narrative of my wanderings amongst
all of these remote people would require a very
large and perhaps tedious book; but, my young
readers, I will not fatigue you by travelling over the
whole ground—I will take a shorter way. I will
introduce you at once to the people themselves and
their modes of living, and afterwards to their
customs, which you will then be better able to
appreciate. After knowing how they look and how
they live, you will more easily and correctly understand how they act—Will you not?

We now take an immense stride of twelve
hundred miles in a moment, from the scenes of my
younger days just described, in the State of New
York, where the Indian tribes have all disappeared
many years since, to the centre and heart of the
great American wilds, where men and animals are
still roaming in their native beauty and independ-
ence, on the great and almost boundless grassy
plains of the Upper Missouri.

In the absence of a pictorial illustration, let me
describe a painting from life, which my portfolio

contains, of a family group, comprising the head war-chief of the great Sioux nation, with his daughter (an unmarried girl) and his wife, with her infant (papoose) slung in its pretty crib, or cradle, ornamented with porcupine quills, dyed of various bright colours. The chief wore a robe made of the skin of a buffalo, with the battles of his life painted on it. His shirt (or tunic) and leggings were made of deer-skins, and the seams embroidered with porcupine quills and fringed with scalp-locks. His moccasins, made of deer-skins, were handsomely embroidered; in his right hand he held his lance; and his head-dress, made of war-eagles' quills and ermine skins, extended quite to the ground, and was surmounted by a pair of horns, denoting his office as head war-chief of his tribe, a curious mode, which I found to be the same in most of the tribes.

The dress of the young woman was made of the skins of the mountain sheep, more light and more soft than deer-skins, and was very prettily embroidered and painted. The costume of the wife of the chief was much the same as that of the daughter; her leggings and moccasins being beautifully garnished.

It will be seen by this description that these people are not always the "poor *naked* Indians;" for in their native state, before white men come to destroy their game, they have an abundance of skins and furs to clothe themselves with; and, except in very warm weather, when it is more agreeable to be partly naked, they are abundantly and comfortably, and oftentimes elegantly, clad.

We discover in this family group, also, a good illustration of the *domestic relations* existing amongst these poor people. Here is the father, the mother, the husband, the wife, the children; clearly showing that these people have the institution of marriage, as we have it in the civilized world. By my observations amongst them I find that they feel and observe those conjugal, those paternal and filial affections as strongly as any people in more enlightened society, some striking examples of which will yet be given in this little book.

The Sioux* is one of the most numerous and powerful tribes in North America, numbering about twenty-five thousand, divided into forty bands, each band having a chief at its head, which chiefs are again subordinate to one head-chief; and with him, in council, they form the government of the nation; and such is the custom amongst most of the other tribes.

There is no tribe better clad, who live in better houses (wigwams), or who are better mounted, than the Sioux. They catch an abundance of wild horses, which are grazing on the prairies, oftentimes in groups of several hundreds, and from their horses' backs, at full speed, they deal their deadly arrows, or wield their long and fatal lances in the chase of the buffaloes, and also in war with their enemies.

These people, living mostly in a country of prairies (meadows), where they easily procure the buffalo-skins, construct their wigwams with them, in form

* Pronounced See-oo.

of tents, which are more comfortable than rude huts constructed of timber, are more easily built, and have the advantage of being easily transported over the prairies ; by which means the Indians are enabled to follow the migrating herds of buffaloes during the summer and fall seasons, when they are busily engaged in drying meat for their winter's consumption, and dressing robes for their own clothing, and also for barter to the fur traders.

From this view (Frontispiece) of a Sioux village, on the Upper Missouri, my little readers will get a very correct notion of the manner in which these curious people live. There were in this village about four hundred skin tents, all built much in the same manner : some fifteen or twenty pine poles forming the frame, covered with one entire piece of fifteen or twenty buffalo-skins sewed together, and most curiously painted and embroidered, of all colours ; presenting one of the most curious and beautiful scenes imaginable.

Inside of these tents, the fire is placed in the centre, the smoke escaping out at the top; and at night the inmates all sleep on buffalo-skins spread upon the ground, with their feet to the fire ; a most safe, and not uncomfortable mode. When you enter one of these wigwams you have to stoop rather awkwardly ; but when you are in, you rise up and find a lofty space of some twenty feet above your head. The family are all seated, and no one rises to salute you, whatever your office or your importance may be. All lower their eyes to your feet, instead of staring you in the face, and you are asked to sit down.

A robe or a mat of rushes is spread for you, and as they have no chairs you are at once embarrassed. It is an awkward thing for a white man to sit down upon the ground until he gets used to it, and when he is down, he don't know what to do with his legs.

The Indians, accustomed to this from childhood, sit down upon, and rise from, the ground with the same ease and grace that we sit down in, and rise from, a chair. Both men and women lower themselves to the ground, and rise, without a hitch or a jerk, and without touching their hand to the ground. This is very curious, but it is exceedingly graceful and neat. The men generally sit cross-legged; and to sit down they cross their feet, closely locked together, and extending their arms and head forward, slowly and regularly lower their bodies quite to the sitting posture on the ground: when they rise they place their feet in the same position, and their arms and head also, and rise to a perfectly straight position, apparently without an effort.

The women always sit with both feet and lower legs turned under and to the right or the left, and, like the men, lower and raise themselves without touching the ground.

When you are seated, to feel at ease your legs must be crossed, and your heels drawn quite close under you, and then you can take the pipe when it is handed to you, and get a fair and deliberate glance at things around you.

The furniture in these wigwams is not much, but it is very curious in effect, and picturesque, when we look at it. The first startling thing you will meet on entering will be half-a-dozen saucy dogs, barking, and bristling, and showing their teeth, and oftentimes as many screaming children, frightened at your savage and strange appearance.

These hushed, you can take a look at other things, and you see shields, and quivers, and lances, and saddles, and medicine bags, and pouches, and spears, and cradles, and buffalo masques (which each man keeps for dancing the buffalo dance), and a great variety of other picturesque things hanging around, suspended from the poles of the tent, to which they are fastened by thongs ; the whole presenting, with the picturesque group around the fire, one of the most curious scenes imaginable.

In front of these wigwams the women are seen busily at work, dressing robes and drying meat. The skin-dressing of the Indians, both of the buffalo and deer-skins, is generally very beautiful and soft. Their mode of doing this is curious : they stretch the skin, as seen in the illustration, either on a frame or on the ground, and after it has remained some three or four days with the brains of the buffalo or elk spread over the fleshy side, they grain it with a sort of adze or chisel, made of a piece of buffalo bone.

After the process of "graining," and the skin is apparently beautifully finished, they pass it through another process, that of "smoking." For this, a hole of some two or three feet in depth is dug in the ground, and a smothered fire kindled in the hole with rotten wood, producing a strong and peculiar sort of smoke ; and over this a little tent, made of two or three buffalo-skins, and so closed as to prevent the smoke from escaping, in which the grained skins hang for three or four days. After this process, the dresses made of these skins may be worn repeatedly in the rain, and will always dry perfectly soft—a quality which, I believe, does not yet belong to dressed skins in civilized countries.

"Drying meat" is done by cutting it into thin slices and exposing it in the sun, hung upon poles (as seen in the cut), where it dries, and is successfully cured, without salt and without smoke.

Men are here seen also coming in from the hunt, with their horses loaded with meat and skins, to keep the poor women at work. It is proverbial in the civilized world that "the poor Indian woman has to do all the hard work." Don't believe this, for it is not exactly so. She labours very hard and constantly, it is true. She does most of the drudgery about the village and wigwam, and is seen transporting heavy loads, etc. This all looks to the passer-by as the slavish compulsion of her cruel husband, who is often seen lying at his ease, and smoking his pipe, as he is looking on.

His labours are not seen, and therefore are less thought of, when he mounts his horse, with his weapons in hand, and working every nerve and every muscle, dashes amongst the herds in the chase, to provide food for his wife and his little children, and scours the country both night and day, at the constant risk of his life, to protect them from the assaults of their enemies.

The Indian woman's life is, to be sure, a slavish one ; and equally so are the lives of most women equally poor in all civilized countries. Look into their humble dwellings in all cities and towns, or in the country, in civilized communities, and see the industry and the slavish labour of poor woman! She works all the days of her life, brings water, makes fires, and tends to her little children, like the poor Indian woman ; and *she may* be *a slave* to an idle husband, who is spending his time and his money, as well as her own earnings, in a tap-room.

The civilized world is full of such slavery as this ; but amongst the American Indians such a system does not and cannot exist ; every man is a hunter and a soldier ; he must supply his family with food, and help to defend his country.

The education of woman in those countries teaches her that the labours are thus to be divided between herself and her husband ; and for the means of subsistence and protection, for which she depends upon his labours, she voluntarily *assumes* the hard work about the encampment, considering their labours about equally divided.

" Slaves to their husbands " is an epithet so often and so inappropriately applied to the poor Indian woman by the civilized world, and so frequently reiterated and kept alive by tourists who have happened to see an Indian woman or two at work when their husbands were asleep or smoking their pipes, that I cannot, in common honesty to you, my young readers, nor in justice to the Indian, consent to pass it by in this place without some further comment.

One of the distinguishing natural traits of the American Indian, that stamps his character as mentally superior to that of the African and some other races, is his uncompromising tenacity for unbounded freedom. All efforts made (and there have been many) to enslave these people, have resulted in failures ; and such an abhorrence have they of the system, that they cannot be induced to labour for each other or for white men for any remuneration that can be offered, lest the disgraceful epithet "slave" should be applied to them by their tribe.

In the relationship of man and wife, in which, as amongst white people, "both are one," they can and do labour for mutual interests and mutual subsistence, without incurring this reproach ; and I do not believe that, among the poorer class of any civilized people on earth, a better and a more voluntary division of the toils of conjugal life can be found than exists amongst the American Indians.

By the custom in all the American tribes, the person of every individual in society, either within the pale of the domestic relations or out of it, is considered sacredly protected from the lash or a blow, which in themselves imply degradation or servitude, and in all cases they may be revenged with death.

If this system should, by possibility, have its

disadvantages, how much does it redound to the credit of the Indian's character, and to the honour of his race, and what a lesson is it for the civilized world, that there never was known to exist amongst them the unnatural brute that has beaten his wife or his little child !

But we left these poor women at their "slavish work," dressing robes and drying meat. Let us go back to them for a few moments yet, lest we should lose sight of a Sioux village before we know all about it, and of course be unable to appreciate some extraordinary and amusing Sioux customs, to be explained further on as we advance.

We here see the Indian women in the full enjoyment of their domestic happiness, with their little children and dogs around them, the villagers dressed in their ordinary costumes, and the little cupids taking their first lessons in archery, which is the most important feature in their education. This happens to be "scalp-day;" the Sioux, like most of the other tribes, having several days in the year for "counting scalps," which are observed somewhat as holidays. The chief on those days passes through an aperture in the side of his wigwam, and erects over it a pole called the "scalp-pole," from which are suspended the scalps which he has taken, which is the signal for all the warriors to do the same ; so that the chief and every person in the village can count them, and understand each warrior's standing and claims to promotion, which are estimated by the number of scalps he has taken.

Amongst the Indian tribes every man is a military man, a warrior, a brave, or a chief. All are armed and ready to go to war if necessary. A *warrior* is one of those who has taken one or more scalps; a *brave* is one who goes to war as a soldier, but as yet has taken no scalps, has killed no enemy.

Taking the scalp is practised by all the American tribes much in the same way, and for the same objects, which, with the mode of taking it and using it, will be more fully described hereafter.

From the Sioux mode of constructing their villages, which I have thus briefly explained, and to which we shall have occasion again to return, we will now take a glance at some other modes practised by other tribes living at great distances from them.

The *Assinneboins*, the *Crows*, the *Blackfoot*, the *Omahas*, the *Shiennes*, the *Camanchees*, and yet several other tribes living in the vicinity of the herds of buffaloes, build their wigwams, and live much in the manner of the Sioux. All of these I would denominate "*skin-builders.*" There are also the *grass-builders*, the *dirt-builders*, the *bark-builders*, and the *timber-builders*, and yet other builders, all of whom will be noticed in their proper places.

How curious it is that these ingenious people, who have invented so many ways of constructing their dwellings, never yet have adopted the mode of building with stone. This is probably not the result of ignorance or want of invention, but from their universal policy of leaving no monuments. All the

American tribes are more or less migratory; and when they move, they destroy all their marks, by burning their wigwams, if they cannot take them with them, and "smoothing over the graves of their parents and children."

The *Pawnee-Picts* (in their own language *Tow-ee-ahge*), a numerous tribe living on the head waters of the Red River, in Western Texas, build their wigwams by a sort of thatching of long prairie grass, over a frame of poles fastened in the ground and bent in at their tops; the structure, when completed, having much the shape and appearance of a straw beehive.

This singular mode, which is only practised by that tribe, and partially so by the *Kiowas* and *Wicos*, smaller tribes subjugated by the *Pawnee-Picts*, is very convenient; they are comfortable dwellings,

easily constructed, and easily demolished when they
are left, by putting a fire-brand to them.

The tribe of *Mandans*, on the Upper Missouri, the
Pawnees of the Platte, the *Minatarees*, and the
Riccarrees, are the only *dirt-builders*, and they all
seem to construct their wigwams much in the same
manner.

These tribes, unlike the Sioux and other tribes
living in skin tents, and who are constantly roaming
about the country, live in permanent villages, and
construct their wigwams with more labour and
more strength, and uniformly fortify them against
the assaults of their enemies, by the bank of a river
on one side, and a stockade on the other. These
wigwams are always made by excavating, in a circular form, some three or four feet into the ground,
for a foundation, from which they make a super-
structure of round timbers lying against each other,

the butt ends placed in the bottom of the excavation, and the smaller ends concentrating near the top, and supported within by beams resting on upright posts; the whole is covered with willow-boughs, to preserve the dryness and soundness of the timbers; and covered again with a foot or two in thickness of a concrete of tough clay and gravel, permitting the whole family, dogs and all, to recline and gambol on the top of it in pleasant weather.

In the Mandan village I measured several of these, and found the smallest to be forty-five feet, and many of them sixty feet in diameter. The fire is always built in the centre, with the smoke escaping at the apex, as seen in the illustrations.

These, then, are the only modes of construction which are confined to any uniform shapes; the *wood-builders*, and the *bark-builders*, and others, like the *timber-builders* and *palm-builders* in Central and South America, using a thousand different shapes in constructing with those materials.

So much for the various modes in which these curious people live. We will now take a little further view of their personal appearance, and then proceed to their actions and usages, from which I intend you shall draw more amusement, and obtain important information in support of the character of these abused people, which, I have fearlessly said, entitles them to a high position amongst the families of the world.

CHAPTER IV.

Warriors—War Dress and War Paint—War Weapons—
Smoking the Shield — Warfare — War-Whoop — War-
Whistles—Flags—Scalps and Scalping—Prisoners of War
—Calumet (Pipe of Peace).

NOW, my little readers, we are soon coming to scenes and events that will be more exciting; skip over nothing, but read every word as you pass along, for we are so far getting a foundation for what is to follow. Don't get impatient for the description of *Scalps* and *Scalping*, for the *Buffalo-hunts*, the *Dog-feasts*, the *Stone-man Medicine*, the *Thunder's Nest*, etc., but learn how the people *look* first; and then, as I have said, we will more easily understand their actions.

In the last chapter I have described to you the family of an American wild man, an officer of the highest rank, the head war-chief of his tribe, in full dress, with his wife and children around him; and I now present to your acquaintance (Plate No. III.) three distinguished Indian warriors, in war dress and war paint, and equipped for war. These I have selected from amongst my numerous portraits painted

68

from the life, and from them you will be able to get faithful and lasting ideas of the appearance of that class of citizens who are found in all the tribes of the American Indians.

These gallant young men were all my familiar and hospitable friends, whilst I was living amongst them ; and ready at all times to afford me any aid or facilities in their power—ready to guard my property and life, even at the hazard of their own. With these fine young men I have smoked, wrestled, run races ; and in hunting with them I have confidently and safely trusted my life with them in our excursions over the prairies, and places far distant from their homes.

These young men are warriors. Warriors, I have said, are those who have taken scalps. The leggings of these men were fringed with scalp-locks taken from their enemies' heads ; and yet they were the last of all people on earth to meddle with mine.

Nothing, my young readers, that I can convey to you of Indian character and Indian modes can possibly be more interesting and more important than the chapter I am now entering upon, of Indian warriors and Indian warfare—the key, in fact, to Indian life and Indian doings yet to be described in the following chapters.

Every Indian tribe is a separate community, surrounded by other tribes with whom they are generally at war, owing to several causes which don't exist to the same extent amongst civilized nations. They have no settled (but always disputed and imperfectly defined) boundaries, over which their fierce hunting excursions often lead them, exposing them to the attacks of their enemies : another, and more frequent cause of warfare, is the popular ambition to signalise themselves, which is felt amongst all Indian warriors, who have but the one mode to rise to enviable distinction in their tribes, that of being a great warrior.

I have already said that every tribe has its civil and its military, or war chief, and that all the young men are warriors and braves.   In war, the war-chief takes the command, and without the least compulsory power *leads* his warriors, who are all volunteers, and at liberty to desert the chief at any time, if they are willing to meet the disgrace that attaches to them on their return.   Of the three warriors shown in Plate II.—

No. 1 represents Om-pa-ton-ga (the Big Elk), an *Omaha* warrior, dressed, and armed, and painted for war—with his bow and several arrows clenched in his hand, and always ready at an instant—his buffalo robe, with his battles painted on it, wrapped around him—and his quiver slung on his back, filled with arrows.

No. 2. Seekh-hee-de (the Mouse-coloured Feather), a *Mandan* warrior, in war costume and war paint— his bow and arrows ready, and his quiver slung on his back ; he wears a necklace made of the huge paw of a grizzly bear, and his leggings are fringed with scalp-locks.

No. 3. Loo-ra-wee-re-coo (the Bird that goes to War), a *Pawnee* warrior, in war paint and war cos-

Plate II.   Om-pa-ton-go, Seekh-hee-de, Loo-ra-wee-re-coo, three distinguished Indian Warriors. — p. 70.

tume—with bow and arrows, and shield, and quiver, and his spear in his left hand; his body is curiously ornamented with his war paint; his ankle ornaments are strings of antelopes' hoofs, which make a frightful rattling noise when he dances or walks; he wears a beautiful kilt made of eagles' quills, and his head is shaved (according to the uniform custom of the tribe) and ornamented with a beautiful red crest made of the hair of the deer's tail dyed red, and horse-hair; in shape much resembling a Grecian helmet.

" *War dress* and *war paint,*" here, is something very curious. It is the invariable custom of the warriors of all Indian tribes in America, to go to war in *war dress* and *war paint;* the *first* consisting in a mode of dressing the person just as each individual may fancy for himself, so as to afford the greatest facility for the free use of his weapons; and, in fact, most generally amounting to (nearly) no dress at all. And the *second*, his limbs being chiefly naked, consisting of a thick daubing or streaking of red and white clay, vermilion, and charcoal, mixed with bears' grease, covering various parts of his body and limbs, as well as his face, sometimes half black and half red, and at other times the whole face black, in such a manner as even to be disguised, oftentimes, from his own familiar friends.

Each warrior has some peculiar and known way of painting, by which he is recognised by his fellow-warriors, at a distance at which they would not distinguish him from his comrades from the natural differences, so great is their resemblance in the open air when naked and in action.

It was one of the curious and unaccountable facts that I met with in my travels, that I never in any instance was able to get a warrior to stand for his portrait until he had spent the requisite time at his toilette (oftentimes from sunrise until eleven or twelve o'clock) to arrange himself in his war dress and war paint. And I also everywhere learned that all warriors apprehended through life, with the greatest solicitude, the possibility and the misfortune of losing their lives when they are not in their *war paint.*

The principal arms (or weapons) of all the American tribes are seen in the portraits of these three warriors—their *bows* and *arrows.* Their bows are short and light, for easy and effective handling on horseback; but they have great power, being mostly covered on the backs with layers of buffalo sinews, giving them great elasticity. Their arrows are mostly pointed with flints, broken in so ingenious a manner, with a point and two sharp edges, as to enable them to enter the flesh of the buffaloes or their enemies, on whichsoever they may use them.

These arrows are carried in a quiver slung on the back, and generally made of the skins of animals adapted in shape and size to hold them. When not in service, their arrows are carried in the quiver with the points downwards, for protection; but when they are going into battle, the arrows are reversed, leaving the points standing out, being thus more ready to be drawn suddenly and without obstruction.

Besides the bow and arrow, the *tomahawk*, already shown and explained, and war clubs of various shapes and materials, and lances, are used in warfare, and shields carried on the left arm for protection. These shields are carried by every horseman, completing his dress and equipments, completely in the classic style of the ancient Roman and Grecian cavalry.

These shields are invariably made of the skin of the buffalo's neck, the thickest part of the hide; tanned and hardened in such a manner with the glue remaining in them, that they are proof against arrows, and even against a gun shot when held obliquely, which they do with great skill. They paint and ornament these shields in a great variety of ways, and add to their picturesque appearance by suspending eagle quills and other beautiful plumes from them, and oftentimes painting the representation of their medicine bags upon them. ("Medicine bags" you will understand in a few moments.)

"*Smoking the Shield.*"—Have you ever heard of "Smoking the Shield?" I believe not. Why, it is one of the grandest and most imposing ceremonies to be seen in the Indian countries. Let's see.—An Indian lad is old enough to go to war—he is sixteen or eighteen years old—he wants a shield—*must have one*—can't go to war without one. Can he *buy* one? He might, perhaps, but "it won't protect him if he does"—he must make it for himself—and how? He must kill the buffalo bull with his own hand. With a gun? No; a smaller boy than he can do

that : he must kill it with an *arrow*, and take the
hide off with his own hand ; and then—Well, then
what ?   Why, he has got to *make his shield*.   Can
he do this privately, and at his leisure ?   No ; Indian
soldiers are counted by their shields.   Indian warriors are the property of their nation.   Can any
Indian lad secretly enlist, and make himself a warrior ?   Have they any newspapers to announce their
enrolments ?   No : the making of a warrior is a
public act, and must be made in a public way : the
warriors help in this.

In the great *Camanchee* village, in 1836, I was
invited to go and see the "*Smoking a Shield.*"   An
immense crowd was assembled a little out of the
village, within which a circle, of a hundred feet or
more in diameter, was preserved by a line marked
on the ground.   In the centre of this circle a young
man had dug a hole in the ground, and over it,
stretched horizontally, a little elevated above the
surface, the bit of bull's hide, of which he was to
forge his shield, tightly strained by a great many
pins driven into the ground, and a fire burning in
the excavation underneath, while the glue extracted
from the buffalo's hoofs, and spread over the skin,
was frying and roasting into it, to give it the hardness and stiffness required.

To witness this ceremony, which they call
"smoking (or roasting) the shield," in order to
insure its success, and legitimately to publish its
owner's change from the phase of boyhood to that
of warrior, all the warriors of the village had assem-

bled at his invitation, in full war dress and war paint, with their shields on their arms, who formed in rings within rings, and danced in circles around the roasting shield; and each one passed it brandishing their war clubs, their tomahawks, and shields over it, vaunting forth the wonderful efficiency of their own, and invoking the "fire-spirit" to give strength and hardness enough to that of the young warrior, to guard and protect him from the weapons of his enemies. Was he then a *warrior?* No; his shield finished, he was a *brave*—a soldier; and this ceremony his enlistment—no more. He can go to war, as you have been told. If he can take a scalp, he *then* becomes a *warrior.*

All the American tribes may properly be said to be warlike. I have explained the principal causes of their wars, and a book might yet be written on their modes of conducting and ending them. Their arms, as I have shown, are not numerous, nor so destructive as those used by civilized nations; and consequently their wars are not so devastating.

Warfare amongst those people is generally conducted by small parties who volunteer under a war-chief, to avenge some wrong or cruelty inflicted by their enemy; and when a few scalps are taken, sufficient for retaliation, they generally return, make a great boast, and entertain the villagers with the scalp dance and other ceremonies.

As these people have fewer and less efficient weapons, they depend somewhat more upon strategy to gain advantages than white men do; and in these they are beyond all conception ingenious and inventive.

In the warfare waged between these people and civilized forces, the Indians are often condemned for their strategy, as "cowardly," because they prefer secret ambuscades and surprises, instead of coming out into the open field and " taking a fair fight " (*i.e.*, coming out and standing before the cannon's mouth, and being shot down like pigeons). This is wrong; the poor Indians know the advantages which white men have, with their rifles, and revolvers, and cannons, in the open field; and their refusal to stand before them and be cut down, under such circumstances, should be called prudence rather than cowardice.

There are no people on earth more courageous and brave than the American Indians, if they can only be assured that they are contending with an enemy with equal weapons. Their sagacity in tracing or reconnoitring an enemy, and evading pursuit if necessary, is almost beyond the reach of comprehension for those not familiar with their modes.

Their signals in war are many, and very intelligent as well as curious. The world-wide notorious (but partially appreciated) war-whoop (or war-cry) is one of these, and is given by all the tribes, both in North and South America, precisely alike, when rushing into battle. It is a shrill and piercing note, sounded long, and with a swell, on the highest key of the voice, with the most rapid vibration possible, made by the striking of the flat of the hand or the fingers against the lips.

There is nothing so very frightful in the sound itself, for many sounds can be produced by the human voice, in themselves far more terrifying than the war-whoop; but none other, perhaps, that could be heard so far, and so distinctly in the din and confusion of battle. It is the *associations* of those who know its meaning and its character, that give it its terror; its being known to be the infallible signal for attack—the war-whoop never being sounded until the rush is made, and weapons are raised for shedding blood.

A person not accustomed to Indian modes might listen to the war-whoop as the Indians were rushing on to him, without alarm, when others, aware of its meaning, would shudder at its sound. No Indian is allowed to sound the war-whoop in time of peace, except in the war-dance and other ceremonies countenanced by the chiefs, lest it should be echoed by their sentinels on the hill tops and their hunting parties through their country, raising an unnecessary and disastrous alarm.

Another signal is the *war-whistle*, which is very curious. Every chief leading in war carries a little whistle of six or eight inches in length, made of the bone of a turkey's leg, the two ends of which have two very different sounds, so shrill and so piercing, and so different from the mingled war-cry and other din in battles, that they can be distinctly heard an immense distance; blowing in one end is the signal

for "*advance—*on*—*on;" and in the other for
retreat. No chief goes into battle without one of
these little war-whistles suspended from his neck and
hanging on his breast; and no warrior goes to war
without knowing the distinction and meaning of
these sounds.

Flags also are used as war-signals. The white
flag is in all tribes a flag of truce, an emblem of
peace, and a red flag the challenge to combat. How
curious is this! All savages are found using the
white flag, and advance with it even into their
enemies' ranks, in the midst of battle, their lives
sacred and protected under it, the same as in civilized
nations. How strange (not that the Indians should
use it, for civilized nations have brought the custom
out of savage life); but how strange that the native
races of all the world should use the same colour as
the emblem of peace; and as sacred and inviolable,
even in the din and rage of battle! Has an American Indian ever been known to violate the sacredness
of the white flag in time of war? No. Have
Christian nations ever done so in their wars with
the Indians? We shall see. Such a disgraceful act
would be *strategy?* No; its better name would be
"*treachery.*"

But then the "*savage cruelty* of *scalping!*"—
savage, of course, because savages do it; but where
is the *cruelty* of scalping? A piece of the skin of a
man's head is cut off after he is dead; it don't hurt
him; the *cruelty* would be in *killing;* and in the
Christian world we kill hundreds of our fellow beings

in battle where the poor Indians kill one! Cutting off a small piece of the skin of a dead man's head is rather a *disgusting* thing; but let us look. What better can the Indian take? He must keep some record. These people have no reporters to follow them into battles, and chronicle their victories to the world; their customs sanction the mode, and the chiefs demand it.

If civilized warriors should treat their fallen victims thus, it would be far worse. There would be no motive or apology for it. It would be almost as bad as taking their watch, or the gold from their pockets!

But the Indians scalp the living? Yes, that *sometimes happens,* but very rarely. The scalp being only the skin with the hair, a man *might* be scalped without injuring the bone, and, of course, without destroying life; and in the hurry and confusion of battle, the wounded and fallen, supposed to be dead, have sometimes been scalped, as the Indians were rushing over them, and have afterwards risen from the field of battle and recovered. I have seen several such. These scalps, if the Indian should ever be made aware of the fact, would not be carried; but would be buried, as things which warriors would not have a right to claim, and which their superstitious fears would induce them to get rid of.

The scalp, to be a genuine one, must be *from an enemy's head,* and *that enemy dead,* and killed by the hand of him who carries and counts the scalp.

An Indian may have sufficient provocation to justify him, under the customs of his country, in slaying a man in his own tribe; but he would disgrace himself in such case by taking the scalp.

Scalps are the Indian's *badges* or *medals,* which he must procure by his own hand; he can neither buy nor sell them without disgracing himself; and when he dies, they are buried in his grave with him; his sons can't inherit them; if they want scalps, they must procure them in the same way as their father got his.

Prisoners of war are made in savage warfare as well as in civilized nations. The cruelty of savages to their prisoners is sometimes terrible, but this has been much exaggerated. Their modes of *torturing* prisoners of war, in the few instances that we know of, have been cruel and diabolical, almost beyond the reach of imagination; but these occurrences have been but very rare at any time, and for the last half-century have not been heard of at all.

All tribes *exchange* prisoners, precisely as is the practice in civilized nations, as far as equal exchanges can be made; the remainder of those not exchanged are adopted into the tribe, where they are captives; and as far as there are widows of warriors who have been killed in battle, these prisoners are compelled to marry them and support them and their children; the surplus are adopted into the tribe, with all the rights and privileges of other citizens, and go to war with them, and make reliable and efficient warriors, even against their own nation.

The *torturing* of *prisoners* is therefore nowhere a general custom, nor a frequent mode, as the world has been led to believe. In the isolated cases which have been known, the relations of persons who have been cruelly tortured by the enemy's tribe, have demanded of the chiefs one or two of the prisoners taken, to wreak their revenge upon ; and the chiefs, after a long deliberation and hearing of the grounds of the claim, have handed over the prisoners demanded, to the women related to the person or persons who have suffered ; and their modes of cruelty have, in some cases, no doubt, been as cruel and fiendish as the accounts we have heard of them.

Wars are ended, and treaties of peace made amongst the Indian tribes, much in the same manner as amongst civilized nations ; but from the causes above named, *peace establishments* amongst them are less solid, and of less duration.

The chiefs and warriors come together in treaties under the white flag, and take their seats in two semicircles on the ground, facing each other, each warrior having his head decorated with two eagle's quills, one white, and the other blood red, informing their enemies that they are ready for war or for peace. In these treaties the *calumet* (or pipe of peace) is used. The calumet is strictly a *sacred* pipe, differing in appearance and in its uses from all others. It is public property, and always kept in the possession of the chief, and only used on such occasions.

For this purpose, in the centre of the circle
formed by the chiefs and warriors seated in treaty,
the *calumet* rests in two little crotches, charged with
tobacco, and ready to be smoked when the treaty
stipulations are agreed upon; when each chief, and
after him, each warrior of the two tribes, in turn,
draw one whiff of smoke through the sacred stem,

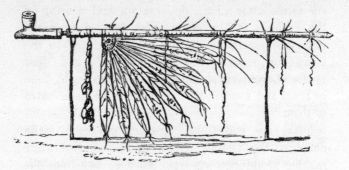

as the solemn engagement to abide by the terms of
the treaty. These treaties are all verbal, of course,
as they have no means of recording them; and the
smoking through the sacred stem is equivalent to the
" signing" of a treaty, which they are unable to do
in writing.

CHAPTER V.

Medicine Men—Looking at the Sun—Medicine Wedding—
Rain Makers — Rain Stoppers — Medicine Lodge — The
"Great White Medicine"—Medicine Bag.

NDIAN life has many phases, and here we suddenly enter upon a new and a different chapter.

Amongst ignorant, and consequently superstitious, people, mysteries are so mixed up with the actions and thoughts of their lives, that it is necessary we should know something of them fully to understand the people and their customs.

The American Indians are all more or less superstitious, and all have their physicians, who deal in roots, and herbs, and other specifics, and also pretend to great and marvellous cures by *mysteries*, or a kind of *sorcery*, which they practise as the last resort with their patients, when all the other attempted remedies have failed.

These Indian doctors were called by the Frenchmen, who were the first traders on the frontiers, "*Médecins*," the French word for physicians; and by

83

a subsequent frontier population, "*Medicine Men;*" and all mysteries, "*Medicine,*" as synonymous with mystery. We shall have, therefore, *Medicine Men, Medicine Drums, Medicine Rattles, Medicine Dances, Medicine Rocks, Medicine Fire,* and a great many other medicine things to deal with before we are at the end of this little book.

To begin. On the title-page we have an illustration of a *Medicine Man,* a *Professor* of mysteries (a Blackfoot doctor) in the full sense of the word; and in the full dress and performance of his mysteries over a dying patient. Here is a gentleman who gains laurels without going to war—who stays at home and takes care of the women and children. His fame and his influence, which often exceed that of the chief of the tribe, are gained without risk of life, by a little legerdemain and cunning, which are easily practised upon a superstitious people, who are weak enough to believe that his mystic arts often produce miracles.

Whilst residing in the American Fur Company's Factory at the mouth of the Yellowstone River, on the Upper Missouri, I had an opportunity of witnessing a Blackfoot doctor's display, in this identical costume (the skin of a yellow bear), over a dying patient, whom he had placed on the ground, and was hopping over and over, and pawing about with his hands and his feet, in the manner that a bear might have done, and who breathed his last under his strange and even frightful gesticulations, and growls, and groans.

The day after this pitiable farce, upon which some hundreds of his tribe were looking, and crying with their hands over their mouths, I painted his portrait as here seen, and also purchased, at an extravagant price, the extraordinary dress, with all its appendages, which has formed an interesting object in my Indian Collection, and been examined by hundreds of thousands of persons in London and in Paris.

Every tribe has its physicians; and all physicians deal (or profess to deal) in mysteries (or medicine). There is nothing but what they will attempt to do by the powers of their *medicine;* and if they fail, they have generally not much trouble in making so superstitious a people believe that something was wrong in the time of day—in the weather—or (what is more probable) in their want of faith, to interfere with their complete success.

Each one of these Indian physicians, during his lifetime of practice, conjures up and constructs some frightful conception for his *medicine dress,* strung with skins of deformed animals, reptiles, and birds —the hoofs of animals—the claws and toe-nails of birds—the skins of frogs, of toads, of bats, and everything else that he can gradually gather to consummate his ugliness, and the frightfulness of the sounds made by their grating and rattling as he dances, with his face hidden underneath them; adding to them the frightful flats and sharps of his growling and squeaking voice, and the stamping of his feet, as he dances and jumps over and around his dying patient.

The doctor never puts on his frightful dress until he goes to pay his last visit to his patient, and when he moves through the village with this dress on, it is known to all the villagers that the patient is dying; and from sympathy, as well as from a general custom, they all gather around in a crowd to witness the ceremony; and all, with the hand over the mouth, commence crying and moaning in the most pitiable manner.

All persons in Indian societies breathe their last under the operation of these frightful mysteries, if a doctor be near; and all the crowd seem to have more or less faith in the efficiency of this *dernier ressort*. From what I have seen and learned (as they are said in some instances to cure), these ingenious jugglers sometimes put on the official garb of monstrosities, and call the villagers together to witness the *miraculous* cure of a patient whose disease they alone have previously discovered to have taken a favourable change.

One such success in presence of the whole village is enough—it gains him presents to last him his lifetime, and a renown that nothing can shake. And on the other hand, if his patient dies, which of course is generally the case, he gets along by condoling with the relations, and assuring them that for some purpose which they are not allowed to know, the Great Spirit has called their friend away; and that when such is the case, his medicines are of no avail.

These jugglers, I have said, exist in every tribe,

and are invariably looked upon by the people as *oracles*, as *sorcerers*, as *soothsayers*, as *high priests*. They officiate in all religious ceremonies, of which they have many ; and are entitled to a seat with the chiefs in the councils of the nation. Their influence, therefore, is very great, and for the traveller passing through their country, it is as necessary to have the good will and countenance of these dignitaries, as it is to have his passport to travel on the continent of Europe. They are a sort of *octroi* to every village, and at one's first entry, after conversing, and smoking a pipe with the chief, the next important inquiry should be for the *great medicine man ;* with a little present given *expressly* in compliment to " his great fame, which you have heard of at a long distance."

The results of this little prudence, at first interview, will be sure to be a kind and friendly welcome everywhere; and most likely, as the author has several times experienced, a regular and formal *installation,* in a convocation of medicine men, as Doctor (or Fellow) of Mysteries, by the presentation of a *shi-shi-quoin !*—a *mystery rattle,* the usual *badge* of that enviable Order.

Some unaccountable cure, or other effect, it matters little what, first entitles an Indian to the appellation of mystery or medicine; and once lucky enough to gain the public confidence in this way, it requires no very great degree of tact and cunning, amongst those ignorant people, to keep it up through the remainder of life.

Medicine men are perhaps more often made by

some mere accident, than by any long and laboured design, which often costs them great pain, with the danger of a great failure, resulting in a disgrace as lasting as their fame would be in case of success. For instance, when I was residing in a large Sioux village on the Upper Missouri, I was one day attracted by a great crowd surrounding a man who was endeavouring to show his people that he was *great medicine.* The custom which is often practised amongst them, and which he was trying, they call " *Looking at the Sun.*"

Here was a man, naked, with the exception of his breech-cloth; with splints about the size of a man's finger run through the flesh on each breast, to which cords were attached, and their other ends tied to the top of a pole set firmly in the ground, which was bending towards him, by nearly the whole weight of his body hanging under it as he was leaning back, with his feet slightly resting on the ground. He held his *medicine bag* in one hand and his bow and arrows in the other, and in this position was endeavouring to look at the sun, from its rising in the morning until it set at night; moving himself around the circle, inch by inch, as the sun moved.

His friends were gathered around him, singing, and reciting the heroic deeds of his life, and his many virtues, and beating their drums and throwing down for him many presents. to encourage him and increase his strength; whilst his enemies and the sceptical were laughing at him, and doing all they could to embarrass and defeat him. If he succeeds, under all these difficulties, in looking at the sun all day, without fainting and falling, " the Great Spirit holds him up," and therefore he is *great medicine,* and he has nothing else to do to make him, for the rest of his life, a *medicine man ;* and compliments and presents are bestowed upon him in the greatest profusion. But if his strength fails him and he falls, no matter how near to his complete success, shouts and hisses are showered upon him, and his disgrace not only attaches to him for the moment, for having dared to set himself up as a *medicine,* but the scars left on his breasts are pointed to as a standing disgrace in his tribe, as long as he lives.

It is easily seen that this is a somewhat dangerous experiment to make, and is therefore more seldom resorted to as the mode of making a doctor than many others that might be named.

Whilst I was residing amongst the tribe of *Puncahs,* living farther down, on the bank of the Missouri, I witnessed another mode of the self-creation of a *medicine man,* which one will easily conceive to have been much more agreeable, and no doubt equally efficient in its results.

Hongs-kay-de, a gallant little warrior of eighteen years, and son of the chief, took it into his head (when his father had told him he was a man, and old enough to marry, and gave him nine horses, and a handsome wigwam to live in, and other presents to start him in the world) to marry four wives in one day. Major Sanford, the government agent, and myself were lucky enough to be present on the merry occasion, and to witness the exciting scene which took place on a little hill just back of their village, where he had assembled the whole tribe to witness the plan which he contrived, and which they as yet but partly anticipated.

It seems he had gone to one of the subordinate chiefs, who had a very pretty little daughter of thirteen or fourteen years of age, and made arrangements for her hand in marriage, for which he was to make him a present of two horses and other things, and the chief was to meet him exactly at noon on the top of that little hill, on a certain day, with his daughter, where the horses would be ready, and the exchange made, according to promise ; but the condition of this was to be profound secrecy until he asked for the hand of the girl at that place.

He then went to a second chief, who also had a beautiful daughter about twelve years old, and made with him a similar arrangement, and also on the same condition of secrecy. He then went to a third, and afterwards to a fourth chief, each of whom had a beautiful daughter, and for whose hands he stipulated precisely in the same manner as with the first, enjoining in each case profound secrecy, and appointing the same hour and the same place for the ceremony, having thus disposed of eight of his horses, keeping one for his own riding.

The appointed day arriving, he invited the whole village to attend his wedding, which was to take place at noon, on the top of the little hill, back of the village, where all the villagers assembled. It was a beautiful scene, the hill was completely covered. The chiefs were all seated around on the ground, leaving a little space in the centre, where the ceremony was to take place.

At the moment appointed the gallant young and new-made chief (for his father had that day abdicated in his favour) presented himself with his waving plumes, in the centre; and addressing himself to the chief whom he had first arranged with, and whose little daughter was sitting by his side in a very pretty dress—" My friend, you promised me the hand of your daughter in marriage this day, and I was to present you two horses; was this so?" " Yes," replied the chief. " The horses are standing here and are ready. I now demand the hand of your daughter."

The chief rose and led up his little daughter, placing her hand in that of the young chief, which was followed by a great shout of applause by the multitude, who were then about to disperse.

The proud little fellow then said to the crowd, " My friends, be patient;" and, turning to the second chief with whom he had arranged—" My friend, you agreed to give me the hand of your beautiful daughter in marriage on this day and at this place, and I was to give you two horses; was this so?" " Yes," replied the chief. " Then I expect you to perform your promise—I demand the hand of your daughter in marriage." The chief then arose and led up his little daughter, and, like the first one, placed her hand in that of the young chief; and precisely in

the same manner he demanded and received the
hands of the daughters of the other two chiefs whom
he had last arranged with, and, taking two in each
hand, he said to the chiefs, " This day makes me
medicine?"   " Yes."   " My father has this day
made me chief of the Puncahs! Am I not a *medicine chief?* " to which the whole tribe shouted with
one voice, " How, how ! "   (Yes, yes!)

Hongs-kay-de then descended the hill triumph-
antly, leading off to the village his four beautiful
little wives in their pretty dresses, two in each
hand, the crowd all following, to his own wigwam,
which was thenceforth the wigwam of the medicine
chief.

I have before said that the *medicine men* will
undertake to do anything and everything by their
mystic operations, however impossible or ridiculous
it may be.   But in these efforts where the results
are in the least uncertain, the constituted *medicine
men* take especial care not to run any risk by making
a second attempt ; but they superintend and manage
the preliminary forms, leaving younger aspirants to
run the chances of failure or success.

In the *Mandan* tribe I found they had "*Rain-
makers*" and also "*Rain-stoppers*," who were reputed *medicine men,* from the astonishing fact of
their having made it rain in an extraordinary drought,
or for having stopped it raining when the rain was
continuing to an inconvenient length.

For this purpose, in a very dry time, when their
maize and other vegetables are dying for want of

rain, the *medicine men* assemble in the *Medicine Lodge* (a large public wigwam built expressly for *medicine* operations, *councils*, etc.), and sit around a fire in the centre, from day to day smoking and praying to the Great Spirit for rain, while the requisite number of young men volunteer to try to make it rain. Each one of these, by ballot, takes his turn to mount on the top of the wigwam at sunrise, with his bow and arrows in his hand, and shield on his arm, talking to the clouds and asking for rain—or ranting and threatening the clouds with his drawn bow, *commanding* it to rain.

One of these young men, who flourishes throughout the whole day in this manner, in presence of the crowds gathered around him, and comes down at sunset without having succeeded, can never, on any occasion, again pretend to *medicine*, "his *medicine* is not strong."

After several days of unsuccessful attempts have passed off in this way, with a clear sky, some one more lucky than the rest happens to take his stand on a day in which a black cloud will be seen moving up, it is reported through the village that "his *medicine* is better," when the whole tribe will gather round him to hear him boast, to see him strut and bend his bow upon the clouds, commanding it to rain; and when he sees the rain actually falling in the distance, to see him let fly his arrow (which by his dexterity, as the string snaps, is turned into his hand with the bow), and pointing with his finger, "There! my friends, you have seen my arrow go, there is a hole in that cloud, we shall soon have rain enough." The rain begins to fall in torrents, the gaping multitude are hidden in their wigwams, but this successful *débutant* in mysteries still stands, sawing the air and commanding it to *continue raining*, until he is completely drenched, that the Mandans may have no further cause to complain. When he comes down he is a "*medicine man*," the doctors give him a feast and a great ceremony, and a shi-shi-quoin (a doctor's rattle).

These manœuvres are very wonderful, and there are two things about them that are curious—the *one*, that when the doctors commence "rain making" they never fail to succeed; for when the ceremony is once begun, they are obliged to keep it up from day to day until rain begins to fall; and the *other*, that those who once succeed in making it rain, in presence of the whole village, never undertake it a second time. "The whole village have seen me make it rain, they all know what I can do, and I would rather give other young men a chance."

Every Indian village has its *medicine* (or mystery) lodge, a sort of town-hall, strictly a *public building*, in which their councils are held, and all their religious ceremonies performed. These sacred places, which are closed most of the year, were generally granted to me as the place to paint my portraits in, which they always looked upon and treated as great *medicine*, and myself as the greatest of *medicine men*, for painting their chiefs and warriors, in whose portraits they often discovered "the corners of the mouth and the eyes to move," considering, therefore, that there must be life, to a certain degree, in them.

Amongst the Mandans I was soon the talk of all the village, from the portraits I had made of the war-chief and the great doctor. My wigwam was filled with the chiefs and warriors from day to day, and the whole village assembled in crowds around it. I was styled the greatest of all *medicine*. I received the doctor's badge, a beautiful shi-shi-quoin, and was regularly named, "*Te-hee-pe-nee Washee!*" (the *Great White Medicine*).

The wives of several of the chiefs brought their beautiful and modest little daughters to the door of my wigwam in splendid, pretty costumes, and the interpreter to explain, to know if I should like to marry ; all of which complimentary and tempting offers I was obliged, from various reasons, to decline. My reasons seemed to be sufficient, and my answers, though a disappointment, to give no offence.

My gun and pistols, with percussion caps, which they had not seen before, were great mysteries, and no one was willing to touch them. The remaining half of a box of lucifer matches I had, was also great *medicine*, and was soon exhausted by one of the *medicine men*, who turned it to great account after I had given it to him, by a mode he soon discovered, of igniting the matches by drawing them between his teeth, and "making fire in his mouth," which he did with wonderful effect, amongst the astonished villagers, until the box was unfortunately exhausted. His *medicine* was much improved for the while by this little lift, but he told me he lost it all when his matches gave out.   The poor fellow seemed losing caste by the unfortunate exhaustion of his matches, and I presented him a little *sun-glass* which I carried in my pocket, by which he could light his pipe anywhere when the sun shone, and which, I explained, he could never wear out.   This, therefore, was a greater wonder to him than the other, and more highly valued.   He gave me a very beautiful pair of leggings for it, and until the day that I left them he had crowds about him to see him " draw fire from the sun ! "

Medicine Bag.—This is one of the most important and extraordinary *medicine* things in all Indian tribes.   This curious appendage to the person pertains not only to *medicine men*, but to every male person in Indian society, whether warrior or brave, over the age of fifteen or sixteen years, the usual time of life when it is first instituted.

A lad of that age is said to be " making his *medicine*," when he absents himself from his father's wigwam for several successive nights and days, during which time no one makes any inquiries about him ; it is enough to know, or to suppose, that he is " making his *medicine*."   During this absence he is fasting the whole time, and the first animal, reptile, or bird, that he dreams of, he considers the Great Spirit has designated, and introduced to him in his dream, to be his mysterious protection through life, his *medicine*.

He returns home, relates his dream to his parents,

who make him a choice feast, to which he invites his relatives and as many of his friends as he chooses, who all compliment and congratulate him on his success. After the feast he starts out and traps or hunts for the animal or bird until he kills it, and obtains the entire skin, which he prepares and preserves as nearly in the size and shape of the living animal as possible. This he carries about his person the most of his life as his *talisman*, a charm that protects him from all harm, and to which he attributes all the good luck of his life; and which he confidently believes is to accompany and protect him in the world to come; it always being buried with him with the greatest care.

To go to battle without his *medicine bag* would be to go with a " faint heart," and under the conviction that he would be killed. To lose it in battle is to live in disgrace in his tribe, as "a man without *medicine*," until he can procure another, *in battle*, by adopting that of an enemy whom he has slain; his *medicine* is then *reinstated;* but by no means can he ever *institute* a second *medicine* if he loses his first, no matter by what means.

No money therefore could purchase an Indian's *medicine bag*, though such things have in several instances been presented to me by warriors who had taken them in battle, together with the scalps of their enemies.

These talismans are of all sizes, from the skin of a mouse, hidden under the dress, to the size of a duck, a loon, an otter, a badger, and even sometimes to the skin of a wolf, and therefore exceedingly awkward to carry.

I recollect that when I was painting the portrait of a Camanchee chief, I inquired his name, which another chief, sitting by, gave me, as *Ish-a-ro-yeh* (he who carries a wolf). I expressed my surprise at his getting such a name, and inquired if he had ever carried a wolf? to which he replied, "Yes, I always carry a wolf," lifting up his *medicine bag* made of the skin of a white wolf, and lying by the side of him, as he was sitting on the ground.

Medicine men and mysteries I need say no more of in this place. I shall therefore end this chapter here, and have something more to say of them and their doings in future pages.

CHAPTER VI.

Indian's Colour and Form—Indian's Painting--Wild Horses and
Buffaloes—The Prairies.

IN the midst of those vast plains denominated
the valley of the Missouri, let us take a
little further look yet at the numerous
tribes and their modes, and the country about us,
before we sweep off across the Rocky Mountains, or
into the ever-green valleys of the Essequibo and the
Amazon, in South America.

Besides the *Sioux* and the *Mandans*, there are the
fierce and terrible *Blackfoot*, and the beautiful
Crows, with their long and glossy-black hair trailing
on the ground as they walk; the *Knistineux*, the
Assinneboins, the *Ojibbeways*, the *Shiennes*, the
Pawnees, the *Omahas*, the *Ioways*, the *Saukies*,
the *Winnebagos*, the *Osages*, the *Camanchees*, and
yet many other tribes, all of whom I have lived
amongst, and studied their looks and their modes.

In general, in their ways of life, in the chase, in
war, and in their amusements, of which they have
many, they bear a strong resemblance to each other,
as well as in their colour and features.

99

Their colour, which has often been described as red, as yellow, and more often as copper colour, is not exactly either; but more correctly described as *cinnamon colour*, the exact colour of cinnamon bark; sometimes a little more dark, and at others more light; but that may with truth be said to be the standard of colour amongst the American tribes.

Their forms are generally very perfect and handsomely proportioned, much more so than those of any civilized people, owing chiefly to the facts that they are so constantly exercising their naked limbs in the open air, free from the enervating and weakening effects of heavy costumes, and also the rigid manner in which all American Indian infants, without exception, are reared in cribs (or cradles),

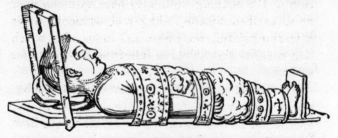

their backs lashed to straight boards for the space of six months or a year, giving straightness to the spine and the limbs, which last them through life.

All the American Indians have straight and black hair, and generally (though contrary to the opinion of the world), exceedingly fine and silky. Their eyes (though their effect is black) are of a deep and reddish-brown, and their teeth, almost without exception, uniform and regular in their arrangement, and white and sound, even to old age.

These people have probably got the appellation of " Red Indians " from their habit of using so much red ochre and vermilion, their favourite colours, in painting their bodies and faces, rather than from their natural colour, which I have already said is not red.

The habit of painting is much the same in all the various tribes. They mix their colours with bears' grease ; and, with the aid of a little bit of broken looking-glass, which they buy of fur traders, they daub the paint on with their fingers used for brushes. Paint is considered by them as a part of their dress ; and few Indians allow themselves to be seen in the morning until they have spent an hour or so at their toilette, oiling and arranging their hair, and painting their faces and limbs, after which they consider themselves in full dress, and ready for society.

This would seem to be a great deal of trouble, and to occupy much of their time uselessly ; but then it will be borne in mind that these people have little else to do, and time is not so valuable to them as it is to other people. They are excessively vain of their personal appearance, and well they may be, for, as I have said, their fine and manly figures, reared in, and used to, the open air, without the flabbiness and emaciation which overclothing generally produces, have a roundness and beauty which the civilized world cannot produce.

The tribes which I have above named, living chiefly in a country stocked with buffaloes and wild horses, also hunt and go to war much in the same manner.

The wild horses, which were no doubt first introduced into America by the Spanish invaders of Mexico, have in time wandered away and spread over the prairies as high as the fifty-first degree of north latitude, affording the Indians, who catch and convert them to their use, the means of killing the buffaloes and other game with more ease, and also of carrying on their warfare with more effect; and what is best of all, a pleasurable and healthful mode of exercise in the open plains, so conducive to strength and manly beauty.

The buffaloes, we have a right to believe, have been created for the use and happiness of the Indian tribes, who exist almost entirely on their flesh, clothing themselves and constructing their dwellings with their skins, and converting almost every part of these useful animals to the supply of their various wants and comforts. Their tongues, when cured, are amongst the greatest of luxuries, and equally so the hump (or fleece, as it is familiarly called) on the shoulders; the rest of the flesh is about equal to the best of beef. Of their skins their comfortable dwellings are made, and their beautiful robes, as already explained. Their sinews are used for strings to their bows, and many other purposes; the bones of the shoulders form the trees for their saddles; their brains are used for dressing their skins; the bones of their legs are broken up for their marrow, which resembles and equals the richest of butter; and their hoofs are boiled up for glue, which they use in the construction of their beautiful bows and other weapons.

These noble and useful animals roam over the same .vast and boundless prairies of green grass where the wild horses graze, and are often seen in herds of many thousands together. One can easily imagine that here is the easiest and most independent region for the Indians to live in; and it is here, and from these causes, no doubt, that the healthiest and most beautiful races of men are found that are to be met with in America, or perhaps in the world.

It is over these interminable carpets of green, dotted with flowers of all colours—where the Indian gallops on his wild horse, his wants all supplied, and his mind as free as the air that he breathes—that man, in the unshackled freedom of his nature, extends, and has extended his hand in friendship, to all strangers in his country, before he has been ensnared by the craft and cunning of the mercenary white man.

A few words must be said of the *prairies*, the dwellings of savage steeds and savage beeves. But, my anxious little readers, what shall I say? I am here beginning to fear that this little book is going to be five times too small for all that I want to describe to you. If we could together leap from the deck of a steamer upon one of the grassy banks of

the Upper Missouri, and clamber up the sloping
sides of the bluff, on our hands and feet, knocking
the bowing lilies of yellow, and blue, and of red, and
the gay sunflowers, from our faces ; and leaving
the purple violets and gushing ripe strawberries
under our feet till we come back, and take a *glance*
from its rounded top over the vast expanse of green
and of blue beneath and around us—of the serpentine
windings of the river above and below us, with its
vast alluvial meadows alternating on one side and
the other; and, back of them, the thousands of shorn
and green bluffs sloping down like infinite ranges
of grass-covered ramparts and redoubts—and, back
of them again, in the east and the west, an ocean of
green, enamelled with all colours at our feet, but
terminating in a horizon of blue—you would get in
that *glance*, a partial knowledge of an American
prairie. But if at this point we could mount our
horses together, and gallop to the east or to the west ;
here a covey of grouse fluttering from under our
horses' feet ; next, the swift antelope bounding over
the surface ; the frightened deer rising and springing
from its lair ; and farther on, the huge white wolf,
with a dogged sauciness and reluctance, licking his
hungry chaps as he walks slowly out of our way, with
the bristles raised on his ugly back as he stands and
scans us as we pass, to smell and follow in our track
behind us—we should then be gathering further
knowledge of the prairie. But we go on ; the noble
elks have " taken the wind," and are sweeping away
to the right or the left ; the stately moose, under his

long and unbroken trot, and his mighty horns, passes
out of sight; the funny little prairie dogs in myriads,
barking from the tops of their mounds of dirt,
dart into their burrows, and our horses are brought
to the ground by breaking into their vaulted under-
ground villages; and the huge and frightful rattlesnakes are seen coiled and ready for a leap—we are
still wiser. And yet farther on, a band of wild
horses, with their rising manes and tails, and starting
eyeballs glaring upon us, put off for a five-mile
heat before they stop; and on—on—on—again, and
far beyond, a straight black line forms all the
western horizon! and over it, to the right, a cloud
of smoke is rising from the ground! "That can't
be a fire?" No, my young friends; we are now
in the midst of a great and level prairie—we are
"out of sight of land;" the black streak you see is
formed by the backs of a large herd of buffaloes,
and the cloud of dust which you see, is raised by
their feet, which shows us they are in motion, with
a party of Sioux Indians with arrows and lances
pushing them up on the flanks and in their rear.
On—on, farther yet; and at length the black streak
disappears, they are all out of sight; but the cloud
still rises—and rises yet, as on we go. And at last
we discover, like mere specks in the distance, here
and there, individual objects moving in various
directions, and evidently nearing us, as we move on.
Next we find the green sward under our horses' feet
cut to pieces, and looking, in the distance, much
like a newly-ploughed field; the herd has here

passed; and in the distance we discover here and
there black specks lying upon the surface, and horsemen galloping to them and dismounting.   We will
rein up our horses to them—don't be afraid : put on
a bold and calm front (the Indians always admire a
bold and daring man), and offer them your hand.

Smiling and exulting, as they shake their heads to
part their falling locks from before their eyes, come
dashing up from different directions, on their puffing
and snorting little horses, with inflated nostrils and
shaggy manes, a hundred warriors astride their
horses' naked backs, with bows and lances in their
hands; they rush up with the friendly hand extended; but our horses, like civilized *people*, have a
dread of the savage—and we must dismount, or be
dismounted.   We are all upon our feet, Indians and
all, and our horses held ; a shaking of hands takes
place.   Next moment we are seated on the ground,
and the pipe is lit and passed round.   Here is a
pause and a rest for all, for all are tired.   A conversation takes places ; and in the midst of this, what
do we see ?   In the distance, a moving, unintelligible
mass, of all colours.   It approaches ; and, at last, we
see it is a phalanx of several hundred women and
children, with three or four times that number of
dogs, coming out from their village to skin the
slaughtered animals, and cut up the meat and trans-
port it to their village.   We see no more, for the
refreshed hunters have invited us to their village ;
and remounted, we fall in their wake, leaving the
women and children to do the rest.

Their village, as I have described, is built of skin-covered wigwams. We are taken to the chief's tent—we smoke the pipe with him, seated on beautifully-garnished robes and rush mats spread upon the ground; we feast with him and the hunters in his hospitable dwelling, and lodge in it during the night. Our horses have been well taken care of by the chief's sons and relations, and brought to us in the morning when we are ready to start back.

But where are we? only one day in the prairie! And so we might go on from day to day, for a month of days, before we should find its end. We have yet to *return*: have we seen all? Not quite—we take a different route.

CHAPTER VII.

Catching Wild Horses—Turning to the Left—Walking the Circle—Buffalo Chase—The Giant Bull.

ILD horses, I have said, are the shyest animals of the prairies, and oftentimes run in immense herds. The wild horse will generally run from the approach of a man at a mile distance, without "getting the wind," such is the power of his eye in distinguishing his enemy man from wild animals, when the elk may be approached within half-a-mile, and the buffalo and deer oftentimes within dead-shot distance for a rifle, before they take to flight.

The Indians have a hard struggle in capturing these animals, which they generally do with the lasso, thrown from the back of another horse, while they ride at full speed. The lasso is a strong cord made of raw hide, with a noose at the end of it, which being open some four or five feet, the loop is dropped over the horse's neck, and being drawn tight chokes the animal; and the Indian, checking his own horse gradually, and drawing on the length-

108

ened cord, at last brings the animal to the ground, which falls for want of breath.

The horse is then completely at its captor's mercy, who proceeds to secure his prey, and then to tame it. For this he hobbles the animal's two fore-feet together, and then fastens a short halter with a noose around the horse's under-jaw, back of the teeth, while its mouth is wide open and it is gasping for breath.

At this moment the lasso is loosened, allowing the animal to breathe; by which, in a few moments, as it is getting strength to rise, it finds the Indian at the end of the halter, prepared to prevent its rising on to its feet. The horse makes a struggle to rise, getting only on to its fore-feet, which are fastened together, and it still remains in a sitting posture.

Before it can rise on its hind feet, it requires to throw its head quite back, which the Indian, standing in front of the animal, prevents it from doing, by leaning back, with the weight of his body on the halter. By a great many useless struggles to rise, the horse remaining yet in its sitting posture, and the Indian approaching nearer and nearer (inch by inch) to its nose, on the shortened halter, and yelling as loud as he can, the animal's fear is increased to the highest degree. The Indian still advances nearer on the tightened halter, and at length begins patting the horse on the nose, and gradually slipping his hand over its eyes, begins breathing in its nostrils, their noses being together.

After a few breaths exchanged in this manner, the

relaxation of the horse's muscles and its other motions, show that its fears are at an end—that it recognises a friend instead of a foe, in its captor; and this compromise being effected, the Indian is seen stroking down its mane, and otherwise caressing it; and in fifteen or twenty minutes he is seen riding it quietly off!

From the moment of this unaccountable compromise, the animal seems to make no further effort to escape, but becomes attached to its master, whom it recognises by the breath: which it always seems fond of exchanging from that moment.

I have witnessed these exciting scenes on a number of occasions, and always have viewed them with great surprise. It requires a severe effort to catch the horse in the first place, and then a struggle ensues which is cruel, and painful to look upon; but the excess of fatigue, of fright, and actual pain, followed by soothing and kindness, seems to disarm the spirited animal, and to attach it at once, in a mysterious way, to its new master.

You have all read of Mr. Rarey's wonderful mode of breaking and taming vicious horses, which I believe, in some respects, is very similar; but Mr. Rarey has not the wild horse *to catch.* It is very likely that an Indian could not break a vicious horse as well as Mr. Rarey; and at the same time it might be equally, if not more difficult, for Mr. Rarey to take the lasso from an Indian's hand when he has got it over the neck of a wild horse, and stop its career, and conquer and break it, as an Indian does.

The judgment of man in guiding his horse enables him, on an animal of less speed, to get alongside of a wild horse, though he seldom is able to overtake the fleetest of them. But here is something more surprising yet—the Shiennes, who capture more wild horses than any other tribe, catch a great proportion of their horses without the aid of a horse to ride ; they overtake the wild horse on their own legs ; which is done in this way : Plunging into a band of wild horses while on the back of his own horse, the Indian separates some affrighted animal from the group, and forcing it off to the right or to the left, he dismounts from his own horse, and hobbling its feet, or leaving it in the hands of a friend, he starts upon his own legs, his body chiefly naked—a lasso coiled on his left arm, a whip fastened to the wrist of his right hand, and a little parched corn in his pouch, which he chews as he runs ; and at a long and tilting pace, which he is able to keep all day, he follows the affrighted animal, which puts off at full speed.

Throwing himself between the troop and the animal he is after, and forcing it to run in a different direction, the poor creature's alarm causes it to over-fatigue itself in its first efforts, and to fall a prey to feebler efforts, but more judiciously expended. In the beginning of the chase, the horse discovers his pursuer coming towards him, when he puts off at the greatest possible speed, and at the distance of a mile perhaps, he stops and looks back for his pursuer, who is coming at his regular pace, close on to

him! Away goes again the affrighted steed, more
alarmed than ever, and at its highest speed, and
makes another halt, and another, and another; each
time shorter and shorter, as he becomes more and
more exhausted; while his cool and cunning pursuer
is getting nearer to him.   It is a curious fact, and
known to all the Indians, that the wild horse, the
deer, the elk, and other animals, never run in a
straight line : they always make a curve in their
running, and generally (but not always) to the left.
The Indian seeing the direction in which the horse
is "leaning," knows just about the point where the
animal will stop, and steers in a straight line to it,
where they arrive nearly at the same instant, the horse
having run a mile, while his pursuer has gone but
half or three-quarters of the distance.   The alarmed
animal is off again; and by a day's work of such
curves, and such alarms, before sun-down the animal's
strength is all gone; he is covered with foam, and
as his curves are shortened at last to a few rods, his
steady pursuer, whose pace has not slackened, gets
near enough to throw the lasso over the animal's
neck.   One must *imagine* the rest; what kindness
and caressing through the night (for they encamp
upon the ground), and what compromise is effected,
for the Indian rides his captured horse into the
village the next morning, having attached his lasso
with a noose around its under-jaw, and having taken
up his hobbled horse in his way.

I have said that the horse and other animals
"generally turn to the *left*."   How curious this fact,

and from what cause? All animals "bend their course." Why bend their course? Because all animals have their homes—their wonted abodes, and they don't wish to leave them: but why bend to the *left?*

I never have forgotten one of the first lessons that I had from my dear friend Darrow, in deer-stalking in the forest. "George," said he, "when a deer gets up, if the ground is level, never follow him, but turn to the left, and you will be sure to meet him; he always runs in a curve, and when he stops he is always watching his back track."

But *man* "bends his course;" man, lost in the wilderness or on the prairies, travels in a curve, and always bends his course to the *left:* why this?

While ascending the Upper Missouri, some years since, on a steamer, the vessel got aground, and there was no prospect of getting it off until the water rose, which might not be the case for some weeks. I was anxious to reach a Sioux village on the bank of that river, about one hundred miles above where we were detained, in order to be using my brushes amongst them. I left the steamer with one man to accompany me, and with my rifle in my hand, and my sketch-book on my back, we started to perform the journey on foot. In our course we had a large prairie of some thirty miles to cross, and the second day being dark and cloudy, we had no object by which to guide our course, having no compass with me at the time.

During the first day the sun shone, and we kept

our course very well—but on the next morning, though we started right ("laid our course") we no doubt soon began to *bend* it, though we appeared to be progressing in a straight line. There was nothing to be seen about us but short grass, everywhere the same ; and in the distance a straight line, the horizon all around us. Late in the afternoon, and when we were very much fatigued, we came upon the very spot, to our great surprise, where we had bivouaced the night before, and which we had left on that morning. We had turned to the left, and no doubt travelled all day in a circle. The next day, having the sunshine, we laid (and kept) our course without any difficulty.

On arriving at the Sioux village, and relating our singular adventure, the Indians all laughed at us very heartily, and all the chiefs united in assuring me that whenever a man is lost on the prairies he travels in a circle ; and also that he invariably turns to the *left;* of which singular fact I have become doubly convinced by subsequent proofs similar to the one mentioned.

The Indian having taken his wild horse in the manner above described, and broken it for the purpose, we see him (Plate III.) in the chase, by which means he supplies his family with food, and in the same manner also he contends with his enemies in battle.

The horse being the swiftest animal of the prairies, the rider on its back is able to come alongside of any animal ; and at the little distance necessary to throw

Plate III.   Buffalo Chase.—*p.* 114.

his arrows, the first arrow is generally fatal; being
sent with such force as to penetrate the heart of that
huge animal the buffalo, and oftentimes (as I have
myself witnessed) sent quite through the animal's
body, leaving a wound resembling that of a gun-
shot.

The bow used for this purpose is very short, being
more convenient for handling on horseback, and
generally not more than two feet and a-half in
length, but made of great strength, and with much
ingenuity: the main part frequently one entire piece
of bone, but more often of wood, and covered on the
back with buffalo's sinews, so closely glued together
as seldom to come apart.

Besides the bow, a long lance is often used, and
perhaps with more deadly effect in the chase than
the arrows; for the Indian, with his horse trained
to "approach," easily rides near enough to the side
of the animal to give the fatal lunge of his lance,
which seldom fails to reach the heart, tumbling the
animal instantly to the ground.

In battle and in the chase, the Indian always has
dragging behind his horse a long cord of raw hide,
which is attached to its neck; a different thing from
the lasso. The object of this cord is, in case he is
thrown from his horse, by the horse falling or stepping into holes, that he may grasp hold of it and
recover his horse, and be again upon its back. This
is called by the French, *l'arrêt* (the stop), and by
some travellers and writers, *larriette*.

Now, speaking of buffaloes, I must be allowed to

say a few words of *myself*, and some of my own
exploits, amongst buffaloes in the prairie country.

The young reader will recollect that I commenced
my early career with a strong passion for guns and
fishing-poles, and will scarcely believe that my hunting propensities lay dormant during the gap that I
have mentioned, from the affair of the "kettle of
gold," to the age of thirty-three, when I have said,
I started on my Indian campaigns; he will easily
believe that during that period, surrounded as I was
with all the temptations, and with my old Nimrod
companion, John Darrow, as my teacher, I was
making constant progress in the slaying art, and in
rifle-shooting; and that I had greatly increased,
instead of diminishing that passion which first led
me to the old saw-mill lick, and which eventu-
ally had its weight in leading me into the great
prairies of the Far West.

Poor Darrow! he was good for nothing else but
hunting; but what a veneration I had for him!
How he could trace a deer or a bear; and how deadly
the crack of his rifle! What music it was to my
young ear when I heard it sing amongst the lofty
forest trees; and how happy were those days when
John Darrow and I, in our white hunting shirts and
white caps, with our rifles trailed, entered the deep
and lonely forests to spend the day in a good "tracking snow!"

But to fight off from these scenes in my native
valley and my boyhood, and to come back to where
I left you, my young readers, in the buffalo range,

and ready for my first buffalo hunt, on the prairies of the Missouri. At the mouth of the Yellowstone River, on the banks of the Missouri, two thousand miles above St. Louis, where the American Fur Company have a large factory, or trading house, I was residing with Mr. M'Kenzie, the chief factor, when it was announced one morning by one of his men, that a large herd of buffaloes had arrived during the night, and were then grazing on a beautiful plain across the river, and but two or three miles distant.

M'Kenzie instantly resolved that he "wanted some meat," and invited me to join the hunt, for which he turned out some five or six of his best hunters, on horseback, and himself took the lead, with a small and exceedingly light and short single-barrelled fowling-piece in his hand.

They furnished me with a tremendously tall horse, called "Chouteau" (for what reason I never knew), said to be a very good animal in the chase. Several others of his men were ordered to follow at a proper distance, with one-horse carts, to bring in the meat, and we all moved off, somewhat like a regular caravan.

When we had arrived within half-a-mile or so of the unsuspecting animals, we were called to a halt, to decide upon the best mode of attack: that decided, all hands started off upon a gallop, at the signal given, ready to make the *dash* as soon as the animals took the alarm. This done, the dust was rising, and we were in the midst of them!

M'Kenzie, Major Sanford, and Chardon were the most experienced, and consequently the most successful in the melée. The repeated flashes of their guns I distinctly saw, as they seemed to be buried in the moving mass of black and dust. These men were hunting "for meat," and of course were selecting the fattest and the sleekest of the young cows for that purpose; but I had quite a different ambition; I saw in the crowd the back and horns of a huge bull towering so high above all the throng that I resolved upon his scalp or nothing.

I made several desperate lunges with old "Chouteau" into the various openings which seemed to afford me a chance of coming near to him: and as often was closed in and jammed along with the moving mass, no doubt with a most imprudent risk of my life; for hundreds on hundreds were plunging along behind me, and ready to have trampled me to death in a moment if I had lost my balance.

I at length saw my way clear, and made a desperate rush for his right side, that I might get my shot from the proper point.

My gun was a double-barrelled fowling-piece. My first shot seemed to have no effect, but the second one brought him down upon his knees, and the herd passed on. I was swept along a great distance before I could extricate myself from the throng, having no further ambition than the capture of this overgrown, and, in fact, giant of the band.

When I got relieved from the herd, I reloaded and rode back to my noble prize, who had risen up and stood balancing his huge carcass on three legs, one of his shoulders being broken. His frightful mane was raised, and his eyes bloodshot with madness and rage, as he was making lunges at me, and partly tumbling to the ground at each attempt.

Here was just the subject I wanted, for all the world : and having my sketch-book with me, I sat upon my horse, in perfect safety, and made my model change his positions as I wanted them. It is impossible to describe the demoniacal looks of this enraged animal when he bristled up and was just ready to spring upon me.

While I was engaged in this operation, M'Kenzie and Sanford came riding up to me, and laughing most excessively at me for attacking a poor old bull which scarcely the wolves would eat. I claimed a great victory nevertheless, and was perfectly satisfied with my first exploit, which, however, had a little drawback to it when Sanford asked me how it was that my horse's head was covered with blood, which I had not observed, and which was found to be issuing from a round hole through one of old "Chouteau's" ears, near to his head, where my first ball had undoubtedly passed.

My sketches completed, I finished the old bull with another shot in the head: and joining M'Kenzie and Sanford, who were looking up and claiming their victims left upon the ground they had run over, I was astonished to find that the former, with a single-barrelled gun, and with a flint lock, had selected and shot through the heart, six fat cows in the run, which was probably not over a mile distance, in which time he must have reloaded his gun five times at full speed! The carts were soon up, in the rear, and conveyed the meat, with the head and horns of my venerable bull, to the factory's larder.

I said at the end of the last chapter, that we had not seen the whole of the prairies—that "we should return by another route." We are a great way from home, so we will leave our horses and take a *canoe*.

CHAPTER VIII.

Stores laid in—The Tame Eagle—Bivouacing—Melting the Coffee-pot — Freaks of the Eagle — Stoop of the Eagle—Grizzly Bears inspecting us—Grizzly Bears overhauling us—Adieu to the Grizzlies.

SEATED in a light and frail canoe in front of the American Fur Company's Fort, at the mouth of the Yellowstone River, Ba'-tiste, Bogard, and I took leave of M‘Kenzie and his little colony, for a voyage to St. Louis, which, by the winding course of the Missouri, was but about two thousand miles ; and the whole of that way without other habitations than the occasional villages of the wild Indians ; and without inhabitants, excepting wild men and the wild animals that roamed over and through it.

Jean Ba'tiste, a Frenchman, and Abraham Bogard, a Mississippian, were two discharged hands who had been for eight or ten years in the employment of the Fur Company, trapping beavers and other furs at the base of and in the Rocky Mountains, and were now returning to St. Louis ; and of myself, more will be learned hereafter.

121

We three, then—the two first of whom with good
rifles, and knowing well how to use them; and myself
with a good double-barrelled fowling-piece, for
ducks, and geese, and prairie hens, and a first-rate
rifle for long range, and a belt with two side pistols
for nearer quarters—took our seats in our little
bark; the first in the bow, the second in the centre,
and myself in the stern, with my steering-paddle,
with which I steered it in safety, but not without some
accidents, amid snags, and sand-bars, and sawyers,
and rocks, to the wharf in St. Louis, whilst the boiling current swept us along, and Ba'tiste and Bogard,
and most of the time all three, paddled.

We had powder and ball in abundance laid in,
and our fishing tackle; some good robes to sleep
upon and under; a tin kettle, a coffee-pot, a frying-
pan, plenty of ground coffee, of sugar, and salt; each
man a spoon, a knife, and a tin cup; and though we
had no bread or butter, the little reader, whose
imagination is pretty strong, will easily see we had
a tolerable chance for enough to eat, and that there
was a glorious prospect for the indulgence of my
sportive passion, as well as the gratification of my
Indian propensities, ahead of me; and he will be just
about as much disposed to skip over the now coming
part of this little book, as I would have been inclined
to have left my little outfitted canoe and the beautiful shores of the Missouri, to have taken a nearer
cut, and footed it over land.

There are now ten thousand things of curious
interest before us, and I must needs again be brief;

for we shall have other rivers, and a great many other things to speak of.

At our starting, we had another "compagnon du voyage," which I had almost forgotten to mention. Mr. M'Kenzie had made me a present of a full-grown, domesticated war-eagle, the noble bird which the Indians so much esteem for its valour, and the quills of which they so much value to adorn the heads of chiefs and warriors. I had a perch erected for it some six or eight feet high, over the bow of the canoe, on which it rested in perfect quietude, without being fastened, silently surveying all that we passed above and below; thus forming for our little craft the most picturesque and appropriate figure-head that could be imagined.

From day to day we thus passed on, surveying the beautiful shores; the grassy and rounded bluffs rising in groups, sometimes hundreds on hundreds, appearing in the distance as if green carpets of velvet were spread-over them; sometimes speckled with herds of buffaloes grazing on their sides, which the crack of a rifle would set in motion: the scattered herds grouping together and running in little and winding paths, seemed in the distance like black snakes drawing their long carcasses over and around the hill sides.

The sand-bars in the distance sometimes seemed as if they were covered with snow, from the quantities of pelicans and white swans that were grouped upon them. The white wolves that were looking at us from the banks got an occasional pill from one of our rifles, and sometimes the terrible grizzly bears, that trace the water's edge for the carcasses of dead fish, and the buffaloes often left fastened in the mud, where large herds have been crossing the river.

We went ashore every afternoon a little before sunset, where we could discover dry wood enough to make a fire with, cooked and ate our supper; and then, leaving our fire, paddled on till some time after dark, hauling our buffalo-skins out, and, scarcely knowing what was around us, quietly spreading our beds upon the grass, lest prowling war-parties might be attracted by the smoke of our fires, and strike a blow upon us in their sudden way, mistaking us for their enemies or for some of the fur traders, against more or less of whom these people have long and just causes of complaint, and for which we are, in such cases, liable to pay the forfeit.

We were generally off again at daybreak, and usually stopped at eight or nine in the morning, to make and to take our breakfast.

At one of these delicious breakfasts, after we had been some days on our voyage, when we had just finished, my two men, observing a herd of buffaloes grazing on a hill at a short distance, took up their rifles and went for some meat.

I remained by the fire, and while making a sketch of a very pretty scene in front of me, I resolved that I would have another cup of coffee before we started, and placed the coffee-pot on the fire to make it hot. The sound of their rifles soon announced to me that they had got some meat (for they made it a rule never to lose a charge of powder for nothing), and the next moment came the throng dashing down the hill near by me. I seized my rifle and ran to a deep and narrow defile where the whole herd were aiming to pass, and placing myself in the bed of the stream then dried up, and behind a small bunch of willows, I stood unobserved, and probably unheard by them (such was the thundering of the throng as they came plunging down one side, and clambered up the other, of the deep ravine), and reloaded and fired until I had shot down some twelve or fourteen of them, each one tumbling down within a few paces from where he was struck, and several thousand passing by me within gun-shot.

This wanton slaughter, which I always regretted, was easy, was simple, and wicked; because Ba'tiste and Bogard had got meat enough to last us for several days. Not even the skins, the tongues, nor the humps, of these poor creatures were taken, but were left for the wolves to devour.

My two men joined me, having heard my firing and when we went to our little bivouac, I found my coffee all boiled away, and the seams of my poor coffee-pot all unsoldered, and the fabric falling to pieces. Was not this retribution? I shot not for meat, nor in self-defence—and I never shot for the mere pleasure of killing after that.

Our tin kettle having fallen overboard a few days before, I made a sort of coffee a few times in the frying-pan, but this was excessively awkward, and proved a decided failure; and Bogard, who had a

rabid taste for coffee, had the privilege of filling his
pocket with ground coffee and sugar, which he daily
ate from the hollow of his hand, while it lasted; and
thus was our luxury of coffee, with that of delicious
soup, which had vanished with the loss of our tin
kettle, for the rest of the voyage at an end.

Our noble and beautiful pet was a picture to look
at: he held to his perch, and could not have been
made to leave us. He was well fed with fresh
buffalo meat, and sometimes with fish. His eagle
eyes gazed upon all around him, and he seemed to be
owner and commander of the expedition. We always
found him on his stand in the morning; and during
the day, as we were gliding along, when he became
tired of his position, he would raise himself upon his
long and broad wings, and spreading them over us,
would hover and soar for miles together, a few feet
above our heads, and in precise progress with the
canoe, looking down upon us, and fanning us at
times with fresh air, and at other times shading us
from the rays of the sun!

Birds of all kinds and wild fowl, as they flew over,
this monarch of the air would gaze at from his
perch; and whenever he discovered one of his own
species soaring in the sky, or even in the clouds,
which was sometimes the case, he commenced a
chattering of recognition which no other excitement
could bring forth, and which they invariably answered.
He knew them, and could easily have gone to them in
a moment, but the perch that he clenched in his feet
he preferred, for there he was sure of his daily food.

One day, while we were passing through what is called the "Grand Detour," a deep gorge through which the river passes, with precipitous clay banks, some hundreds of feet in height, on each side, our royal guest rose suddenly, and unusually high from his perch, and flapping his long wings, flew back some distance, and kept rising, when we all of one accord exclaimed, "He has gone! he has taken final leave!" but he made a circuit or two in the air, and then a stoop, just grazing the side of the ragged clay bluff, from which he lifted a huge snake, that was writhing and twisting in his deadly grasp as he was coming towards the boat. "Sonnette! sonnette!" exclaimed poor Ba'tiste, as the snake, when the eagle was on his perch, was to hang right over his head!

It happened, luckily perhaps, not to be a rattle-snake, but a harmless reptile, probably better known to eagles than to us, which the eagle's eyes had discovered basking in the sun as we had passed, and which he had gone back for, and now on his perch, directly over poor Ba'tiste's head, was regularly making a delicious meal of. Ba'tiste soon got over his fright, and admitted that "it was all right,—that we were all hunters and adventurers together."

Annoyed to agony, and sometimes almost to death, by the mosquitoes that infest the shores of that river in some places, we generally selected a barren sand-bar or sandy beach as the place of our bivouac, for they generally fly only as far as the grass extends.

Having one night selected such a beach, and

drawn our canoe well on to it, we spread our robes
on the soft sand, and got a comfortable night's rest ;
and a little after daylight in the morning, I heard
Ba'tiste exclaim—" Voilà, Mr. Caltin ! voilà Caleb !"
(as the trappers of these regions habitually call the
grizzly bear) "regardez, Mr. !" I raised myself
up, and found Bogard and Ba'tiste rising gradually,
with their hands on their rifles, and their attention
fixed upon a monster of a grizzly bear, sitting a few
rods from us on the slope of the prairie, regularly
reconnoitring us ; and at a little distance farther,
the female with her two cubs ; about enough altogether for us three to have furnished a comfortable
breakfast, for which they were no doubt, with some
impatience, waiting.   (Plate No. IV.)

The time had passed heavily with them while
they had been waiting for us to wake up, for it is a
curious saying of the country, and probably a true
one, that "man lying down is *medicine* to a bear"
—that grizzly bears will not attack a man when he
is asleep, although they are sure to attack him if
they meet him on his feet.   We all alike knew the
motto of the country, yet I believe none of us were
quite disposed to go to sleep for our protection.

A council of war was the first thing that was
necessary ; and as we discovered, on looking around,
that these terrible beasts had been in our canoe and
hauled every article out of it on to the beach, and
pawed them open, and scattered them about ; and
that our poor eagle was gone, and swallowed, no
doubt ; and knowing the danger of attacking them,

Plate IV

Grizzly Bears overhauling us. — *p.* 128.

we agreed that our canoe was the first thing ; the scattered remnants of our property (if we could have time to collect them) the next—preferring to have our battle afterwards. We simultaneously arose, moved our canoe into the water, and got our paddles into it, and our guns safe in our hands.

The animals made no move towards us in the mean time, and we began to gather our robes and other things which were strewed in all directions. Some packages were carried several rods from the canoe, and everything excepting a couple of large portfolios of drawings which they could not untie, and a roll of canvas which had stood the test, but was sadly pawed about in the mud, were as regularly unrolled and looked into (and smelled) as they would have been in passing a custom-house in France or in Brazil, with a doubtful and suspicious passport.

We had three or four days' supply of fresh meat laid in, and some delicious dried buffalo tongues, and a quantity of pemican, all of which were devoured. My paint-box was opened, and nothing left in it—the brushes were scattered over the beach, and many of the bladders with colours tied in them, chewed, and the contents scattered and daubed, in strange mixtures of red, and green, and all colours, over everything. Two packs of Indian dresses, safely tied with thongs, were as regularly untied as if done by human hands ; and shirts, and leggings, and head-dresses, and robes, were daubed in the mud and spread out upon the beach as if to dry, or to be disposed of in lots at an auction sale. What an unprincipled overhauling this!

In taking up our sleeping robes, the enormous footprints sinking two or three inches into the hard sand, showed us that these stupid and terrible beasts had passed many times around and between our beds, which were not more, perhaps, than two or three feet apart. Was not here enough to shake one's nerves a little?

Our things thrown in confusion into our canoe for a better arrangement at a more agreeable place, we pushed out a little from the shore, and felt again at ease, knowing that the grizzly bear will never enter the water for anything.

The moment our canoe was afloat, with the accustomed flappings of his wings, the long and yellow legs of our illustrious passenger were reaching down for their perch, whilst he was drawing in his long wings, and seemingly shrugging his shoulders with satisfaction at being back to his old stand, and out of danger, as he was casting his piercing eyes around and over the gathered wreck, which he seemed to be aware of. From what hill-top or ledge this noble creature descended, or where he got his night's lodging, no one had the least knowledge.

Now we were ready for the attack—we were brave—we could flourish trumpets. Bogard and I levelled at the male—he being the nearest to us—Ba'tiste reserving his fire, which he gave to the female as she came, in all fury and with horrid growls, to the water's edge; she received his ball in her breast, and, galloping off, followed her companion, which had got our two rifle balls, and entered a thicket of high grass and weeds.

We were now floating down stream again, and though I urged my two companions to go back with me and complete the engagement, they both had fears, and most likely very prudent ones, of following those creatures into a thicket; so we left them to die, or to cure their wounds if they could, in their own way.

CHAPTER IX.

Mandan Singularities— Mandan War-Chief—Lance of the Riccarree Chief — Mah-to-toh-pa and the Crow Chief — Indian Belles—Singular Names—Tradition of the Flood— Destruction of the Mandans—Taking leave of the Mandans —A Silent Gift.

WE are now at the village of the kind and hospitable Mandans (or, as they call themselves, See-pohs-ka Nu-mah-kah-hee, *People of the Pheasants*), two hundred and fifty miles below the mouth of Yellowstone, from which we started: a tribe of two thousand, living in a village of clay-covered wigwams, on the west bank of the Missouri. My canoe and all my things are carried up by the women to the chief's wigwam, where they are to be kept in safety until I want them, and I a welcome guest while I stop—not a sixpence to pay.

The Mandans (of whom I have shown you one of their warriors in Plate No. III., and of whose *medicine* operations in *rain-making* and *rain-stopping* I have before alluded to) I considered one of the most interesting tribes that I visited, inasmuch as their language and many of their customs, as well

132

as personal appearance, were so decidedly different from all other tribes in America.

As they were not a roaming, but a stationary tribe, they all lived in one village, which was effectually protected against Indian assaults by a high and precipitous bank of the river on two sides, and a stockade of large timbers set in the ground, on the back part.

This tribe, not following the migrations of the herds of buffaloes, like the Sioux and other tribes, secured themselves against want by raising considerable fields of maize (which they always kept hidden) in sufficient quantities to answer them when the buffaloes might for a time leave their vicinity.

The most striking singularities in the personal appearance of these people were those of complexion, and the colour of their hair and eyes. I have before said that black hair, black eyes, and cinnamon colour were the national characteristics of all American savages; but to my great surprise I found amongst the Mandans, many families whose complexions were nearly white, their eyes a light blue, and their hair of a bright, silvery grey, from childhood to old age!

This singular appearance I can account for only by the supposition that there must have been some civilized colony in some way engrafted on them, but of which neither history nor tradition seem as yet to furnish any positive proof.

From having found several distinct Welsh words in use amongst them; their skin canoes round like a tub, and precisely like the Welsh coracle, and their mode of constructing their wigwams like that in use at the present day in the mountainous parts of Wales, I am strongly inclined to believe that this singularity has been caused by some colony of Welsh people who have landed on the American coast, and after having wandered into the interior, have been taken into this hospitable tribe.

The Mandans I found to be a very peaceable people, not engaging in warfare except to defend their village and preserve their existence, for which they have had many hard struggles with the Sioux and Crow Indians.

When I was with the Mandans, there were living amongst them two chiefs of great distinction, the Wolf chief, head civil-chief, and Mah-to-toh-pa (the Four Bears), head war-chief of the tribe. I painted the portraits, at full length, of these valiant and proud men ; and the latter, who became very much attached to me, I shall always consider one of the most extraordinary men who has lived amongst the American tribes.

He was in every way graceful, elegant, civil, and polite, and at the same time most gallant and invincible as a warrior. After I had painted his portrait, with which he was much pleased and astonished, he presented me his robe, with all the battles of his life painted on it, his wife being allowed time to make him an exact copy of it.

On this extraordinary robe he was represented, at full length, in fourteen battles in which he had been

victorious, and for which he had the scalps as proofs
which no one could deny.   When he gave me the
robe, lest it should be unappreciated by me, he
spread it upon the ground, and inviting me to sit
down by the side of him, he proceeded to explain to
me each group, the place where the battle was
fought, and the manner in which he gained his
success ; and for each battle he showed me and
placed in my hand, the scalp.

Several of his most celebrated warriors, who were
familiar, of course, with his military exploits, were
listening to his explanations, and nodded assent to
every scene which he described, and which I wrote
down, word for word, in my note-book; and amongst
those fourteen achievements there was one which he
described in this way :—

"This spear," said he, taking it up from the
ground behind him, and laying it on the robe—a
spear of some eight feet in length, and ornamented
with a number of red and white eagles' quills, and
with a long blade of steel,—"this spear once belonged to the war-chief of the Riccarrees (a tribe
about equal in numbers to the Mandans, and living
two hundred miles below them on the same bank of
the river).   The Riccarrees have always been making war upon us, and in one of their cowardly midnight attacks upon our village, when a great many
of our young men, as well as women and children,
were killed, my brother, younger than myself, was
missing ; and three days after the battle, in which
we had driven our enemies away, I found the body

of my brother amongst the willows, with the blade
of this spear remaining in his body. I recognised
the spear as belonging to the treacherous war-chief
of the Riccarrees, having seen it and handled it
when we had sat together and smoked the calumet
in a treaty of peace but a few months before; many
of my warriors also recognised the spear. I preserved it, with the blood of my brother's body dried
on its blade, and I then swore to avenge my brother's
death with my own hand.

"I kept this spear for three years, and no opportunity occurring, and unwilling to spill the blood of
the innocent by bringing the two tribes into conflict,
I resolved to get my revenge in another way. For
this purpose I put my body and face into war paint,
which a chief, by our custom, is not in the habit of
doing. I took parched corn in my pouch to last
me several days, and without other weapon than
this spear in my hand, I started off, unknown to
my people, for the Riccarree village, travelling over
the prairies by night, and lying secreted during the
day.

"In this manner I came near to the Riccarree
village on the sixth day. I secreted myself during
the last day, and when it was dark I approached
and entered the village without danger of being detected. Knowing the wigwam of the war-chief, I
loitered about it, and often peeped in and saw him
seated by the fire smoking his pipe.

"His wife at length went to bed; and after he
had sat and smoked out another pipe by himself, he

went to bed also.   The time for me had then
arrived; the fire was almost out, and the wigwam
quite dark.   I gently opened the door and walked
in with the spear in my hand, and sat down by the
fire.   There was a pot hanging over the fire with
some meat in it, which I commenced eating, as I
was almost starved to death.   Whilst I was eating
I heard his wife ask him what man that was eating
from the pot in their wigwam; to which the chief
replied, 'No matter; I suppose the man is hungry.'
After I had satiated my hunger, I very gradually
stirred the fire a little with my foot, until I just got
light enough to see my way to my enemy, when I
arose and drove the lance to his heart.   I darted
from the wigwam with the lance in one hand and
his scalp in the other, and made my way as fast as
possible towards the Mandan village, without their
knowing where the enemy was from, or which way
he had gone.

"I travelled fast all that night, and lay secreted
during the following day, and so travelled night after
night until I entered the Mandan village in triumph,
with the scalp of the war-chief of the Riccarrees
resting on the point of his own spear.   This, my
friend," said he, "is the scalp of that enemy, and
this is the spear which I drew from the body of my
brother, and with which, I believe, it was the will of
the Great Spirit I should avenge his death.   You
see, my friend, that I have done it, and the blood of
both is now dried upon its blade.

"This, my friend, was unlike the deeds of Mah-to-toh-pa; but I went to slay a dog, who died as he deserved. Though he was a war-chief, and had many scalps, he was not an honourable man; he hung about our village like the sneaking wolves in the night, and even scalped our women and children when they were bathing on the shore of the river. If he had been an honourable man, Mah-to-toh-pa would have given him a chance for his life in equal combat; but as his life had been that of a coward, it would not have been just that he should die the death of a brave man."

Now, the rest of this little book might be filled with the exploits of Mah-to-toh-pa; but I will describe *one more*, and then we will pass on. While sitting upon the robe, Mah-to-toh-pa showed me the scalp of a brave man—a celebrated chief of the Crows; and, pointing to the illustration on the robe, dictated while the interpreter described in this way:—

"The Crows have long been our enemies; their war-parties have often attacked our village and our hunting-parties when they have been upon the plains. A few years since, many hundred Crow warriors appeared on the prairies, not far distant from the Mandan village, when Mah-to-toh-pa, with his warriors, went out to meet them. When the two war-parties were coming near to each other, on a level plain, and just ready for battle, they halted, and the war-chief of the Crows sent a white flag to the Mandans, with this message:—'Is Mah-to-toh-pa, the war-chief of the Mandans, there? He is a brave man. If he leads the Mandan war-party to-day, let him come out alone, and he and I will decide this combat, and save the lives of our brave warriors. Hora-to-ah, war-chief of the Crows, sends this message.'

"To this Mah-to-toh-pa replied—' Hora-to-ah is a chief and a brave warrior, and worthy of Mah-tó-toh-pa. Mah-to-toh-pa leads the Mandan war-party this day. Mah-to-toh-pa is glad to meet the war-chief of the Crows, and save the blood of his brave warriors. It is Mah-to-toh-pa, war-chief of the Mandans, who sends this reply.'

"After the messenger had returned, the Crow chief was seen galloping out upon the plain, on a milk-white horse, with a shield on his arm and a gun in his hand.

"Mah-to-toh-pa was not slow to meet him. They passed each other twice, and fired with their guns without effect; but Mah-to-toh-pa's powder-horn was shot away; he held it up, and showing that he had no more powder, the Crow chief drew his powder-horn from his neck, and flung it to the ground and his gun also, and drew his bow, his shield and quiver being slung upon his back. Mah-to-toh-pa did the same, and the combat was now with bows and arrows. Many were the passes that were made, and many the arrows that were shielded off. Each chief was wounded in the legs, and the horse of Mah-to-toh-pa fell, with an arrow through its heart. Mah-to-toh-pa was on his feet, but his bow and his shield were before him.

"The Crow chief was a gallant and brave warrior and was worthy of Mah-to-toh-pa; he sprang upon the ground, and driving an arrow through the heart of his horse, stood before his antagonist. The battle here began again, but was near its end, for at last the Crow chief raised and shook his empty quiver, and throwing it to the ground, drew and brandished his terrible knife. Mah-to-toh-pa's quiver was also hurled to the ground, and he said 'Yes!' as both were rushing on. His knife was not in his belt! but it was too late, they were in each other's arms! The wounds of Mah-to-toh-pa were several; the two-edged blade of his antagonist's knife was twice drawn through his hand, but he at length wrested it from his enemy's hand and plunged it to his heart. Thus fell Hora-to-ah, the war-chief of the Crows. The scalp of that chief and his war knife, with his own blood dried upon it, belong to Mah-to-toh-pa, and here they are; and the right hand of Mah-to-toh-pa, as you see, is crippled for the remainder of his days."

The women in the Mandan tribe, like those of most of the neighbouring tribes, were comfortably, and oftentimes very beautifully, clad with skins, extending from the throat quite to the feet. They were generally modest and timid, and observed exceeding propriety in their conduct. Some of them were very beautiful, of which the Indians seem to have a correct and high appreciation.

Amongst the Mandans, the reputed belles when I was there were *Mi-neek-e-sunk-te-ca* (the mink), and

Sha-ko-ka (mint), daughters of two of the subordinate chiefs; amongst the Riccarrees, *Pshan-shaw* (the sweet-scented grass); and amongst the Minatarrees, a few miles above the Mandans, *Seet-see-be-a* (the mid-day sun). These were all very beautiful and (then) unmarried girls. I painted their portraits full length, in their soft and white dresses, made of the mountain sheep-skins, and fringed, not with scalp-locks, but with ermine, and beautifully embroidered with porcupine quills.

How curious their names, and how pleasing! The sweet-scented grass is a sort of grass with a delicious odour which these little girls gather in the prairies, and which they wear in braids amongst the strings of beads on their necks.

And also amongst the Assinneboins, *Chin-cha-pee* (the fire-bug that creeps, or glow-worm). Amongst the Shawanos, *Kay-te-qua* (the female eagle); of the Ioways, *Ru-ton-ye-wee-me* (the strutting pigeon); and among the Puncahs, *Hee-la-dee* (the pure fountain), and *Mong-shong-shaw* (the bending willow). Among the Pawnee-Picts, *Shee-de-a* (wild sage); and amongst the Kiowas, *Wun-pan-to-mee* (the white weasel).

All of these have been brought to me to paint, by the chiefs and braves, as their most beautiful and modest girls, and whom I have painted, amongst the hundreds of female portraits which I have made in the various tribes.

And the names of the *men* also; how infinitely various, and sometimes how droll! They have no

family names, as we have in the civilized world, nor
Christian names, like John and George, etc.; but
every one has a name, especially and entirely his
own. As in the few examples selected amongst the
chiefs and braves whose portraits I have painted :
*The Thunder — The Thunderer — The Roaring
Thunder—The Whirling Thunder—The Red Thun-
der—The Yellow Thunder—He who comes on the
Thunder — The Cloud — The White Cloud—The
Flying Cloud—The Black Cloud—The Driving
Cloud—The Strong Wind—The Steep Wind—The
Walking Rain—The Hail-storm—The Moonlight
Night—The Deep Lake—The Round Island—The
Hard Hickory—The Earth Standing—Both Sides
of the River—To fix with the Foot—The Man of
Sense — The Busy Man — The Mouse-coloured
Feather—The long Finger-nails—The very sweet
Man—He who sits everywhere—He who travels
everywhere—The Smoke—There he goes—No Fool
—He who carries a Wolf—New Fire—Tobacco—
Stone with Horns—He who fights with a Feather—
The Wolf tied with Hair—Hair of the Bull's Neck
—The Bow and Quiver—The Handsome Bird—
The Flying Gull—The Bear's Fat—The Bear's
Shoulder—The Buffalo's Back-fat—The Bird of
Thunder—The Grizzly Bear—The Bear's Track—
The Yellow Bear—The White Bear—He who drinks
the juice of the Stone—The Grass, Bush, and Blos-
som.* And yet ten thousand others, as they may
get them from some achievement, some resemblance,
or some whim or accident of their lives, and which

are, from these circumstances, often changed and
new ones taken; and it matters little to these poor
and happy people how often their names are changed,
or what their names are, as they are nowhere en
rolled in tax schedules, nor have they ever to sign
their names to contracts or promissory-notes or bonds.

The Mandans related to me a very curious and
distinct tradition they have of the Deluge, teaching
that all the human race were destroyed by the rising
of the waters, excepting one man, who landed his
big canoe on a high mountain, not far from their
village, and was saved, and that all the present
human family have descended from that man.

The name of this "first, or only man," was *Nu-
mohk-muck-a-nah;* and they held an annual religious
ceremony, lasting four days, in commemoration of
the event, lest it should happen again. This strange
ceremony they called *O-kee-pa*, and have an immense
wigwam kept solely for this purpose, called the
Medicine Lodge. This strange man, Nu-mohk-
muck-a-nah, professes to come every season (about
the middle of June) and open the Medicine Lodge,
and to commence the celebration by appointing a
medicine man, whom they then call *O-kee-pa-ka-see-ka*
(the conductor of the ceremonies), and then returns
over the prairies to the high mountains, where he
professes to dwell, telling the people they may be
sure he will reappear the next year, to open the
ceremonies again.

The appearance of this personage is very grotesque
and curious; he, no doubt, is a medicine man who

goes out upon the prairies the night before, and enters the village at sunrise, from the mountains in the west, where he tells them he has resided from the time that he landed in his big canoe. He wears a robe made of four white wolf-skins, his head-dress is made of two raven-skins, and his body, otherwise naked, is covered with white clay, and his face and his cheeks painted, apparently, to personate a white man.

I was fortunate enough to be present during the four days' ceremony, in which the young men were suspending their bodies by splints run through the flesh on the shoulders, and breasts, and arms, and otherwise torturing themselves in various ways, as a religious penance, almost too shocking to describe, and entirely too long to be fully explained in this place. I consider it altogether the most extraordinary and curious of all the customs I have met in the savage countries.

It was pitiable to see so kind, so hospitable, and apparently so happy a people, under the influence of ignorant superstition, practising such self-inflicted cruelties; but it was a part of their religion, and, like all religious customs, would have required time and patience to have corrected. But, poor unfortunate people, they are all gone, and their errors are done away with!

The second summer after my visit to them, one of the American Fur Company's steamers, ascending the Missouri River to trade with the various tribes, and to supply their trading establishments with rum and whisky, and other articles of commerce, imprudently stopped in front of the Mandan village while there were two of their men sick with small-pox on board.   The disease was soon taken into the Mandan village, and, in the space of three months, the two thousand Mandans were reduced to the exact number of thirty-two.   This I give to the world on the authority of a letter in my possession, written by a Mr. Potts, formerly of the City of Edinburgh, in Scotland, and at that time a clerk in the Fur Company's factory at the Mandan village, and who says—" At the moment I am writing, there are but thirty-two of these poor people in existence, and they mostly women and children."

What an illustration is this of the wickedness of mercenary white men, who push their commerce into the Indian country, calling these poor people up to trade under the cannon's mouth, and selling rum and whisky to them, as these poisons were sold at the Mandan village at that time, at eighteen dollars per gallon, and other articles of extravagance and luxury at similar ruinous prices !

There was a government Indian agent on board of the steamer when this unfortunate occurrence took place, a staunch and honourable man—Major Dougherty—who remonstrated against the steamer's advancing to the Mandan village with the small-pox on board, and ordered the commander to turn it back; but he was two thousand miles beyond the reach of the laws, in a country where brute force was the law of the land, and what could he do?   He could do nothing against the weight of a solid cargo of rum and whisky, and so the poor Mandans suffered ; and the disease went to the Blackfeet, of whom twenty-five thousand perished, and how much farther towards the Pacific, and how many other thousands perished, no one knows, for newspapers are not received from those regions, and fur-traders are not the most reliable sources for information.

The last I saw of my friends the Mandans, was at the shore of the river in front of their village. My canoe and all my packs were brought down in safety to the water's edge—my canoe placed in the water— the whole tribe upon the beach. My friend, Mah-to-toh-pa, the Wolf chief, and the *Great Medicine*, all successively embraced me in their arms ; the warriors and braves shook hands with me, and the women and children saluted me with shouts of fare-well ; and Ba'tiste, and Bogard, and myself were again afloat, and on our way for St. Louis.

At this exciting moment, when we had got too far into the current to stop, and well under way, a gallant young warrior whom I recognised followed opposite to us, at the water's edge, and, leaning over, tossed safely into the canoe a parcel which he took out from under his robe; and seeing me attempting to unfold it, he waved his hand and shook his head, and made a sign for me to lay it down in the canoe, which I did. All now was done, and we were off.

After we had got a mile or so from the village, I took in my paddle and opened the parcel by untying a great many thongs, and, to my great surprise, found the most beautiful pair of leggings which I ever had seen, fringed with a profusion of scalp-locks, and handsomely garnished with porcupine-quills.

These I instantly recognised as belonging to the son of a famous chief, the "Four Men," and the identical pair I had been for some time trying to purchase, and for which I had offered the young man a horse, but got no reply, excepting that "he could not sell them, as the scalp-locks were so precious as trophies, and his fellow-warriors would laugh at him if he sold them."

What a beautiful trait this! Having parted with me without the least prospect of ever seeing me again, he compels me to accept as a *present* what he could not *sell* to me the day before for the price of a horse! and envelops it in an intricacy of thongs which he had intended I should not be able to untie until the current had wafted me beyond the possibility of my making him any compensation for them! and how much like the gift of the saddle of venison left in my father's wood-house, containing the eagle plume, by the unfortunate On-o-gong-way, and which so opened the eyes and the heart of poor Johnny O'Neil!

CHAPTER X.

Indian Signal—An Excitement—Fort Pierre—The Sioux
Doctor—Sioux Portraits—Jealous Sioux Chiefs—Story of
the Dog—Death of Mah-to-chee-ga—Pursuit of the Dog—
Death of the Dog—The Author Challenged.

ON—no—still glides our little boat, as Ba'tiste
and Bogard paddle and I steer; the un-
ceasing banks of greensward, enamelled
with beautiful wild flowers, and the countless sloping
hills and knolls, with their verdant sides, are still
before, around, and behind us. The river still winds
in its tortuous course, and at every turn a new and
cheerful landscape is presented, with here and there
beautiful meadows, with tufts and copses of trees,
and many of the hill-sides dotted with solitary oaks;
the whole presenting a continued and never-ending
view as of an old and beautifully cultivated country
greensward, instead of ploughed fields, with the
houses and hedges removed.

Such are yet the American prairies, and more must
still be said of them before they will be fully understood. Night after night, and for weeks of nights,
148

Plate V.

Shooting Buffaloes. — *p.* 149.

our little craft is hauled ashore, and our robes spread upon the grass or upon the barren sand-bars, while the silvery, but discordant notes of the bands of howling wolves are hourly serenading us as we are getting our night's rest.

The great tribe of Sioux are below us, and there are probably some days yet between us. Our larder was low, and a lazy little herd, quietly sleeping and grazing on the right bank, tempted us ashore, where we silently landed our canoe, and nicely approaching in a deep ravine (Plate No. V.) we got our three tongues and our three fleeces (or humps) without the slightest trouble, and continued on; I having stopped a few minutes to make a sketch of the snug little box in which the band were luxuriating.

Whilst we had enough to eat, and our paddles were constantly at work, it was natural to sing, and to whistle, and to tell stories for amusement; and whilst Ba'tiste and Bogard were relating to me some exciting and amusing stories about the Crows and the Blackfeet, in whose countries they had been trapping and trading, bang! went a gun on the shore opposite to us, and skipping, skipping, came a bullet across the water, a rod or so ahead of our canoe! An Indian was standing at the water's edge, alone, and making signs and calling to us to come ashore.

The shot fired ahead of us was the usual friendly mode of inviting parties ashore on that river, but is generally the *second* invitation, the *first* being by signals and by calling. Bogard was anxious to go ashore, but I did not exactly like the mode of invitation, nor the position of things; for this man could scarcely be supposed to be there alone; and he had placed himself on the shore just above the sudden bend in the river, where the current running in very swift, would bring us in quite near to a rocky shore, in case we drifted with it. In this place his companions, if he had any, would naturally conceal themselves in case they had any unfriendly design upon us, as they might easily have; there being then existing many unsettled feuds between some of that tribe and some of the fur-traders, for which I or any other traveller might be liable to suffer.

The river was very wide where we were, and I steered the canoe nearer to the opposite side, to prevent floating with the current into the bend. Bogard, who was a drunken fellow, and I believe thought it might be an opportunity for getting something to drink, said in rather an authoritative tone, " We will go ashore;" and Ba'tiste said, " Oui, oui;" and I said, " No; the canoe is mine, and I won't go ashore —I don't like the look of things ashore;" when both drew in their paddles and violently threw them down in the bottom of the canoe, and were evidently looking over their shoulders for their rifles, which were lying under a buffalo robe between them and me.

I instantly seized my double-barrelled gun, and cocking both barrels, laid it across my lap, having their backs, luckily, towards me. They perfectly understood the meaning of this movement, and, from my looks, what would have been the instant conse-

quence if either of them had reached for his gun.
I then commenced paddling the canoe myself, and
succeeded, by a violent effort, in not allowing it to
fall into the current near the shore, and in forcing it
towards the opposite side. Just at this time, and
when the two men were snarling and growling at
me for " being afraid of one, poor, solitary Indian,"
some twenty or thirty naked warriors, seeing that
we were not coming in, rose from behind the rocks
where we should naturally have landed if we had
gone ashore, raising the war-whoop, and running
down the shore to meet us below the bend.

"Il faut combattre ! " exclaimed Ba'tiste, as he
seized his rifle. " No," said I, " on ne combattre
pas. Il faut *ramer ! ramer !* " " On *rame !* " said
Ba'tiste, laying down his rifle and taking up his
paddle, and all three paddled with all our might.

Bogard, who was a desperate and sullen fellow,
said, " We must knock over some of those fellows."
I said, " No ; we have nothing to do but to row, and
every man to ply his paddle." I kept the canoe
about in the middle of the river, in order to take
advantage of the strongest current, and the Indians
were running on the beach and sounding the war-
whoop, which showed us beyond a doubt what their
object was. Notwithstanding all our exertions, they
were in a little time some distance below us, when
some eight or ten of them sprang into the water and
came swimming towards us, holding their bows and
arrows in the left hand above the water.

Seeing them thus ahead of us, and nearing the boat,

I then said to my men, " Now, take up your rifles, but
don't fire unless I give the word." We all took in
our paddles, and with our rifles in our hands, and
cocked, I beckoned to them to go ashore ; but still
coming nearer, and some of them within a few rods,
I raised my rifle as if to fire, when they sunk almost
entirely under the water, and commenced returning
towards the shore. Those on shore were still running
and yelling, and setting them on us again, when
several of them approached us a second time ; but
in a similar manner were turned back. Seeing that
they were armed with only bows and arrows, though
they use these with great effect in the water, I felt
no further alarm, and resolved not to use any unnecessary cruelty upon them. If they had begun
upon us, however, we should have been obliged to
fire, and could easily have killed every one of them
as they approached our boat.

Getting ashore, the whole party followed opposite
to us for several miles, but finding the chase unprofit-
able, they turned back, and we paddled on till after
dark, and bivouaced on the opposite side of the
river without further molestation.

Who these people were, whether Sioux or Riccarrees, or what was their design, I never was able to
learn ; but it has been a source of continual gratification to me that we had the forbearance not to fire
upon them.

A few days more of paddling brought us to Fort
Pierre, a large trading establishment amongst the
Sioux, with fifteen hundred skin wigwams of Sioux

Indians grouped upon the plains around it. Hundreds
on hundreds of horses were grazing on the prairies,
and as many children and dogs guarding them.

I have shown you how the Sioux Indians build
and ornament their tents, and you can easily imagine
now how picturesque and beautiful a scene was
around us. My canoe, as amongst the Mandans,
was carried by the squaws (as they call their women);
a tent was prepared for my painting operations, and
I was soon at work with my brushes, and plenty of
picturesque subjects to paint.

Ha-won-je-ta (the One Horn), head civil-chief of
the Sioux, was the first whose portrait I hit off, the
size of life, in a beautiful costume. All had been
quite silent about my wigwam, and my advent but
little cared about or known, until this private operation, known only to the chief and his doctor, was
finished, and his portrait, held by the corners of the
frame, was elevated above the heads of the crowd by
the *great medicine*, crying to the gathering multitude in front of my tent: "Look, my friends! we
have now got two chiefs—when the one is dead the
other will live—look at him and be ashamed! he
smiles upon you and is alive; to-morrow you will
see *me*. Be patient, my friends! I am but a little
boy." (I had made a dead colouring of the old
doctor, and set it by to dry.) "Mine is put in a
box, to grow over-night; to-morrow, *my* face will
shine upon you. This is the wonderful work of a
great white *medicine man;* he is now sitting and
smoking with the chief; you cannot see him, but

perhaps he will sometime walk through our village, and then you can look at him. The Great Spirit has shown him how to do these things, and you must make but little noise. He says I can do the same thing, and I think so, my friends!"

The doctor's harangue was long and very curious, and, through some little crevices in my tent, the astonished multitude was one of the most curious sights I ever beheld—an interminable mass of red and painted heads, of eagles' quills, of ermine-skins, of beads and brooches, spears, lances, shields, and quivers. Some were mounted on horses, and others raised upon the shoulders of their friends, and all gazing in wonder and astonishment at the one object—the chief "that had a little life" (as they said); the corners of whose mouth many of them could see to move, and the eyes of which actually turned and followed all as they changed their positions. Oh, for a photographic lens! what a picture or two I could have got!

" My friends," said the doctor, "you see the chief's eyes move! if any doubts that, let him walk round and look at the chief again. My friends, our chief is a great chief! but here is a chief whose eyes are on you all at the same time; he sees you all at one time alike. What chief can do that? My friends, put your hands over your mouths and be silent; to-morrow you will see *me!*"

Mr. Laidlaw, the factor at that fort, in whose house I was made welcome, brought into my wigwam several of the most distinguished chiefs and warriors to be painted, and I had full employment. The chiefs and warriors were seated round the sides of the wigwam and smoking their pipes while I would be at work at one, and each one waiting patiently for his turn to come.

This time they seemed to while away very merrily, relating all the anecdotes, creditable or otherwise, of his life, whilst he was under the operation of the brush, with his mouth shut, and unable to deny anything that was said. The scene was one of continual merriment and laughter, and the laughing and fun was increased when the operation was over and the portrait placed before them, when they were not sparing in criticisms on its good looks and in anecdotes of his life, which " it reminded them of."

In the meantime the door of my wigwam was guarded by a warrior with a lance in his hand, a sort of police placed there by the chief, with orders not to allow any one to enter except those whose rank entitled them to admission ; and the facetious old doctor had enough to do outside, magnifying my wonderful powers, and the importance of *medicine*, whilst he was keeping back the women and children and dogs, and hushing them into respectful silence.

Thus progressed the mystery operations inside and outside of my wigwam from day to day; and I had but one difficulty which I could apprehend before me, which was this : It had been represented to these chiefs and warriors that I was a great chief in my own country, that I had heard they had some very distinguished chiefs and warriors amongst them, and had come a vast distance to see who they were, and to obtain their portraits to hang on the walls alongside of the great men in the civilized world. This made it necessary that they should be painted in order, according to rank. I had begun with the head chief, and gone on until I had painted nearly the number that I cared about painting, and from necessity, some of the ugliest looking men I ever saw; and finding new subjects waiting in my wigwam every day in full dress, and ready to take their turn as decided by the chiefs, and knowing that the Sioux tribe contained forty bands, with forty chiefs, and ten times that number of medicine men and great warriors, I began to apprehend a serious difficulty approaching. Some remonstrances were also being raised by several of the jealous chiefs, as to the right of the *great medicine* being painted next to the head chief; but that was a *fait accompli*, and the chief decided that it was all right.

In the midst of these growing difficulties, and amongst these jealous spirits, Mr. Laidlaw brought into my wigwam a fine young man in his war dress and war paint, and fully armed and equipped, and said—"Mr. Catlin, I have brought in a friend of mine for you to paint—Mah-to-chee-ga (the Little Bear); he is not a chief, but he is a young warrior of such distinction, and of so good a character, that I am sure the chiefs will agree that he shall be painted." To this the chiefs all agreed, and he taking his position, I put a canvas on my easel and commenced immediately. His first attitude was beautiful, and what I wanted. He was looking off, towards the sides of the wigwam, as if gazing over a boundless prairie; the face was, therefore, what we painters call a "three-quarter face," one-half of it thrown into shadow.

While I was painting, and had the portrait pretty well advanced, one of the secondary chiefs, by the name of Shon-ka (the Dog), and whose portrait I had painted some days before, rather a surly-looking fellow, and somewhat sarcastic, crept round behind me, and for a while overlooked the operation of my brush, having a full view of the portrait. Being an evil-disposed man, disliked by most of his fellow-chiefs, and jealous of this rising warrior, he addressed to him this insulting remark—"I see that you are but half a man." "Who says that?" said Mah-to-chee-ga, in a low tone of voice, and without the change of a muscle or the direction of his eye. "Shon-ka says it," replied the Dog. "Let Shon-ka prove it," replied Mah-to-chee-ga. "Shon-ka proves it in this way; the white *medicine man* knows that one-half of your face is good for nothing, as he has left it out in the picture." Mah-to-chee-ga replied, "If I am but half a man, I am man enough for Shon-ka in any way he pleases to try it."

Here a sharp repartee took place for a few minutes, the Dog keeping his eyes upon the portrait, and those of Mah-to-chee-ga still stretching over the distant prairie. In this dialogue, which was carried on to the great amusement of the chiefs, Mah-to-chee-ga seemed to have the advantage of his adversary, who sprang upon his feet, and wrapping his robe violently around him, suddenly darted out of my wigwam, evidently in a rage.

The chiefs seemed, from the change in their manner, to be apprehensive of the result, while my subject still stood without a change or apparent emotion, and so stood until the portrait was finished, when he deliberately took off from his legs a beautiful pair of leggings, fringed with scalp-locks of his own earning, and asked me to accept them as a present.

After sitting down and smoking a pipe with the chiefs, and hearing their comments on his portrait, with which they were all well pleased, he got up, shook hands with me, and went out, passing into his own wigwam, which was but a few paces from mine.

Apprehensive of what might happen from the last expressions of the Dog, as he had left my wigwam, he took down his gun and loaded it in a hurried manner, which excited the apprehensions and inquiry of his wife, to which he made no reply, but set his gun aside, and prostrating himself upon the ground, his face to the dirt, according to their mode when danger is near, he prayed a moment to the Great Spirit; and during that moment, to prevent mischief, his wife extracted the ball from his gun without his knowing it, and set it down ; and at the next moment, the voice of the Dog (who had gone to his own wigwam, and returned with his gun in his hand) was heard in front of his door—" If Mah-to-chee-ga is man enough for Shon-ka, let him come out and prove it." Like a flash of lightning, Mah-to-chee-ga was upon his feet, his gun in his hand, and the instant he rushed out, the two guns, lapping over each other, were fired! Mah-to-chee-ga fell, weltering in his blood, that side of his face entirely blown away which had been "left out" in the painting, and decided by the Dog to be "good for nothing;" and the Dog, with his face a little blackened, and the thumb of his left hand carried away, fled to the outer part of the village occupied by his band, where he called upon the warriors of his band to protect him.

At the firing of the guns, the chiefs all rushed out of my wigwam, each one raising the tent behind where he sat, and disappearing in an instant. I was left alone; not a word for some time, but footsteps running and leaping were heard in all directions. I peeped through the crevices in my *medicine* house, and saw women, and children, and men running in all parts; the horses were caught and brought in at full gallop from the prairies, the twilight was approaching, and the dogs were howling.

I was slipping my pistols into my belt, and examining the caps of my double-barrel, when Laidlaw dashed into my tent. "Now we shall have it!" said he; "now for the pictures! That splendid fellow, the Little Bear, is dead! all that side of his face you left out in the portrait is shot off! Hang the pictures! I have been afraid of them. I have urged these people to sit for these pictures, and they are saying everywhere that you are the cause of the Little Bear's death. The warriors of the Little Bear's band

are all arming, and, if they can't kill the Dog, they
have said they will look to you for satisfaction."

At this moment guns were heard firing in the out-
skirts of the village.

" Leave your tent as quick as lightning," said
Laidlaw, " and come into the fort; you know it is
all open; it is but half-finished, and we may all be
cut off before morning." I followed with him, leaving all behind me excepting my arms and ammunition. Most of Laidlaw's men were off on the prairies
at the time, and our position therefore was extremely
critical.

One of Laidlaw's clerks, by the name of Halsey,
and myself, took possession of one of the un-
armed bastions, a small log building, barricading the
windows and doors as well as we could, and receiving
from the Company's stores some two or three dozen
of muskets, which we loaded, and stood listening and
waiting results during the greater part of the night
in almost breathless anxiety. We kept our quarters
darkened, and could hear the constant trampling
and running in different parts of the village, and now
and then the flash of a gun or two, and at last a
rapid succession of flashes on and over the prairies,
convincing us that the Dog was retreating, protected
by his warriors, whilst the warriors of the Little
Bear's band were pursuing him into the country.

On the following morning all was quiet, but
the village and fort had assumed quite a different
appearance. All was silent, and seemed sullen.
Several fine young men on both sides were reported

killed, and the Dog, though wounded, was still retreating, and pursued. My wigwam was found
solitary and unentered, just as I had left it. My
paintings and all things were speedily packed. We
joined together in burying the remains of the fallen
warrior, raising an honourable monument over his
grave; and made liberal presents to his widow and
all of his relations, which saved us perhaps from
violence.

The chiefs treated me with friendship afterwards,
apparently satisfied that I was in no wise to blame;
but the *medicine man* was of a different opinion,
notwithstanding all his kindness and attachment to
me. He had "just learned that my *medicine* was
too great," and that I "must have known that that
side of the warrior's face was good for nothing, or I
would not have left it out in the portrait; and if
I had not left it out there would have been nothing
said about it, and that therefore the Little Bear
would still have been alive." There was no metaphysics amongst these people to rebut such con-
clusive reasoning as this; and though we had
mended the breach as well as we could, I thought
the safest way was to be on the water again as quickly
as possible; which it is easy to imagine I lost no
time in effecting.*

* I learned from Mr. M'Kenzie in St. Louis, who descended
the Missouri some months after this affair, that in pursuing the
Dog, the friends of Mah-to-chee-ga had, by mistake, killed
Tah-tech-a-da-hair, a brother of the Dog, but a very fine man,
and whose portrait I had also painted, and afterwards, near the
base of the Rocky Mountains, they succeeded in killing the Dog.

Thus ended one of the most exciting and lamentable affairs growing out of my interviews with these curious people; strongly illustrating, from its beginning to its end, the high and chivalrous jealousy existing in their society, and a striking instance of the extent and certainty to which they are sure to carry their revenge.

Another brief anecdote, growing out of the unaccountable process of my portrait painting amongst these people, will help to show further how far their superstitions will sometimes carry them, and may be worth relating.

While ascending the Missouri River on a subsequent occasion, and stopping in the tribe of *Omahas*, after having painted several of the chiefs and warriors, I painted the portrait of a fine young man, who was not a warrior, but a brave. The portrait was recognised and approved by all; but I had observed him for several days afterwards, coming in and sitting down, and looking at his portrait a while, and going off, apparently in a somewhat surly and melancholy mood. One day he brought in the interpreter, and said "he did not like his picture; it was not good; it looked ashamed, because it was looking the other way."

The portrait was a three-quarter face, and the eyes looking off. He said "I had painted all the others right, looking straight forward. He had been always in the habit of looking white men in the face; but here they would all see him with his face turned the other way, as if he was ashamed." He requested me to alter it, and make his eyes look straight forward. The chiefs were all pleased with it, and advised me not to do so.

He had learned a few days afterwards that I was not going to change his eyes in the portrait, and the interpreter came into my wigwam, and said I had got to fight; that the young man was in front of my wigwam, and ready, and he believed there was no alternative.

I went out with my palette in my hand, and to be sure, here he was, entirely naked and ready. I explained to him that I was very much surprised, and that I loved him too much to fight him : and also, that I had not thought he was so much offended with his portrait, which the chiefs all liked so much ; and if to alter the eyes of his picture was all that he wanted, I would do it with the greatest pleasure the next day. This prevented all necessity of our meeting; and the next day, with some water colours mixed on my palette with some dry white lead, and he sitting a few minutes, I painted him a new set of eyes, staring in a prodigious manner across the bridge of his nose, which pleased him exactly, as they were looking straight forward. He shook hands with me, seeing what I had done, and made me a present of a pair of leggings as an evidence of his satisfaction.

On my return to St. Louis, a year afterwards, a piece of sponge with some clean water took off the new pair of eyes, and the portrait now stands as it was originally made, one of the most interesting in my collection.

CHAPTER XI.

Canoe Stolen—Pawnee War-Party—Falls of St. Anthony—
Fox and Wisconsin Rivers—St. Peter's River—Pipe-stone
Quarry—Stone Man Medicine—The Thunder's Nest—
Descent of St. Peter's—Packs Stolen—The Root Diggers.

BUT, my little readers, we need not go on all
the way to St. Louis; it is a long distance,
though Ba'tiste and Bogard and I *did* jog
on, through smoke and through fire, for the fall
season was approaching, and the broad prairie
meadows, with their waving grass eight or ten feet
high, were now in flames; and our long beards in
constant danger, for my razors were lost in the
unfortunate affair of the tin kettle, and for six
months our beards had had their own way.

My poor little canoe, so safely taken care of by the
Mandans and the Sioux, was stolen from me at the
wharf at St. Louis within two hours after our arrival;
and my beard being thoughtlessly shaved off, so that
my friends might know me, rendered me a laughing-
stock for the space of two or three weeks, until the
sunburnt redness of the upper half could be made to

164

harmonise with the death-like paleness of the nether portion of my face.

From the Sioux, on the Missouri, it is but a step of two or three hundred miles to the Platte River, on the banks of which dwell the numerous tribe of *Pawnees.* Oh, what a terrible, and yet beautiful-looking set of warriors they are; their heads all shaved, and painted blood-red, and surmounted with the beautiful red crests, as I have before described to you! When a war-party of them, on their war horses, are prancing along over the prairies in the distance, with the blades of their long lances glistening in the sun, they look like a bed of red poppies mingled with the silvery heads of barley, bowing and waving in the wind.

These are the gentlemen who catch such vast quantities of wild horses, their country abounding in countless numbers of them, and also in the most numerous herds of buffaloes.

Shon-ha-ki-hee-ga (*the Horse chief*), oftentimes called *Wee-tar-ra-sha-ro*, is the head chief of this tribe, a very dignified and hospitable man. It was in this man's wigwam that the Hon. Charles Aug. Murray was entertained, protected, and made welcome on his visit to the Pawnees in 1833. Mr. Murray, for several subsequent years, was Master of her Majesty's Household. (Have you read his " Prairie Bird," and his " Tour on the Prairies " ?)

We are now near the base of the Rocky Mountains, but the smoke is getting too bad here too. All is gloom; the fires are all around us; the prairie hens are flying in all directions ; the deer are all in motion ; the frogs and reptiles are looking for their burrows; the black and smoking plains are strewed with bleaching bones, and shrouded nature has lost its charms.

Imagination (how lucky) can waft us in a single moment to the falls of St. Anthony, on the Upper Mississippi ; the distance is but a thousand miles, where perhaps there is a clear sky. This dashing, foaming cataract, second only to Niagara, which was discovered and christened after his patronymic saint by the good old Father Hennepin in 1860, has been a dividing boundary line, and consequently hostile ground, for centuries past between the Sioux and the Ojibbeway tribes, and the vicinity around is strewed with human bones, which indicate the destructive scenes which have been enacted there.

With Corporal Allen, seated in a beautiful birch-bark canoe, he paddling while I steered, I started from this beautiful scene, in the summer of 1834, wending our way amidst the towering cliffs and grassy plains of the mighty Mississippi to St. Louis, a distance of nine hundred miles, drawing our light little craft upon the beach at night, and supplying our little larder from day to day with rock bass taken from the rocky eddies, and wild fowl and deer, which we killed with our rifles.

The Indian tribes which we saw on the banks of this river were the *Sioux*, the *Winnebagos*, the *Menomonies*, the *Saukies*, the *Foxes*, and *Ioways*. My paintings were made, and we were treated by them all with kindness. My little bark canoe, which was beautifully painted, was always taken care of by them while we stopped, and placed in the water when we were prepared to proceed on our way.

When we arrived at the wharf at St. Louis, our luggage was lifted and sent to my hotel, and, for the sake of safety, with the captain's permission, I had my pretty little canoe lifted on to the deck of his steamer lying at the wharf, to remain for a few hours until I could find a place to store it; and when I came for it it was gone. I never again could hear of it.

In the next succeeding summer, with an English gentleman, Mr. Wood (now residing in Philadelphia), I ascended the Fox River, from Green Bay to its source, also in a bark canoe. At the head of that river, in making the portage to the head of the Wisconsin, which we were to descend to the Mississippi, we had but a distance of two miles over a level prairie.

My companion said, "But what are we to do here?" "Well," said I, "we have got to take turn about with our little canoe; it has carried us a great way, now we have got to carry our canoe."

"Oh, but, my dear sir, what shall I do with my dear little wife?" (meaning his beautiful little guitar, which he played with great taste). "Never fear," said I; "if you will carry the pack which I have now made up, I will take the canoe on my shoulders and your guitar case under my arm." Turning the canoe bottom upwards, raising it

upon one end, and getting the middle beam on my
shoulders, I very easily carried it the distance, and
laying it on the clear waters of the Wisconsin, there
but a few yards wide, we took our seats, and, paddles
in hand, commenced our descent of some hundreds
of miles to the Mississippi, encamping at night upon
its grassy and picturesque shores.

After we entered the Mississippi we had some
hard work against its boiling current before we
reached Prairie du Chien; and from that to the
Falls of St. Anthony, a distance of four hundred
and fifty miles, some "up-hill work" again. Men
in these regions sometimes have to use their arms
as well as legs in travelling.

"Up-hill work" we all know the meaning of, and
I have had much of it to mar my progress in life; but
"up-*river* work," with a somewhat similar meaning,
is a term less perfectly understood. The difference
between them is, that the one *may* be very hard
work, and the other is *sure* to be; but in the latter,
like the boy who drags his sled with hard labour up
the hill, we are encouraged by the pleasure we anti-
cipate in riding down.

From the Falls of St. Anthony we ascended the
St. Peter's River one hundred miles, to visit the red
pipe-stone quarry on the Grand Côteau des Prairies,
where the Indians procure their red stone for making
their beautiful pipes. This place we found to be one
of great interest, not only from the Indians' tradi-
tions about it, but from the peculiar features of the
country, and the singular character of the pipe-stone,

a species of steatite, but differing from any other sort found in America, or perhaps in the world.

Many of the contiguous tribes have no doubt been in the habit of visiting this place to procure the red stone for their pipes, protected from the weapons of their enemies, under the belief they all have that the Indians were made from the red stone, it being precisely their own colour—" that it is a part of their flesh—that the Great Spirit gave it to them expressly for their pipes, and it having been given to them all alike, the Great Spirit would be angry if they raised their weapons against their enemies going to or returning from the red pipe-stone quarry. The Great Spirit told them it was their own flesh, and must be used for no other purpose than the bowls of their pipes."

The Sioux, in whose country this quarry is, stopped and detained us several days, and made great resistance to our going there, asserting that no white people had been there, and that none were permitted to go, because it was a sacred place. They said they believed we were sent by the government to see what it was worth, so as to try to buy it from them, and they did not wish to sell it.

Assuring them, however, that we were but two private persons, who had only curiosity to see it, and that we would respect all their feelings, they permitted us to go and see it, provided twenty of their warriors could accompany us; probably to see that we committed no sacrilege about the place.

While at the pipe-stone quarry the Indians told

us we were within twenty miles of the "*thunder's
nest!*" "Thunder's nest! why, what on earth is
that?" "Why," said one of the *medicine men*, "it
is the place where the thunders are hatched out."
"The thunder comes out of an egg, then, does it?"
"Certainly." "It must be a pretty large bird to lay
such eggs?" "No, it's *very small*." "How large?"
"Why, about as large as the end of your little finger;
most of the medicine men of the Sioux have seen it."
"Well," said my friend Mr. Wood, "we must go and
see that *by all means*. I have heard a great deal
about it, and I venture to say it must be something
very curious to see."

Our interpreter and guide, a half-breed, told us
that this strange place was on the highest ridge of
the côteau, and the Indians believed that in the very
hottest days, previous to the thunder-showers, the
bird was sitting on her eggs, and when they hatched
out it made the thunder. He told us that on our
way to the thunder's nest he would take us a little
to the west, and we would see the "*stone man medicine.*" "This," said he, "is a great curiosity—a
place where every Indian who is going—" "Never
mind," said Mr. Wood, "don't tell us all about it;
that will spoil it all; let's go and see it." So we
took an early start the next morning, on our way to
the "*thunder's nest*" and the "*stone man medicine.*"

We rode off at an early hour with three of the
Indian party, and spent the day in looking at these
wonderful places, the last of which we found on the
top of a high and rounded bluff, covered with short

grass, and from the top of which no tree or bush could be seen: all around was a mass of rolling and sloping hills of green stretching off to the horizon. On the top of this mound, which has, perhaps, a couple of acres of slightly rounded surface, lay the "*stone man medicine.*" It was the figure, in tolerably good proportions, of a man lying on his back, his arms and his legs distended, of some three or four hundred feet in length, composed entirely of flat stones, which had been brought by Indians, probably through centuries, and deposited there; and, what was singular, I could not discover another stone the size of a pigeon's egg for several miles on either side of it.

Whatever led to the beginning of this strange monument no one knows; but the Indians tell us that no Indian going on a hunting excursion, or on a war-party in that direction, has any confidence in success unless he stops at the "*stone man medicine*," and adds a flat stone to the figure; no matter how far it be out of his way, or how far he has to carry the stone.

There is nothing of the character of a barrow in this strange mass, no one stone lying on the top of another, and the number may well be said to be countless; exhibiting, by size and different colours, the features of the face, and even the fingers and toes of a human figure.

Our Indian companions having each deposited their stone offering, and explained all they could to us, we started for the "*thunder's nest.*"

This terrible-sounding mystery we reached after a hard ride, and found it, like the other, on the top of a high prairie mound, where we observed a small bunch of hazel bushes, thickly matted, and as high as a man's waist, occupying some two or three rods of ground.

The leader of our little party at this time was a very droll old fellow, called the "*Blue Medicine*," extensively known to the officers of the United States army in the vicinity of the Falls of St. Anthony; and when we were ascending the side of the mound, and near to the wonderful place, the doctor requested us all to dismount and wait a little. The Indians took all the plumes out of their heads, and placing them under their robes, smoothed down their long glossy-black locks, and with their little looking-glasses took a squint at their own faces, to see if the paint was all right, and then, with their robes wrapt around them, and the doctor leading the way, all marched slowly towards the bunch of bushes, leading the horses by their halters.

Within some two or three rods of the bushes the Indians halted, and each one tossed a plug of tobacco into the grass, which, forward of us, showed no sign of human trespass; but, under our feet and behind us, seemed much trodden down by the frequency of passing visitors.

I gave the reins of my horse to my companion, and with my gun in both hands, as if to shoot upon the wing, I started to walk into the hallowed ground and see if I could put up the little bird; and hear-

ing a deep groan behind me, I looked back, and
seeing the poor Indians all with their hands over
their mouths, and evidently in great distress, I
retreated and came out without seeing anything
excepting some hundreds of bits of tobacco, lying
in the grass, that had been thrown by the poor
superstitious children of the forest as sacrifices to the
Spirit they there invoke—"*The Thunder Spirit*," in
dread of whom they always live.

These are but two of the numerous shrines to
which the poor Indians travel out of their way, and
at which they throw their hard earnings as pro-
pitiatory offerings.

_____

At the "Traverse de Sioux," at the base of the
côteau, Mr. Wood and myself left our horses, and
seated ourselves again in our little canoe, and down
stream (not down *hill*, but a little like it) we were
wafted off, and oh how happy! for we could paddle
when we pleased, or fish when we pleased, or alternately sleep when we pleased ; or listen to the sounds
of his "dear little guitar," accompanied with his
rich tenor voice, which he told me had echoed for
many years on the stage of the Italian Opera-house
in London. And our canoe was still going on—on
—on—as the hills resounded and echoed with
"Away to the Mountain's Brow," etc.

Thus we descended the St. Peter's River, to its
junction with the Mississippi at the Falls of St.
Anthony, and then the mighty Mississippi again, as
Corporal Allen and myself had descended it the

summer before ; spreading our robes upon the grass, and supplying our larder in the same manner ; often bivouacing on the identical spots, and as often lifting our beautiful rock bass from the same eddies, and from under the same rocks.

The day before we reached the city of St. Louis, being fatigued with paddling nine hundred miles, and having a strong wind against us, we hailed a steamer descending the river, and with ourselves had our little canoe and its contents lifted on board.

I related to the captain my former misfortunes in losing my canoes at St. Louis, and told him I should take more care of this. He laughed at me heartily, and said, "You have been very unlucky, but you shall at least be sure of one." We arrived at St. Louis too late in the evening to remove my canoe, and in the morning I was saved the trouble ; and on this occasion, with it had departed for ever a large package which I had left in the cabin, with my name on it, containing several very beautiful articles of Indian costumes, pipes, etc. For the loss of these things on his vessel I remonstrated with the captain, and severely so, for the parcel taken from the cabin of his steamer with my name on it. For this he laughed at me in the face again, and said, "Why, don't you know, sir, that if you leave a box or a parcel in any steam-boat on the Missouri or the Mississippi, with George Catlin marked on it, it is known at once by all the world to be filled with Indian curiosities, and that you will never see it again unless it goes ashore with you ?"

This accounted for the losses I had met with on former occasions of boxes and parcels sent by steamers and other boats, from various remote places in the Indian countries, to St. Louis, containing one-third at least of all the Indian manufactures I ever procured, after I had purchased them at exorbitant prices; and oftentimes the poor Indians had stored them, and carried them over rivers, and transported them over long distances in safety for me. What a comment is this upon the glorious advantages of civilization!

But we are yet at the Falls of St. Anthony; the Indians are many around us, and their modes are curious, but much like what we have seen. The prairies are yet here, they are everywhere. Everything here is gloom; the country is everywhere steeping in smoke and ashes, and let us be off to something new; more fresh and more congenial. Where shall we go?

In the Rocky Mountains there are the funny little fellows, the "*Root Diggers*," who burrow amongst the rocks, and live by digging roots and killing rabbits and pheasants with their short clubs (*bengtwas*), which they throw very dexterously; they have no guns and no horses, and therefore never venture out upon the plains, nor can the horsemen overtake or injure them amongst the rocks and crags in which they live.

Beyond them are the *Banaks*, the *Kayuses*, the *Kayuls*, the *Paunches*, and the *Snakes*, on the Snake

River; and below them, on the Columbia, the Flat Heads, who squeeze the heads of their very young infants between boards until an unnatural and distorted shape is given, and their eyes stand out like those of a rat caught in a dead-fall.

I can show these, and the Nayas, who wear great round blocks of wood, several inches in diameter, passed through their under-lips "to add to their good looks." I can show you the terrible Apachees, with their long lances, and their lasso always in hand, before whom the Californian gold-diggers are constantly trembling; the Arapahos, the Navahos, and half-a-dozen other "hos" living west of the Rocky Mountains. Shall we take a look at these? no, not at present. If we have space, we may take them on our way back; their countries are all prairies, and like those we have just seen, are probably, at this season, fuming in smoke and cinders.

I know of a country that is always fresh and green, that has no smokes, no fires, no winters; whose birds and insects always sing, and fruits and flowers are always growing.

America has two hemispheres; we have seen the wild people and their modes in the one, why not take a peep into the other? *Allons!*

CHAPTER XII.

Ride to the Camanchees—Charley Bought—Deer Stalking—
The Author Decoyed—"Booh! to you, too!"—Story of
the Panther—Walking the Circle—Creasing a Wild Horse—
Indians About!—Stampado—A False Alarm—Indian
Honesty.

BUT stop!—we are travelling very fast.
There are yet the bold and daring *Camanchees,* who hang on the sides of their
horses on their fields of battle; the tall and manly
Osages, with their shaved and crested red heads
(like the Pawnees); the *Konzas;* the *Pawnee-Picts*
(who, I have before said, build their wigwams of
grass, in the shape of straw bee-hives); the *Kiowas;*
the *Wicos,* and a dozen other "os" and "was" in
Western Texas.

And then the *Senecas,* the *Oneidas,* the *Onon-
dagos,* the *Mohawks,* the *Mohigans,* the *Delawares,*
the *Potowatomies,* the *Kickapoos,* the *Kaskaskias,*
the *Weeahs,* the *Peorias,* the *Shawanos,* the *Musko-
gees,* the *Chocktaws,* the *Cherokees,* the *Seminolees,*
and yet others, all of whom I have lived amongst,

177

and of some of whom I must say a few words before we wander too far away from them.

In the spring of 1836, a regiment of mounted dragoons, under the command of Colonel Henry Dodge, was ordered to start from Fort Gibson, on the Arkansas River, seven hundred miles west of the Mississippi, on a visit to the Camanchees, the Pawnee-Picts, and other wild tribes on the western borders of Texas, to make a first acquaintance with those tribes, and to put a stop to border difficulties, which were at that time becoming very alarming on those parts of the frontier.

This favourable opportunity of seeing those remote and hostile tribes I took advantage of, by obtaining from the Secretary-at-War the privilege of travelling under the protection of the regiment, with my faithful friend, Joseph Chadwick, of St. Louis, a young man who was strongly attached to me, and willing to give his time and risk his life for me, for the pleasure of shooting, and of seeing the Indians and their country.

Armed and equipped, Joe Chadwick and myself were on the spot, at Fort Gibson, and ready. We had proposed to travel and maintain ourselves quite independent of the regiment, only asking for their protection. We had, therefore, supplied ourselves with a mule to carry our packs and our culinary and other requisites, and with our own weapons and horses.

For this expedition I had purchased the finest horse then known in that section of the country,

belonging to Colonel Birbank, an aged officer of the
garrison at Fort Gibson, who had become a little
afraid to ride him on parade, where he attracted the
attention and admiration of all the officers; but by
his flourishing gaiety and prancing, he had too much
excited the nerves of his rider, who was willing to
sell him for the price of two hundred and fifty
dollars, which I gave for him.

"Charley" (the name he answered to) was an
entire horse, a mustang, of cream colour; his black
tail sweeping the ground, and his black mane nearly
so. He had been taken and broken by the Camanchee Indians, who take great care never to break
the spirit of those noble animals.

I rode and galloped Charley about, gradually
beguiling him into the new relationship, for some
weeks before the regiment was ready to commence
the march; and my friend Joe, on his nimble,
slender-legged little buffalo charger, which he had
bought of an Indian hunter, was everywhere my
companion.

Colonel Dodge had employed two famous Delaware Indians, semi-civilized, with several of other
tribes, as hunters and guides for the regiment; and
while resting in the encampment for the regiment
to start, they amused Joe and me by the ingenious
preparations they were making for their different
modes of decoying and entrapping game.

Amongst these there was one that attracted our
particular attention, a sort of whistle, made of the
bark of a young sapling, of two or three inches in

length, and which they carried in their pouch, by blowing in which they would precisely imitate the bleating "ma!" of the young fawn; so that whenever they discovered a deer on the prairies at too great a distance to shoot, by sounding this, and lying secreted in the grass, they would invariably bring the deer up to them, led to their certain death by the natural sympathy which that animal has for the calls of the young, and the perfect imitation produced by that curious instrument.

Joe and I, from our impatience for the pleasures ahead of us, became exceedingly fatigued with the delay of the dragoons, and to shorten weary time, we resolved to shorten one day at least, by taking a day's amusement at deer-stalking on the " Maple Ridge," a range of hills and heavy-timbered country, some eight or ten miles from the garrison, which was said to be full of deer and turkeys. So the next morning, at an early hour, we mounted our steeds and galloped off, rifles in hand and our luncheons in our pockets. Leaving our horses with a half-breed Indian who lived at the foot of these mountains, we entered and traversed these dark and solitary haunts, laying out and carrying out our numerous *drives* and *meets,* and other schemes for the accomplishment of our designs.

We drove, we approached, and we met, many times, and without success; we saw their white flags a number of times, but had got no shot, and about the middle of the day, having for a long time lost sight and knowledge of Joe, I came to the edge of a small prairie, and stepping a little into it, I heard the sudden bleating of a fawn, which was several times repeated "ma—ma—ma!" From its direction I was sure the little creature was in the shade of a small copse of bushes farther in the prairie, and at too long a distance for a dead shot, so I dropped myself upon my knee in the grass, resolving to wait a while until it might come out.

I kept my eye fixed upon the place, and presently it called again, and I then began to creep slowly and carefully, on my hands and knees, towards the bushes, and getting near, it called again, and at last again; and believing that one or both of its parents was with it, I felt sure that I was going to get a shot.

I kept creeping on, but with greater and greater caution, until I got quite close to the copse, with my rifle cocked and drawn to my shoulder, when, to my inexpressible surprise, the poor little thing called out "ma!" right *behind* me, and on turning my head slowly around, but without changing my position, I beheld, within ten feet of where I had passed, lying concealed in the grass, and heartily laughing at me, the two Delaware Indian hunters.

My hunting pretensions were a good deal cut down by this little occurrence, but I sat down with these good-natured fellows, and learning from them that there was not the slightest use in stalking at that hour, as "no game at that time of day was moving," we spent an hour or so in the shade, and

I then entered the timber again. I often sounded my whistle for Joe, but heard nothing of him.

I travelled on and on, and saw no game; but descending a gently-sloping hill, through an open but dark and gloomy forest of large timber, I espied Joe sitting on a large log, with his back towards me and his rifle standing by his side, while he was engaged eating his lunch, which he had brought in his pocket.

As I had had *my* shock, and there seemed little chance of getting any game, I thought jokes would be better than nothing; so I resolved on giving *Joe* a little shock. I started in a straight line towards him, and as slowly and cautiously as I could step, not to make a noise in the leaves to startle him, and thus advanced with my rifle in my left hand: and after creeping in this manner for some thirty or forty rods—gradually and carefully setting one foot and lifting the other, until I had got very near to him, and laughing at the jump he was to make if I could only get a step or two farther without his hearing me—which accomplished (as he was chewing away), I let my right hand fall upon his shoulder with a *"booh!"* at which instant came a heavy red paw on my own shoulder, with a *"booh! to you too!"* Poor Joe! he made *his* leap near twenty feet, and I made *mine* nearly as far in a different direction. And in the very tracts that I had left, stood smiling at me, a huge Osage Indian, with his rifle in his left hand, and his right still remaining in the air where my shoulder had left it.

We all straightened up, and the good-natured expression of the Indian's face set us all right; but when he related to me, that, knowing my object, he had stepped his foot into every one of my tracts in the whole of that distance the instant that my foot was lifted out, I felt more ashamed of my hunting abilities than I ever had felt before in my life.

The Osage was a good-natured and harmless Indian, and spoke a little English, and having shared our lunch with him, and a little canteen of brandy which Joe had in his pocket, he related several of his hunting feats, which amused us very much.

I told him that notwithstanding my friend and myself had killed nothing that day, we had sometimes had better luck, and that we had hunted many days together. "One day last winter," said I, "when this young man and I were on a steamboat, going from the mouth of the Ohio to St. Louis, on the Mississippi, one of the wheels got broken and they stopped the boat at the shore, by the side of a great and dark forest of cotton-woods, and the captain told us it would take all day to mend the wheel.

"My friend here and I both had our rifles with us, and we went ashore into the woods to hunt; there was a fine tracking snow, about four or six inches deep, and there were a great many signs of deer. My friend and I separated after we got a little way into the woods, and took different directions. The day was very gloomy and dark, and after I had travelled a long distance without getting a shot, I fell into the track of a man who had just gone along ahead of me, with a large dog following him : 'That can't be my friend Joe? no; he had no dog with him.' I followed on, and walked pretty fast, in order to overtake him.

"After a long walk I stopped, and brushing the snow from a large log, I sat down, but the forest being so dense, and the day so thick, I began to think I had missed my bearing and was lost. I then started on again, resolved to overtake the person on whose track I was following, who could, probably, put me on the right course.

"After walking a long distance farther, and following the track, I at length found another man's track coming into it. '*That's* Joe! Very likely; he is lost perhaps, and he is following that man with the dog, as I am; I'll push on and overtake him. But stop; this can't be my friend Joe, for *he* has got a dog also. Never mind, I'll push on and over-take him, for I know I am lost and going wrong.' I continued on, and at length came to a large log where the snow was brushed off. 'The man has been sitting down! Yes; and this is the very log I brushed the snow from and sat upon half-an-hour since! It *can't* be—it *must* be—and that is my own track! I am lost!—I am walking in a circle! But that dog? He steps in my track—he is stalk-ing me! I have no dog!—a panther's track is like a dog's!' I was at this moment sitting upon the log, and had leaned my rifle against it by the side of me. I took it deliberately into my hands and cocked it, to lose no time if there should be need for it behind me; and rising slowly, and looking back on my back track, at the distance of some six or eight rods I discovered the head of a huge panther raised over the top of a log, as he rested his fore-paws upon it, and was staring me in the face, without winking or moving a muscle!

"One of my old, boyish 'shivers' began to rise as I was raising my rifle to my shoulder; 'But,' said I, 'that won't do—it won't do to miss this time.' And by the time I had got my barrel levelled, my nerves were perfectly steady, and the little black wrinkle between the gentleman's eyes so snugly took the bead, that when he fell behind the log, I just walked up as confidently as I would have walked up to a target, knowing exactly where the bullet had gone. This fellow made no more '*tracks*.'

"With his heels tied together, and slung on my back, I was able to walk under his weight, heavy as it was; and hearing the carpenter's blows on the boat at this time, I was enabled to lay my course to it. I met Joe near the boat, coming in with a saddle of venison on his back, and he told me he had dressed and hung up two more, for which he was just sending two men from the boat, on his back track, to bring in.

"My panther was laid upon the deck of the steamer, and its length, from the end of the nose to the end of its tail, was measured, and found to be nearly nine feet. Both Joe and I were compli-

mented by the officers of the boat, and also by the
passengers, for our day's work."

My story pleased the good-natured Osage Indian
very much, and we shook hands and parted. Joe
and I got back to our horses, and galloped home.
So ended *that* day of our amusements.

The dragoons were at length on their march,
stringing off over the prairies and through the
timber two by two, their usual mode of marching;
and Joe and I, with our little pack horse, were
hanging on one or the other wing, and so encamping
at night; our buffalo robes spread upon the grass,
our saddles for our pillows, and our horses picketed
by our heads.

After a week or two of days and nights thus
passed, we had forded the "Little Blue," and swam
the "Canadian," and were now creeping along on
the dividing ridge between the Canadian and the
Red River, and near to their sources. Bands of
wild horses were running from us, and from herds
of buffaloes the rifles of our Delaware hunters were
supplying us with a daily abundance of fresh meat.

While moving on and on in this manner, from
day to day, Joe and I espied one day, at too great a
distance to the right to be frightened by the
dragoons, a band of wild horses grazing, and placing
our pack-mule in the leading of one of the soldiers,
we galloped off towards them for a nearer reconnais-
sance. On nearing them we discovered a ravine,
near the banks of which they were grazing, and
throwing ourselves into this, we rode till we sup-

posed we were near their vicinity, and dismounting, we fastened our horses to some alder bushes, and commenced our ambuscade march on foot. We successfully approached behind some tufts of hazel bushes on the brink of the ravine, to within a fair rifle-shot of them without being discovered, notwithstanding their exceeding shyness.

I had always in my pocket a powerful operaglass, which gave us, as we lay concealed, a perfect view of them, displaying all their blemishes and all their beauty. There were perhaps some two or three hundred in the group, and, like a kennel of hounds, of all colours, from jet and glossy black to snow white. Some were chestnut, some were iron, and others silver, grey; others were pied and spotted and striped, with two, and sometimes three, different colours intermingled. Their tails generally dragged on the grass, and their long and shaggy manes, which seemed generally to cover their eyes, fell from both sides of the neck, and oftentimes were under their feet, and dragged on the grass as they were feeding.

Poor Joe and I saw no way of encompassing or appropriating this noble and beautiful stud; nor had we approached them with the least mercenary view; but a thought instantly suggested itself. We both had heard of the mode which the Spaniards and other frontier hunters often use, who cannot take them in the usual way with the lasso, that of "creasing" them, which is done by shooting them with a rifle through the fleshy (or rather gristly)

part of the neck, on the top of the shoulders, by
which the animal is stunned for the moment, and
falls ; and the hunter having advanced and fastened
the halter upon it, and hobbled its feet together, it
rises again, to be subjugated by its cruel master.
" Let's crease one !" whispered Joe. " Well," said
I. But here was a difficulty again : to travel light
and handy, both Joe and I had left our heavy rifles
at Fort Gibson, and armed ourselves with light
and short single-barrelled fowling-pieces, as better
adapted for our daily support, by throwing shot as
well as ball, and being more easily carried and
reloaded on horseback than our rifles.

There was no certainty of sufficient accuracy with
them, at that distance, for creasing, but we resolved
to try ; and one of the handsomest and noblest of
the troop, a beautiful silver grey, turning himself
round to a fair broadside, I fired, and he tumbled
down, as the herd were off, as if by a blast of wind.
" Beautiful ! beautiful !" said Joe, as we arose and
approached the animal, to find, as we did to our
horror and shame, that the ball had fallen from my
aim, and passed through the animal's heart ! Poor
Joe ! his heart was too tender and too noble to stand
this ; he was younger than I, and had more tears to
shed, and he wept bitterly over the fate of this noble
creature, which we did not mean to injure, and leave
for the wolves to eat. We had the best of reasons
for keeping this adventure a profound secret, and it
was never known to any of the regiment.

Joe and I were soon remounted, and alongside of

the dragoons again; and though in our long, long
travels over the prairies and through the oak openings we had many a fine chance for a rifle-shot, our
light little fowling-pieces, which were easy to handle
and deadly in the chase from our horses' backs, were
but a poor reliance, and it became a motto in such
cases, "Crease him, Joe," or "Crease him, Cat."

About this time began to be heard through the
regiment, "Indians! Indians! Indians about!"
Their signs were fresh; and at last their waving
plumes and the glistening blades of their long lances
began to be seen, now and then dodging about over
the tops of the grassy hills, announcing to us that
we were under the gaze and reconnoitring of a war-
party of Camanchees.

Most of the men in the command, and probably
many of the officers, never had seen an Indian, and
were now undergoing something like the pulsations
and vibrations which a *certain little boy* once under-
went at an old saw-mill lick.

The Camanchees—one of the most powerful and
warlike tribes in America, and undoubtedly the most
bold and efficient warriors on horseback, and heretofore considered hostile to the whites—were now
hovering around us, and their villages, evidently not
a great distance ahead of us. For several days'
march, and as many uneasy nights of bivouac, these
hordes of mounted horsemen were gathering around
us; and during the daytime, constantly more or less
in full view, in squads of flying cavalry, in front and
in rear of us, reconnoitring us at a distance, and dis-

appearing over the hills as we approached them. With my glass, which brought them nearer to me than they thought for, they were beautiful to behold; the fierce and manly expression of their faces, the grace and elegance of their movements, and the fierceness and elasticity of their horses, were altogether one of the most beautiful sights I ever beheld.

We kept moving on, and bivouacing in the nights in the open prairies, the companies forming into hollow squares, the men laying their knapsacks and saddles on the ground, close by the side of each other, for their pillows, with their horses picketed inside the square, and each within its owner's reach, in case of a sudden surprise.

A *picket*, in that country, is a small stake of iron or of wood, made to be driven into the ground, to which the horse is fastened, and is generally carried during the day attached to the saddle or crupper, to be always ready when the encampment is to be formed.

"*Stampado*"—Did you ever hear of a stampado, my little readers? No; well, then, we'll have it. Stampado is a Spanish word, meaning "a trampling," or (what is much the same, and perhaps more intelligible), a tremendous scrambling and scampering, when a party of some hundreds of bold and furious Indian warriors, mounted on their darting war-horses, with brandishing lances and war-clubs in hand, in the stillness and darkness of midnight, when wearied soldiers and their horses are fast asleep, dash at full speed, like a flash of lightning with the thunder following, into and through an encampment, mingling the frightful war-whoop with the unearthly sound (not unlike theatre thunder) of their parchment robes shaken in the hands to frighten the horses. The instant flash of a few guns begins the frightful melée, and in the confused *escampétte*, the affrighted horses, *en masse*, dash against and over each other and their owners, and are off like a whirlwind upon the prairies at the highest speed, with their enemies behind them; leaving the scientific warriors with broken arms, with broken legs, and broken guns, upon their hands and knees, gazing through the dark in vain for some moving object to "draw a bead" upon.

Such is a *stampado*. It is like a tornado that's passed on. And where is it?—did it stop?—is it coming back? No. No scalp was taken, and none was looked for; none was wanted or thought of;— *horses* were wanted; and where are they? Why, twenty miles off—run and pressed to the last breath, and by the daylight next morning an easy prey, and a play spell for the Camanchees' lassos before breakfast.

A stampado had been apprehended and feared for several nights past, from the surrounding appearances—as we learn from the dark and gathering clouds and their electricity that a storm is gathering and preparing to break forth. All were talking of stampados, all preparing for them, and every precaution in the regiment was made for the event. Every man slept with his rifle in his arms, and his horse picketed within his reach; and poor Joe and I, notwithstanding we were invited to sleep in the officers' quarters, in the centre, preferred spreading our robes, and laying our own saddles a little outside of all, and on the *uphill side*, for reasons which the world will never guess.

These were trying times for Joe and me, for I knew that the Camanchees were thirty thousand, and had at least ten thousand of the most desperate mounted warriors in the world; and we resolved whatever deaths we might die, not to be *trampled* to death, nor to lose our horses if we could help it. We therefore drove their pickets close to our heads, and hobbled them at the same time, and took the precaution while on dangerous ground, to spell each other in our sleeps during the night—one sitting straight up and awake, whilst the other was taking his nap.

My lorgnette was a pretty good night-glass, and we doubtless had, therefore, a better sort of clairvoyance of the vicinity of the bivouac than anybody else in it.

About midnight, on one starlight night, a few days after the Indians had ceased to show themselves on the hill-tops, and the whole caravan, excepting my friend Joe and I, had begun to think they had left the vicinity, and therefore to relax a little in their nocturnal discipline; Joe happened to be ogling with the spy-glass, and I was fast asleep—when flash and bang! went a gun, close by a little bunch of hazel bushes, within a few rods of where we were lying, and where a sentinel had been walking his rounds, instantly followed by a struggling and rustling in the bushes, from which came a deep and frightful groan! And in the camp, oh, awful! the snapping of cords, the trampling of hoofs, the sounds of grunting, of groaning! Now and then the flash of a gun, but no war-whoops nor rattling of parchment skins, only a vanishing of steeds, that carried terror and confusion as they fled and disappeared, with their elevated tails and manes, like a fleet (but swifter) under full sail disappearing in a mist!

In the camp all were *à genou*, or "lying close," cocked and ready, or groaning with their wounds. When I awoke, my friend Joe had Charley's halter in one hand, and that of his little charger in the other. Charley stood, when I arose, with his mane and his tail spread—a picture in himself to look at; his eyeballs glaring and his nostrils raised, as he was trembling and alternately glancing his eyes over the flying mass, and turning his head to smell my breath, to know if I was frightened. A moment of silence ensued, and then said Joe, "Here, Cat, hold my horse; it's that fool of a fellow yonder who has done all this—he has shot a poor horse there, in the bushes." Saying this, Joe walked into the camp amidst pointing and aimed rifles and fixed bayonets, exclaiming, "Don't shoot! don't shoot me! there are no Indians!" Poor Joe, at some risk of his life notwithstanding, succeeded in arriving at the officers' quarters, where a sort of council of war was held, and Joe made his report, *to wit*, that "a sorrel horse, belonging to the commissariat, had got loose, and after he had observed the poor creature feeding about for some time, it presented its head and breast out of a little bunch of hazel bushes near to one of the sentinels, who took it, of course, for a Camanchee Indian, and after not learning ' *Who's there ?*' and getting no countersign, blazed away and shot the poor brute through the heart."

The sentinel was put under arrest, and also three or four others, whose guns had gone off accidentally or otherwise in the *melée,* and also Corporal Nugent, who fired at Lieut. Hunter and missed him, as he was holding on to his horse, because he wore a fur cap, and was mistaken for a Camanchee Indian.

Joe and I soon after, and our horses, went to sleep, and the rest of the caravan, excepting those whose wounds were being dressed during the rest of the night by the surgeons and their assistants. Here, of course, a halt for some days was ordered, and it lasted for some weeks, as well as I can remember, and that from necessity ; for the horses, though not all gone, were so reduced in numbers that they must be recovered or replaced before the regiment could proceed.

The poor affrighted creatures had taken the direction of their back track in their flight. Some were retaken within twenty miles, some within fifty miles. some were never taken ; and a great many were brought in by the Indians, taken with the lasso, and carefully and most honestly brought to the camp, and delivered to their owners, by the very people whom we had been sleeping, and even marching, in dread of, and who knew by the flight of our horses what had taken place, and that we stood in need of friendly assistance.

CHAPTER XIII.

Grand Review—Pawnee-Picts—Fort Gibson—Charley saddled for St. Louis—Cherokees and Creeks—Seminolee Treaty—Death of Seminolee Chief—"Dade's Massacre"—Capture of Osceola—A Sad Story—Death of Osceola—Charley's Freaks—A Shake and a Roll in the Grass—Bivouac with Charley—Thunder Storm on the Prairies—Shooting the Buck—Charley Tracking the Buck—Crossing the Great Osage.

THE reader can easily imagine, from the close of the last chapter, that there was little difficulty in making acquaintance with the Camanchees after this; for it was soon learned that there was a mutual good feeling, and a wish on both sides to "shake hands," which was done in a few days, with two or three of the secondary chiefs who were sent out to meet us with a hundred or more of their most beautiful and celebrated warriors, all mounted on fine horses, and fully equipped and painted for war. As they came galloping and dashing up, with their long lances in hand, and their beautiful white shields on their arms, they presented one of the most thrilling and exciting scenes that I ever beheld.

196

After a general shake of the hand with the officers, they invited us to the great Camanchee village, some three or four days' march, to which they conducted us, and showed us daily, as we passed along, their astonishing feats in slaying the buffaloes, by which they furnished the regiment with daily food ; and, in the meantime, they gave also to the officers and men, what they never before had seen, an exhibition of their powers of taking and breaking the wild horse.

Arrived on the summit of a hill, overlooking an extensive and beautiful valley, they requested the regiment to halt, and pointing, showed us the great Camanchee village, at the distance of three or four miles, with eight or ten thousand horses and mules grazing on the plains around it. They then led us into the valley, and at the distance of a mile or so from the village, requested us to halt again, for the chief and the cavalry of the tribe were coming out to meet and welcome us.

Colonel Dodge formed his regiment in three columns, himself occupying the front, with his staff ; and after resting an hour or so in that position, two or three thousand horsemen were seen, in real military order, advancing towards us. The chief was in advance, with his body-guard around him, and his colours flying on each side—the one a white flag, a flag of truce, and the other blood red ; showing that he was ready for either war or peace, whichever we might propose.

The white flag was seen waving in the hands of

each of our ensigns, and the red flag was lost sight
of. The chief now advanced, shook hands with
Colonel Dodge and the rest of the officers, and then
formed his army in a double column of nearly a mile
in length, dressed and manœuvred with a precision
equal to any cavalry manœuvre I ever saw, himself
and his staff taking their position in the centre, and
facing the officers of the dragoons.

After an exchange of friendly feelings between
Colonel Dodge and the chief, the whole Indian force
passed in review, each one extending his hand to
Colonel Dodge, and then to all the other officers as
he passed.

The chief then indicated a suitable spot for our
encampment, and we were soon settled for a residence
of two weeks, which afforded the writer of this and
his faithful friend, Joe Chadwick, amusement enough,
and plenty to do, in studying their manners and
customs, in a beautiful village of twelve hundred
skin tents, on the banks of a clear stream.

Here was material enough for the remainder of
this little book—horse-racing, ball-playing, dancing,
buying and selling horses, councils, etc., but we
must go on.

Everlasting peace and commerce with the United
States was agreed on, and the pipe of peace was
smoked, and we went to the *Pawnee-Picts*, their
allies, eighty miles farther on, where I have said
their wigwams were made in the form of straw bee-
hives, and thatched with long grass. Peace was
made with them also, and the officers were embraced

in the arms of the venerable chief *Wee-tar-ra-sha-ro.* We saw also the *Kiowas,* the *Wicos,* and the *Arapahos ;* all were friendly, and peace with all was easy, and was established, as with the Camanchees, " to last for ever." The mission of the dragoons was accomplished, and also the *far more important* designs of the author; for under the treaty of friendship and commerce came rum, and whisky, and a thousand abuses, the consequences of which were, that in one year after, the whole ground that we travelled over in peace and friendship became hostile ground, and has remained so ever since; whilst the works that I did have not faded or changed, but remain as fresh as the day they were made.

Back to Fort Gibson was a long and yet an interesting journey, but its incidents need not be recounted here—*sufficit,* that Charley was as fat and sleek on our return as he was when we started, though I had rode him more than two thousand miles ; and our familiarity and mutual attachment, from a great variety of circumstances, had grown to a perfection which but few horses or few men have felt, or could probably fully understand.

I at this time was taken extremely ill with bilious fever, and went to bed, and Charley went to pasture in a large field overgrown with white clover and other delectables.

During my illness of two months, and until I was in a convalescent state, my ever faithful friend and companion, Joe, was constantly by me, and afterwards left for the Mississippi, where his business called him. Charley I could not see during this siege of two months; but I heard reports of him often, and learned that he was doing well, and that he had got so wild and so independent that no one could get near him.

I was anxious to take Charley to St. Louis, but to send him down the Arkansas seven hundred miles, and then up the Mississippi nine hundred, by steamer, would be a heavy expense, and I resolved that just as soon as I should be able to ride, Charley and I would start for St. Louis by a shorter route, by crossing the intervening country of prairies, which are entirely wild and without roads, a distance, in a straight line, of five hundred and forty miles.

I knew the point of compass, and with a little compass in my pocket, and a clear sky, and plenty of ammunition, I felt no apprehensions whatever for the result. So one morning in the beginning of September, feeling sufficiently strong to mount Charley with a little aid, and having prepared my little outfit, I sent for Charley to be brought up and saddled; but the answer was soon brought back, that "Charley couldn't be caught, and that no one could get near him."

An old schoolmate of mine, from the Valley of Wyoming, Dr. Wright, then surgeon of the port, and who had attended me through my illness, started with me to the field where Charley was busily grazing, and on entering the field I called "Charley!" at which the noble animal, evidently recognising my voice after two months' separation, raised his head, and also his beautiful black tail and mane, and with his mouth full of grass, which he forgot to chew, instantly replied with a " eegh-ee-e-hee !" and started walking towards me, and soon increasing his pace to a trot, and then to a gallop, came up to me with another "eegh-ee-e-hee !" etc., and with the grass still hanging out of his mouth, commenced smelling my breath, which had always seemed a pleasure to him, and held his head down, and opened his mouth for the bridle which I put upon him, and with which I led him to my quarters.

In half-an-hour's time, with a couple of buffalo robes for my bed, a small coffee-pot and a tin cup tied to my saddle, with plenty of ground coffee and sugar, and about the half of a boiled ham, and some salt, my pistols in my belt, and my fowling-piece in my hand, I was ready to mount Charley and be off ; but here were the *Cherokee*, the *Choctaw*, and the *Creek* (Muskogee) chiefs assembled to take leave of me. What have I told you of them ? Nothing.

The *Cherokees*, of 25,000 ; the *Creeks*, of 21,000 ; the *Choctaws*, of 15,000 ; and the *Seminolees* of 12,000 ; are located in this vicinity, 700 miles west of the Mississippi, and 1200, and 1400, and 1800 miles from their former localities in the States of Georgia, Alabama, and Florida. These people are semi-civilized—in their own countries many of them were owning large plantations, and were raising extensive fields of cotton and corn, and lived in comfortable houses, built school-houses and churches, and printed and published several newspapers in their own language and English. But how came they here, in this wild and desert region ? there's *medicine* in this. No, not at all; all is easily explained, but is too long to be detailed in this place.

These people owned and occupied vast tracts of the best cotton-lands in Georgia and Alabama, and were therefore rich. "These lands were too valuable for Indians to possess, and the Indians were bad neighbours." General Jackson was elected President at that time; he decided that all the Indian tribes should be removed west of the Mississippi, and *it was done.* It took a long time, and was cruel ; they were forced to leave the graves of their parents and their children, and their houses and lands, and their crops growing in their fields, for a country given to them here, with a boundary line on the east, and the north, and the south, but none at the west ; meaning, that they must not trespass on their white neighbours on the east, but that they might, with their rifles, destroy as many of the buffaloes and wild Indians to the west of them as they pleased.

With the Seminolees in Florida, the process of moving them was a very disastrous one on both sides. The draft of a treaty for the chiefs to sign, by which they were to agree to exchange their lands for a country west of the Mississippi, was laid before the chiefs in council, who all refused to sign it, assigning as their reason that their parents and their children were buried around them, and that the country was their own, given to them by the Great

Spirit, and that they would therefore never remove from it.

The treaty was several times urged upon them without success; but it being announced to the eleven subordinate chiefs one day, that Charley Omatla, the head chief, had agreed to sign the treaty the next day—which they could not believe—they all assembled, and went to the Government agent's office, where it was to be done, with their rifles in their hands, to see if their chief was going to do so treacherous an act. With these chiefs came Osceola, whose name you all have probably heard; he was not a chief, but a desperate warrior, and of great influence in the tribe. The treaty was spread upon the table, and Charley Omatla, according to his promise, supposing the other chiefs would follow him, stepped forward, and leaning over the table, made his signature to the treaty, and as he was rising up from the table, the bullet from Osceola's rifle, and then six others from the chiefs, were through his body before it was to the ground, where he fell a corpse.

This treaty was sent by an express to Washington, "signed," (!) to be ratified by the Senate (then in session) before the news of the *manner* of signing should reach there, a distance of 1800 miles, and no railroad or telegraph in those parts at that time. The treaty was ratified; and though it was subsequently proved on the floor of the Senate that the chief Charley Omatla had been bribed with 7000 dollars, still the tribe was removed by force under the treaty, as we shall see.

Osceola fled into the wilderness, the chiefs following him as their leader—for, by the custom of all American Indian tribes, he who kills the chief in his own tribe is, *de facto*, chief, as long as they allow him to live : if his act is approved, no one can object to his lead; and if it is not approved, he is at once destroyed.

One hundred United States troops were then sent into the forest to commence a war upon the Seminolees, and to move them, by force of arms, under the treaty. Major Dade, a very meritorious officer, had command of this invading force ; and in a few days the news arrived that Major Dade and his whole force, with the exception of one man, had been destroyed by the Indians, who had lain in ambush, and gained an advantage by springing upon them before they could use their rifles ; much in the manner of the "Wyoming massacre," mentioned in an early part of this little book.

This was echoed through all the newspapers in the United States, and of course across the Atlantic, as a "*horrid massacre ;*" and so was every successive battle for six years afterwards when the Indians had the best of the fight; and whenever, by an equal or more cunning stratagem, a number of the Indians were killed, the announcements were headed "glorious victory !"

The gallant Osceola, at the head of his Spartan band of warriors, retiring before some 10,000 disciplined troops, kept them at bay for six years, bravely disputing every foot of ground. He was at last captured, however (or rather kidnapped), with four of his principal chiefs and 200 of his warriors, by a stratagem too disgraceful to have ever been practised by an Indian tribe. They were called up by a flag of truce, and as Osceola advanced, with a white flag in reply in his own hand, and their weapons left behind them, they were encompassed by an order from the officer in command, and, pinioned and fastened on horses' backs, were made prisoners of war, and sent to Fort Moultrie, at Charleston in South Carolina.

Here, my little readers, we have arrived at last to a definition of "*Treachery in Warfare.*" This disgraceful act was condemned by every officer in the United States army, and it is probable that the shame and repentance of the one who was guilty of it, have sufficiently punished him for it. The Administration discountenanced the act, but the chiefs were too valuable a prize to be released, notwithstanding; and all were sent, as "PRISONERS OF WAR," through the States, to the wilderness frontier, where we now find them.

Thus was broken the spirit of the Seminolees, and thus ended the Seminolee war, after an expense to the Government of 32,000,000 of dollars, the lives of 28 officers and 600 soldiers, as many Indians, and 2000 innocent and defenceless men, women, and children, living exposed on the borders of their country, whose lives are always known to be imperilled when an Indian war is waging in their vicinity.

From the city of New York to Charleston, a dis-

tance of 1500 miles, I travelled with my canvas and
brushes to paint the portrait of this extraordinary
man, Osceola. Though a humble prisoner in the
fort, I found him an easy, affable, and pleasant man,
but broken-hearted. He was a half-caste, and spoke
English enough to describe to me many of the
interesting events of the war, and the shameful
manner in which he had been entrapped. I painted
his portrait full length, and also those of *Mic-e-no-pa*,
Co-a-ha-jo, *Cloud*, and *King Phillip*, the four chiefs
captured with him.

There were at Fort Moultrie at this time 250
men, women, and children, who were taken with
Osceola, and all held as prisoners of war.

One of the young men of this party, and one of
the handsomest men I ever saw, was one morning
accused by a white man, a producer of poultry and
vegetables, living in the vicinity of the fort, of having
stolen a chicken from him the night before. The
complaint was laid before the chiefs, who took
cognisance of it, hearing the proofs advanced by the
accusing party, which he made out to be very con-
clusive, while the young man accused had no evidence
to give, only asking the chiefs, "Did any Seminolee
ever know *Chee-ho-ka* to steal?" However, the
white man's evidence was so strong that he was
convicted, and the sentence of the chiefs, though
prisoners of war (they being partly civilized), was,
by the custom of their country, that he should be
publicly whipped the next morning at nine o'clock.
At seven o'clock, however, the next morning, his

body was found suspended from a spike in the side of the wall of the fort, by a thong of raw hide, with a noose around his neck, and quite dead. And a little time after, while the officers of the garrison and the Indians were in a group around him, the *fiend* came up who had sworn against him, with the chicken under his arm, and alive, and confessed that it had not been stolen!

This wretch was standing right by my side at the moment, and from an impulse quicker than thought, I seized him with both hands by the throat with an iron grip, that I never was capable of before or since; and *lynching*, without waiting, must have been expressed in my face, for several of the officers stepped forward and begged me to use no violence; and what had ten times more effect, the soft and delicate hand of Osceola was laid lightly on my shoulder, when he whispered, "Don't, don't, my friend, don't hurt him; don't strike a dog!" I let the monster go, and the women and children hooted and hissed him out of the fort, and gave him his chicken to carry home.

After these events I returned to New York, and to my great surprise on my arrival in that city, I learned that Osceola was dead. The news, by express, had passed me on the road. He died the next day after I left the fort, and his disease was announced as a sudden attack of the quinsey.

––––––

But this is an awful long time to keep poor Charley waiting under the saddle, for, like myself, when he was ready, he was always impatient to be off. Well, I took leave of my old friend, Dr. Wright, the officers of the post, and the chiefs who, I said, had gathered to bid me good-bye. These *good-byes* were for ever, and therefore were sorrowful—but my farewell to the *country* was quite the reverse—for the officers and men of the garrison were dying at the rate of six or eight per day, and of the Indian tribes in the vicinity almost an equal proportion, from a deadly fever raging at the time.

Charley and I mounted the grassy hills back of the fort, and soon disappeared. The country for five hundred and forty miles ahead of us (about twice the breadth of England), of hills and dales, of meadows and grassy plains, with brooks, and rivers, and oak openings, was vast, and apparently tedious ; but as my departure from the deadly atmosphere of Fort Gibson was a sort of *escape*, and myself in a state of convalescence, with the bracing air of autumn around me, I entered upon it with a pleasure that few can appreciate who have seen and felt but the monotones of life.

Charley and I, though heretofore the best of friends, had always before had too much company with us to know how much we loved each other ; we both required the solitary and mutual dependence we were now entering upon to fully develop the actual strength of sympathies that had long existed between us, and the extent to which such sympathies may be cultivated between an animal that works for an object, and another that labours without one.

There was another advantage we had that took
much of the apparent hardships of our coming campaign from our shoulders; that arising from the fact
that Charley and I were old campaigners together,
and knew exactly how to go at our work. And
there was *yet another* advantage that cheered the
way very much. Twenty-five days is a long time to
be entirely *mum*, without the power of speaking to
any one, or hearing the cheering sound of any one's
voice; and from a long familiarity and practice,
Charley and I had established a sort of language
which was at times very significant—at all events
better than none—and therefore very cheering in
breaking the awful monotony of a solitary campaign
on the prairies. As, for instance, when I went to
the field to catch Charley, as I have before mentioned, after a separation of two months, when I said,
"Charley, is that you?" he instantly replied, "Eegh-
ee-e-eh" (yes); here was an affirmative, distinctly;
some might call this *gibberish*, but still it had its
meaning; and if he sometimes used it in a wrong
sense, he was nevertheless sure to be right, provided
I put him the right sort of questions; and certainly
he had one agreeable peculiarity which by no means
belongs to all travelling companions in those desert
countries, that of answering immediately either
night or day, to any question I put him. But we
shall see.

I said we had set off; we were now wending our
way over the prairie hills and knolls, crossing beautiful green fields, passing through forests of timber,

leaping and wading brooks, and, when night overtook us, bivouacing in the grass.   By the sun,
while it shone, we easily kept our course ; and when
it was obscure, our little pocket compass showed it
to us.

I was feeble, having just risen from a bed of sick-
ness, but meeting a cool and bracing autumnal wind,
I was every hour gaining strength, though I had
every alternate day an ague chill and fever, and
for these, as I felt them coming on, I dismounted
from Charley, and lay in the grass until they
were over.

Charley profited by these halts, as his saddle and
packs were taken off, and he had an hour or two to
luxuriate on the prairie grass, of which he was very
fond.   He got a good roll or two in the grass in the
meantime, which seemed to be a great luxury to
him ; and these rolls he took a peculiar pleasure in
performing as near to me as he could without rolling on to me.   The shake and the fever, the bait and
the roll all over, and Charley saddled again, we
would start on our course.

Carrying one of my barrels always charged with
shot, ready for grouse or other small game, and the
other with ball, our larder was easily supplied from
day to day with fresh food without the trouble of
dismounting, except to tie it to my saddle for my
supper and breakfast where I encamped.   Grouse
were many times a-day rising under Charley's feet,
and now and then a fine fat doe was gazing at us,
little thinking that in five minutes the choicest part

of her rump-steaks would be suspended from Charley's saddle-strings.

With the exception of one night in the twenty-five I managed to bivouac on the bank of some little stream or river, where there was water to make my coffee, and wood to make a fire. We generally halted a little before sundown, so as to give Charley abundance of time to get his supper before I took him up; that is, before I took up his picket and brought him in. The moment his saddle was off I drove down his picket where the grass was plenty and fresh, and gave him the full length of his lasso to feed around.

I would then gather my wood and make my fire; and that well going, I would dress my prairie hen or prepare my venison steak, erecting them on little sharpened stakes before my fire, and get my coffee-pot on the coals, and spread out all my little traps, such as a tin cup, a bowie-knife, an iron spoon, a little sack of salt, some sugar, and a slice or two of cold ham.

I was in the habit (and this was a habit of long standing with Charley and me) of leaving my little bivouac just at such times and going to Charley with a little treat of salt, of which he was very fond, and which he no doubt took with an additional relish from the fact that I always stood by him, while he licked it out of my hand. This might perhaps have been one of the causes of Charley's affectionate attachment to me; and on this occasion I had taken care to lay in enough to keep up friendly feelings between us during our campaign.

Charley was in the habit, also, of receiving this little attention at that particular time when his meal was about half enjoyed and mine about ready; and he had learned the time so well, that if I was not ready at the moment, his head was up and his tail spread out like that of a turkey-cock, while he would stand gazing at me. I did not ask him on these occasions what he wanted, for he might have been perplexed to answer emphatically, but I would say to him, "Charley! do you want your salt?" "Eegh-ee-e-eh!" (yes). He never failed to answer me in the affirmative on these occasions, and I never failed to carry it to him.

After finishing my supper, and just at dark, having brought in and driven his picket close by the side of me, I was in the habit of spreading one of my robes upon the grass, and using my saddle for a pillow, with the other robe drawn over me, head and all; thus sleeping soundly and comfortably until day-light, when Charley became restive; getting up and moving his picket, I generally got another good nap of an hour or so before rising for the day. Fire built, breakfast eaten, and Charley saddled, we were jogging along again.

In one instance we crossed a large prairie of many miles in extent, without a tree or a bush in sight, all the way covered with a short grass of some six or eight inches high, and the country all around us, when we were in the middle of it, perfectly level, and the horizon a perfect straight line, "out of sight of land," as it is termed in those regions. Night

overtook us in the midst of this, and we were obliged
to bivouac without water, but not without fire. We
had no coffee, of course, that night; but a venison
steak I cooked very nicely with a fire which I made
of dried buffalo dung, which I gathered on the
prairie.

I was awoke in the middle of the night by thunder
and lightning approaching in a terrible thunder-
storm. I got up and drove Charley's picket doubly
strong, and folding up my nether robe to keep it
dry, and laying it on the saddle, I took my seat upon
it, and spread the other one over my head; it falling
to the ground all around me in the form of a tent,
sheltered me and all my things perfectly from the
rain. The rain fell in torrents, and the flashes of
lightning seemed to run like fiery snakes over the
surface of the prairie, as if they were hunting for
something to strike; and I feared at every flash
that Charley and I might be snapped up for that
purpose.

The rain continued until morning, and I got some
sleep, but not of the most satisfactory kind, as I was
obliged to keep my upright position all night.

The monotony of these broad and level prairies
sometimes became exceedingly tedious, and even
doleful. I repeatedly fell asleep while riding, and
waking, I always found Charley not only going
along, but keeping on the course. Sometimes for
hours together, creeping along, without a moving
bird or beast in sight, while both were in deep
thought and contemplation, I have said, " Charley ! a

penny for your thoughts." "Eegh-ee-e-eh!" Charley
would reply; both bracing up our nerves, and
evidently moved along with a new life, and consequently increased speed.

One day, while we were thus jogging along, each
one wrapped up in his own thoughts, suddenly sprang
up from his lair, right before us, and within eight or
ten rods, a stately buck, with a pair of horns that
looked as if he had a great chair on his head!
Charley raised his head suddenly and stopped, and
was gazing at him, while I was getting my left barrel
to bear upon him, and he was trembling so from
fear or anxiety, that I had difficulty in getting my
aim. When I fired the deer staggered back a little,
but recovered, and bounded off, but without "showing his flag," by which I knew I had struck him
right. A few rods took him over the top of a little
hill, and he was out of our sight. I pushed Charley
up to the spot where he had stood, and I saw a profusion of blood on the grass, showing me that all
was right. While I sat reloading, Charley had his
nose to the ground surveying the bed where the
animal had been lying, and also smelling of the blood
upon the grass.

I then guided Charley along on the track, which
I could easily follow by the traces of blood.
Getting over the hill, the deer had gone into a
meadow of high grass which came quite to the top
of Charley's back. We entered the high grass on
the animal's track, and observing the extraordinary
excitement that Charley was under, which I could

feel by his motions as well as see, and observing also
his disposition to trace the deer, I had curiosity to
slacken the rein and let him take his course. He
went on in an unnaturally fast walk, snuffing and
smelling along at the blood, keeping the exact track
as precisely as a hound would have done, and so
followed it for half-a-mile or more; and finally
breaking out of the high grass at the foot of a small
hill, he suddenly turned his elevated head to the left,
and his ears pointing forwards, exclaimed, "Eegh-ee-
e-eh!" (here he is, evidently); for I looked in the
direction, and at twenty or thirty rods from us, on
the side of the hill, lay our noble buck, with his
frightful horns, quite dead!

I never straightened the rein even then; but
Charley started upon a trot, with his head and tail
up (oh, I wish I had a picture of him!), and brought
me within a few paces, and stopped. I then pushed
him up, and he smelled of the animal's nose and
the bleeding wound. "Are you sorry," said I,
"Charley?" "Eegh-ee-e-eh" (yes). "Oh, no," said I,
"Charley, you are not. I put the question wrong;
didn't I, Charley?" "Eegh-ee-e-eh." "That's
right." I dismounted, and Charley looked on
while I cut out a nice steak, and looked and smelled
back at me as I was tying it to his saddle, and
knew, no doubt, as well as I knew, that he was
going to carry it, and that I was to cook it for my
supper.

The almost incredible attachment of this noble
animal, and the rest of the curious incidents of this

journey from Fort Gibson to St. Louis, enough for a
book of themselves, have been written, and must be
omitted in this place. One incident, however, may
be necessary here, to inform the young reader how
we travellers in those rude countries get across
rivers which we often meet, where there are no
bridges or boats.

The greatest difficulty Charley and I had apprehended on our route was the Osage River, which it
was absolutely necessary to cross. We came to it—
it was half-a-mile wide, its banks full with a freshet,
and its muddy and boiling current pouring along at
the rate of five or six miles an hour. Here poor
Charley and I both looked chapfallen—give it up
we can't, we cannot go round it, and *cross* it we
must.

I got Charley's packs off, and put him out to
graze with his picket, and then, laying down my
gun, I followed up the river-shore for full a mile,
picking up drift-wood that I could find near it, and
laying these at the water's edge. Having gathered
enough in that way to form a raft sufficiently large
to carry my saddle and other things dry above the
water, I began following the shore down; accumu-
lating and floating these as I advanced along, and
getting them all together, I formed them into an awkward raft. I then took up Charley's picket, and
leading him to the water's edge and taking off his
lasso, I said, "Do you know what you have to do,
Charley?" "Eegh-ee-e-eh." There was no mistake
about this, as it was a thing he was used to.

I pointed to the other bank and drove him in, and off he started for the other shore. The current swept him down a considerable distance, but he got to the bank and out upon the prairie, and then he turned about and looked at me with a tremendous eegh-ee-e-eh! meaning this time, no doubt, " I am safe over, and I wish you the same." Charley then went to grazing, and I went to work, arranging my things on my raft; laying my saddle on it first, and then my robes, and my gun, and my clothes, which were all taken off.

I moved my raft into the stream, and swimming behind it, with one hand on it I propelled it, but very slowly, as the stream wafted us down. I laboured steadily and hard, however, and was at length nearing the other shore, but with two alarming apprehensions : the dried logs and sticks with which my raft was constructed were many of them rotten, and, absorbing the water, were sinking so low as to bring some of my things into the river ; and the shore where I was to land was lined with logs and tree-tops extending into the water.

But I had no alternative ; " I must force it against them and hold it from pulling to pieces, and get *myself*, at all events, and, if possible, my things ashore." Some of the long timbers of my raft, as I had no axe to make them of equal lengths, caught in the limbs of a tree lying in the water, whirling it round, and thereby threatening to pull it to pieces, and throwing me out again quite into the stream. A second effort, however, brought me to a little better place for landing, and at length I got my feet upon the ground and my traps all safely landed.

I was then in front of a dense forest, and full a mile below where I had lost sight of Charley standing with his head and tail up, and watching me as I disappeared behind the point of timber. Getting my clothes on and all things ashore, and preparing to start through the woods for Charley, I was startled by a cracking noise in my rear, and as I turned round, "Eegh-ee-e-eh!" said Charley, as he was crowding through the thick weeds and nettles behind me.

I have said that Charley was a "noble animal," and that "he loved me." Was he a noble animal? and for what? Could I repay Charlie for such affection? I gave him a double ration. "Ration! of what?" Of *salt*, of course.

CHAPTER XIV.

NOW for the fields and forests of everlasting
and never-ending green, of all Nature's
uninterrupted joy, of bloom, of gaiety, and
song! where dreary winter's blasts are not known,
and leaves are dropping, and buds and flowers are
growing at the same time! I have said that I knew
such a place as this. Who has breathed the delicious
air, seen the gaudy colours, and heard the sweet notes
of this flower-garden, this music-hall, this aviary of
the world—the grand and boundless valley of the
Amazon—and who will not, if his life and his purse
be long enough, go there and see it?

But we are not quite in it yet—*Caracas* is not in
the valley of the Amazon, nor is it the beginning,
exactly, of South America, but it is not a great way
from it. It is in Venezuela, on a sandy, scorching

219

coast. It was there that I first landed, and it is there we will begin.

From some unknown accident in the giant furnace that is burning underneath that region of country, a terrible shock and a shake were given in the beginning of this century, destroying ten thousand inhabitants; and, back of the town, and for a long distance on the coast, you may still see the frightful chasms which were opened at that time.

Natural things are on a large scale in the country now ahead of us. What is forged in the mighty furnace underneath us, and how long it has been worked, nobody knows. It formerly threw out its smoke and its cinders at the top of Chimborazo, only 19,000 feet high. Chimborazo (Tchimboratho) is "laid up;" the chimney now at work is Cotopaxi (Cotopassi), of equal height; its groanings and bellowings can be heard only 600 miles off! and a block of granite of 327 cubic feet it was able to project a distance of only nine miles!

The Orinoco is a large river not far from us—the Amazon is much larger—larger than the Missouri, but not quite so long; at the head of tide water it is but thirty miles wide; it has but about 1500 islands, and the largest of them, occupied by individual nabobs, contain only 50,000 head of horses and cattle! Naval engineers who have surveyed the bed of the Amazon at the expense of the United States Government report that the "Pennsylvania," a 140 gun-ship, built in Philadelphia, could go only as high as Tabatinga in low water; that is, only 1800 miles from its mouth! and ordinary passenger steamers could go only 1000 miles higher, without being liable to get aground, if the water was low! These distances are not very great! The valley of the Amazon is rather large; but it could not possibly hold with comfort more than the populations of England, France, Belgium, and the United States put together: for putting more than that number in might make some men's farms rather too small!

The precipitous wall of rock just back of the town of Caracas is only 6000 feet in height! and in the "shakes" it "shook and shuddered so that the stones and trees were tumbling down from its reeling sides in all directions." Can one climb it? No. But by a hard day's work you may get to its summit by going a great way round. And then, where is the town? and where the ocean? If the day is perfectly clear and sunny, you can see neither. If the weather is thick and overcast, you may see a little strip of white sand and some little red patches at your feet, if you can venture near enough to the brink; but the sky and the ocean are one, and you can't divorce them; and on the top—the cloud-capped summit—what's here? Here is a pebble! a sea-shore pebble! worn round by the waves on the sea-shore; not in the bottom of the ocean, for there are no waves there, the waters lie still in that place. What bird could have brought this here?— but stop, here's another, and another, and then thousands of others!

These pebbles are flint—they contain silicified zoophytes! Everything has a life and a death; these have lived—zoophytes live and grow only in the sea; their beds have been cretaceous. We are only 6000 feet above the sea, and looking into it at our feet. When were these pebbles rolled by the waves of the sea? Where, for thousands of years, to be rounded as they are? In what cretaceous bed lay they for thousands of years, and perhaps for thousands of centuries, to be changed from the living animal, with all their curious and intricate tentaculæ, into silex before they were rolled? and how long have they lain here? and then, how came they *here?* or where has *here* been? But don't let us go mad; let us get down from this place, we are too high. No; it's too much trouble to get back again; we are now on the top of the "Scylla," the grand plateau that sweeps off to the Orinoco. There are Indians on these plains, and I, of course, must cross them. Have any Indian tribes ever escaped me? Yes. Shall I ever see them all? I don't believe so.

How easily the reader travels! how soon he is across the Atlantic! how quick upon the summit of the Scylla and the plains of Venezuela! His sea voyage don't cost him fifty pounds—his knees don't ache like ours. He sits at home, while he reads and smiles at our tugging and groaning; but he loses much that we see. He carries no knapsack; and the escape from one rattlesnake, from one tiger, or from one drowning produces, perhaps, in one minute, more pleasure than he enjoys in a month. This *may* be so—who can contradict it?

My knapsack is heavy, but I have resolved to carry it. Dr. Hentz, a German botanist, and his man, are with me. We have no horses, but we resolve to cross these beautiful plains on our legs; may be the Gauchos, with their mules, will help us. Angostura is on the Orinoco; it is but a hundred and fifty miles—that's nothing.

The prairies in this country are *pampas;* in shape and distant appearance they are much like those which Charley and I passed over between Fort Gibson and St. Louis, rolling and sloping about in all directions, with beautiful clear streams winding through them, and copses and bunches of timber and bushes on their sides and along the banks of the streams.

But those bunches and copses when we come near to them, oh, how lovely! There are the beautiful bananas, the pennated, lofty, and dwarf palms, and, at their feet, palmettoes; acres on acres of geraniums in flowers of all colours and of various odours; of wild roses, and fifty kinds of flowering plants. The meadows are filled with lilies of various hues; the hedges are bending with wild plums and wild grapes. The orange and fig-trees are on every little hillock, and yellow with fruit, and still white with sweet blossoms. Pinks of a hundred colours and patterns, and violets of all hues are under our feet, and now and then a huge rattlesnake!

The busy little humming-birds are buzzing about

us, and ten thousands of beetles and other clumsy
flyers, that no one stops to inquire about, are
knocking and butting against us. Spathes of palm-
flowers are opening, and these swarm in myriads
about them.

The sun looks as it does at home, though perhaps a little smaller, and more over our heads; we
have to bend our necks more to look at it. Man
begins here to feel less than he does in England,
his shadow is shorter, it don't follow him so exactly,
and so far behind him.

The Indians; are there any? Yes; but not many.
Small-pox, and rum, and whisky have destroyed the
most of them. Here are the *Chaymas* and the
Goo-wa-gives, semi-civilized, mostly mixed with
Spaniards. Some full-bloods; colour and character
much like the Ojibbeways in North America;
rather small and slight in stature, but quick and
powerful men, beautifully formed, and no deformities
amongst them.

Who is the happiest man in the world just at this
time? Why, Doctor Hentz, while he is gathering
these beautiful plants and lovely flowers, and packing them in his large books, which a Chayma is
employed to help to carry to Angostura. And who
the next happiest? Why, I, of course, who am
putting these beautiful scenes into my portfolio; and
yesterday, that beautiful dance! What dance?
Why, the *mach-ee-o-a* (handsome or glad dance),
glad, or thankful, because the Indians are pleased
with us, and perhaps have received some valued

present, and also because the *medicine man* has told
them that I am *great medicine.* What! medicine
men here too? in South America? Yes, exactly the
same as in North America. The chief's portrait
was held up by the corners in the same way, and
the medicine men had a grand dance around it.
And then the warriors danced the war-dance, and
gave the war-whoop. What! the war-whoop here
too? Precisely the same. And then; and then, what?
Why then came the *handsome dance.* The young
women dance in this country, but not often.   Three
young and beautiful women were selected by the
chief to give this dance; it was an extraordinary
compliment paid to my *medicine;* for many years
it had not been seen. Was it beautiful? The most
beautiful thing I ever saw. How were these girls
dressed?   Each one had a beautiful tiger-skin
spread under her feet, upon which she danced; their
hair, fastened by a silver band passing around the
head, was falling down in shining tresses; long pins
of silver were run through their under lips, and
strings of blue and white beads were dangling from
them; large and small beads hung in great profusion around their necks, and polished brass bands
were worn, with strings of blue and white beads on
their slender wrists and ankles; their cheeks were
painted red, and their bodies were coloured white
with white clay.

Did they raise their feet from the ground when
they danced? No, not quite, their toes were always
on the tiger-skins. Did they separate their big

toes? Not an inch. Did they dance to music?
In perfect time to the beat of the drum and a chant
of the chief's. Were they graceful? Yes.

Nothing can be more beautiful of their kind than
the rolling plains between Caracas and the
Orinoco. They are abundantly stocked with wild
horses and wild (not buffaloes, but) cattle, which
answer all the same purposes for food to the
Indians as well as to white men. These are taken
both by the Indians and the Spaniards, not with
the bow and arrows or lance, but with the deadly
bolas.

The bolas is a cord of raw hide, branching three
ways from the centre, each branch being some eight
or ten feet in length, with a leaden ball of half-a-
pound or so in weight at its end. One of these
balls the rider holds in his right hand, while his
horse is at full speed, and the other two are swing-
ing around and over his head until he is in the
right position, when he lets go the ball in his hand,
giving them all a sling at the same time. The three
balls keep their respective opposite positions as they
are whirling about in the air, till one of the cords
strikes the neck of the animal, around which and its
legs the cords instantly wrap themselves, and the
animal falls upon its head and becomes an easy and
certain prey to its assailant, who, with a long lance
from his horse's back, or with his knife, by dismounting, does the rest.

This mode is used only for "killing." The wild
horses are killed in this manner for their skins and

their hair, and the wild cattle for their flesh, their skins, and their horns.

In taking wild horses for their *use*, this mode would not answer; for in nine cases out of ten the fall of the horse while at full speed, and entangled in the folds of the bolas, would break the animal's neck, or disable it for life.

For *catching* the wild horse, therefore, the *lasso* is used by these people much in the same way as it is used by the Indians in North America, which has been described; only with the difference, that when the horse is arrested by the lasso, and its speed is stopped, they strike it with a short baton (loo-tank) loaded with lead (something like a " life-preserver"), on the back part of the head, which stuns the animal, and it falls to the ground. The captor then places a bandage around its eyes, and gets upon its back. The horse, recovering from the blow, and rising, soon yields to the wishes of its cruel master, not daring to run with its eyes blinded.

By the effects of this mode of breaking, which I have seen and closely studied, I believe the natural spirit of the animal is irretrievably lost, to such a degree as greatly to diminish its value.

At the small town of Chaparro, about sixty miles from the Orinoco, we learned that a large armed force of insurgents in the civil war at Venezuela, which had suddenly broken out, was marching on Angostura; and by the aid of mules which we employed of the Gauchos, we got posted on to San-Diego, and from that to a point thirty miles below

Angostura, to the banks of the Orinoco; a canoe took us to Barrancas, and from that we got a steamer to Georgetown, Demerara, in British Guiana.

But stop; we did not come to Demerara in a moment, we *could not,* and why *should* we? What did we see, and what did we do? Why, we saw from our little "dug-out" the stately and dark forests overhanging the shores of the Orinoco. Is there anything like them on earth? I don't believe it.

"Stately," did I say? Yes, and lofty. The towering mora, the miriti, with its tall and elegant shaft, the tough hackea, the green-heart, the ebony, the copal locust, the beautiful hayawa, and the olow, with their sweet gushing resin, and the graceful banana, the queen of the forest, and twenty others, mingled and intermingled with cordage and ropes of creeping, and climbing, and hanging vines; with clumps and bouquets of beautiful flowers of all colours and at all heights; and chattering monkeys leaping from branch to branch, with their little ones on their backs, cunningly ogling us as we passed.

The solitary tocanos bowing to us from the withered tops of the lofty moras, and saluting us— "Tso-cano, tso-cano! no, no, no! go on there, go on there!" The beautiful white swans by hundreds, and pelicans also, as white as the snow, were flapping their long wings and on the air before I could get "Sam" to bear upon them. "Sam! who's Sam?" Why, *Sam Colt,* a six-shot little rifle always lying *before* me during the day, and *in my arms* during the night, by which a tiger's or an alligator's eye, at a hundred yards, was sure to drop a red tear—but don't interrupt me. The last of these were everywhere basking in the sun and plunging off from their slimy logs as we approached. The timid turtles were shoving down from the banks of sand, and the tortoises, with their elevated heads, came pacing out of the forest where they roam, taking shelter under the waves whilst their enemies passed.

It is easier to fly over the water and between these hundreds of islands, with their matted, and twisted, and almost wedged foliage, than through them; and these crooked avenues, for birds and wild fowl, are what the Strand and London Bridge are to the Londoners.

There are all sorts, and all sizes, and all colours on the wing; some slow and some fast; some actually loungers, and some evidently expresses, as they dart through the crowds like a shot. Many are gossipers, for they chatter as they travel. So there is din as well as motion; and in the midst of this, once in a while, a flock of wild geese must pass (an omnibus!); the crowd must give way! they fly in a triangle; their leader is a "*conductor*," and distinctly cries, "Get in, John! get in, John! Paddington! Paddington!" while the beautiful tocano turns his head sideways, and rolls his piercing eye down from the tops of the mora, as he echoes, "Go on, John! go on, John! go on! go on!"

"Here's a swarm of bees ahead of us," said Dr. Hentz; "we shall be stung to death!" "No, Doctor, its only the opening of a spathe; and you know what a spathe is better than I; that's in your line, Doctor." "Well," said the Doctor, "that's true, and I'll tell you."

"There are over two hundred different varieties of palm-trees in this country, and each sort has its blossoms and its fruits in its own shape. The fruit of all palms grows just where the leaves and branches start out from the trunk; and before the fruit comes immense large sacks or spathes, containing the flowers, are visible for weeks, and sometimes for months, before they are sufficiently perfected to open. These spathes on some palms are large enough for the back-loads of three or four men, and, when opened, present from ten to one hundred thousand fragrant and honey-bearing flowers of purple, of pink, and other colours, perfuming the atmosphere for a great distance around them.

"The honey-sucking birds and insects generally get a few days' previous knowledge of these important approaching events, and gather in myriads around them, ready for the onslaught, when a bright and clear morning shows them their feast opened and spread before them. That is the scene now before us. You see in the midst of that whirling cloud of insects the spadix of a palm in full bloom, and here is now just going on the 'set-to,' and pell-mell for honey. There's no danger of being stung now, I admit. These busy little creatures,

though most of them with stings, are all at work;
they have their little ones to feed, and no time now
to sting; let's step and look at them a while."
Thank you, Doctor. This was a short lecture in
botany; the Doctor had given us many.

We stopped our canoe, and looked at the busy
group. Through my opera-glass the scene was
indescribably curious. Whilst thousands of honey-
bees, of humble-bees, of beetles, and humming-birds,
and other honey-sucking insects were whirling
around it, like all other riches and luxuries of the
world, it was easily seen that these were divided
amongst the lucky few. The surface of these clusters
of flowers seemed chiefly engrossed by the swift-
darting and glistening little humming-birds, of all
sizes and all hues, whose long and slender bills
entered every approachable cell, as they balanced on
their trembling wings, ready to dart away when
danger comes. These seemed masters of the feast.
But there were others apparently even more successful; the busy, fearless, little bees, and humble bees,
and others, that crept between and through the
winding maze of flowers, and culled their choicest,
freshest sweets, where others could not enter; but
then, where were they? Like too many of the
world who enjoy the sweetest things, the nearest
to eternity.

The sharp claws of the bright-eyed little bee-
hawk suspended him from these mats of flowers; he
loves honey, but sucks it not; he gets it in a shorter
way; he picks up these little labourers as they come

out with their rich loads, and puts them in his crop.
His feast finished, he flies, but heavily, with his
plundered prey, and knows the gauntlet he too has
to run; *his* enemies are of his own kin, but stronger
and fleeter on the wing. *They* sit like silent
sentinels on the dry limbs of overhanging trees,
and stoop upon him and snatch him up as he passes
through the open air. Amidst these incongruous
masses of contending and jealous insects, with their
deadly weapons, many conflicts and many deaths
ensue; and many such, with their accumulated
treasure, drop to the ground beneath, in the grass,
and there—("Let's go ashore," said the Doctor,
"and I'll show you") and he did show me. "There,
do you see that little green snake, and that white
one too? they are both of one species, though their
colours are different; they both are honey-eaters,
though the world don't believe it. They know just
as well as these insects when a spathe of flowers is
opened, and here they are. They take the honey-
loaded carcasses of the unlucky combatants that fall."
"How did you learn this curious fact, Doctor?"
"From the Indians."

"Doctor," said I, "next to the Indians, the thing
I wish most to see is a cocoa-nut tree, and to hear
your description of it." "I don't think there are
any near here," said the Doctor; "the cocoa-nut is
not a native of America, but it has been introduced,
and we shall probably see many of them before long;
but I have not met one yet."

Well, we were jogging along on the Orinoco, were

we not? Look, next time you go to the Museum, for the beautiful *cotingas;* there are several sorts of them, a size larger than the humming-birds, and equally beautiful in plumage. They are all here, and in great numbers are darting about amongst us.

And the *campanero* (strange bird!), their notes exactly like the tinkling or tolling of a bell. They give the forest the most singular character. They are solitary birds, I take it, for we never see them. We hear their strange notes, and then, from some mystery in sound not yet explained, we can't tell which way they are; if we go one way or the other to look for them, it's all the same; the sound is equally near, and all around us; it seems a mile distant, but it may be within a few yards; it tolls only just at night, when it is too late to see it, or just at daybreak, when the difficulty is the same. There's *medicine in this!* It's like the thunder-bird of the "thunder's nest." I never could see one, though I am a "*medicine man.*" *Is* it a bird? or is it some sort of *mirage of sound?* Is it not a distant cow-bell? It's not a *phantom;* phantoms "fly before us;" this does not fly; it's all around, before, and behind us, and travels with us; but we'll drop it, and perhaps hunt for it again.

Though these forests and these lovely river-shores are constantly ringing with song, still one-half of animal nature seems to sleep during the day; for when one set of songsters are done, another begins; but how different! The songs of the day are all joyous and cheering, if we could understand them,

characteristic of the glow and warmth of sunshine ;
but in the dark, how emblematic of the gloom and
loneliness about us, and characteristic of that stealth
with which the animals of the dark steal upon their
sleeping, unprotected, prey! The frequent roar we
often hear of the hungry jaguar ; the doleful howl-
ings of the red monkeys ; the hooting of owls ; and
every night the inquisitive *goat-sucker,* who lights
upon a limb as nearly over us as he can in safety,
and shocks our nerves, in his coarse and perfectly
masculine and human voice, "Who are you? go
away! go away!"

Well, we'll *go* away; we'll jog on ; we are stopping too long in this place ; but then, one word
more before we start. What great ugly beast is
that I see yonder, hanging under a branch of that
hayama tree? That ? That's a *sloth,* sir, the laziest
animal of all the world, and perfectly harmless ; it
hasn't the energy to stand upon its legs, but hangs
all day without moving, and, fast asleep under the
limb of a tree, hangs by his long toe-nails. What!
hangs and sleeps all day? Well, that's easier than
to *stand* and sleep ; its like sleeping in a hammock.
What a gentleman ! Sleeps all day! But he is a
fat looking fellow. I believe he is up all night ;
and if you have a hen-roost I advise you to beware
of him, he seems well fed ; the world is full of such
gentlemen. He can't move—ha ! hand me " Sam."
I'll prick him up a little, and see what he's made of.
Bang ! he falls into the river ! but he swims ! and
now upon the bank ! and at one leap upon the side

of a tree! and at another of forty feet, upon another tree! and the next, out of sight! That's your lazy gentleman, ha! Why, no alligator could catch that fellow in the water; no dog could catch him on the land; and amongst the trees, few monkeys would be a match for him. I believe he is a great rascal.

We are at Barrancas now; Barrancas is a large town; but what are large towns to us? London is considerably larger. This steamer goes to Demerara; just where our little canoe can't go, and where we *must* go. "A good chance to overhaul and air your plants, Dr. Hentz."

"First-rate, Mynheer."

"This is a strange looking place, captain. What a vast number of islands there are ahead of us! We are at the mouth of the Orinoco?"

"Not quite."

"It has a hundred mouths, I am told?"

"No; only fifty."

"How grand and magnificent the forests around us! Those thousands and tens of thousands of lofty palms, their trunks standing in the water, actually! Why, they seem like a grand colonnade, or portico of some mighty edifice!"

"Yes, they are truly so; but they don't look exactly so in low water. The tide is getting well nigh up now. I see you are an Englishman, sir?"

"No, captain, not exactly; I am an American; that's not far from it."

" Give us your hand, stranger ; you know who I am ; we'll have a long talk after a while."

" But, captain, before you go below, what sort of birds' nests are those in those trees on the shore, and on that island ahead of us ?   They are too large for·rooks, I think."

" Well, *don't* now !   You'll make me smile, sir, if you don't take care.   They are a large sort of bird, sir, and you'll see them hovering about us in a little time.   These birds fly upon the water, sir ; not in the air ; they live upon fish and oysters ; and I ex- pect some fresh supplies from them by-and-by.

" These, what you call birds, sir, are Indians, *Guaroanes* (Caribbees) ; they build their houses in the trees, and go up to them by a ladder from their canoes, and never venture out except when the tide is up, and that always in their canoes ; when the tide is out, all is deep mud and slime about them, which nothing can walk through."   (Plate No. VI.)

" Captain, I would give almost anything if we could stop near some of these for a little time."

" That's quite easy, sir, for I've got to lie-to a little till the tide gets high enough to take us over the bar, and you may have a first-rate opportunity to see them, and *visit* them too, if you wish, for I am going to send the yawl to one of them with that Spanish gentleman and his two daughters sitting in the bow yonder, who are going to them."

" Splendid ! captain, splendid !"

Plate VI.   Wig-wams in the Trees. — *p.* 286.

CHAPTER XV.

Demerara—Paramaribo—Rio Essequibo—Howling Monkeys—
Village—Treachery of Interpreter—Indian Hospitality—
Indian Superstition—Showing Revolver to the Indians—
The Old Minié—The Young Revolver—Hill of the Shining
Stones—Picking up a Rattlesnake—A Bed of Poppies.

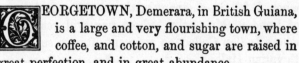

EORGETOWN, Demerara, in British Guiana,
is a large and very flourishing town, where
coffee, and cotton, and sugar are raised in
great perfection, and in great abundance.

One could stop a long time, and, in fact, spend
his life here, with pleasure; but, as I have said, we
are not travelling to see large towns and cities—we
have no time, and everybody knows what they are;
but it is not all the world who knows what's before
us. And no better key to that can be given at this
place than the following extracts made from a series
of letters written at Para, in Brazil, by a fine young
man of the name of Smyth, who (like my faithful
friend, Joe Chadwick, in North America) accompanied
me across the Acary (or Tumucumaque) Mountains
to the valley of the Amazon. These letters were

237

written to his brother in Berkshire several years
since; and, since my return, I have been permitted
to make these extracts, which so graphically and
correctly describe scenes and country we passed, that
I consider them well deserving of this notoriety.

"PARA, BRAZIL, 1854.

"DEAR BROTHER,—You will have thought, perhaps, from my long silence, that I had been killed
by a tiger, or swallowed by an alligator before this.
I arrived in Georgetown, Demerara, one year since,
and I am sorry to say I found it not to be the
thing it was said to be. I lounged about there for
six months without making a sixpence. My tin
was about all out, without my knowing what to do,
when I fell in company with an old acquaintance
of London, Mr. Catlin, whom you will remember,
whose Indian Collection we went often to see in the
Egyptian Hall.   *   *   *

"I one day espied a crowd in the street, amused
at the red heads of some Caribbee Indians, looking
out of a chamber window. I ventured in, and finding myself at the top of the stairs, I got a peep in
and saw what was going on. There was a great
crowd in the place, and at the farther end of the
chamber I recognised the old veteran, with his
palette and brushes in his hands, painting the portrait of an Indian chief, who was standing before
him. He didn't observe me, and I backed quietly
out.

"An hour or so after, when the crowd had cleared

chiefly away, and the chamber was pretty much
empty, I entered again, and advancing, offered my
hand. I said, 'You won't remember me, sir; it is
over six years since you saw me;' but he called my
name in an instant.

*　　　*　　　*　　　*

"There was a German Doctor with him, and they
had just arrived from Angostura, on the Orinoco
River, their noses and faces tanned and burnt almost
to the colour of Indians. A large table in the room
was loaded with plants and skins of animals and
birds, and the sides of the room around lined with
Indian portraits and views of the country.

"I soon learned they were going to start in a few
days for a journey across the Tumucumaque Mountains into the valley of the Amazon, in Brazil, just
the place precisely where I wanted to go of all
others. I proposed to the gentleman, that if he
would pay my expenses and furnish me with powder
and ball, as I had a first-rate Minié rifle with me, I
would go with him, hunt for him, and protect him,
at the risk of my own life if it was necessary. This
offer saved him the expense of hiring a worse man,
and suited him exactly, and the arrangements were
soon concluded. 　　*　　　*　　　*　　　*

"You know the 'old Minié' well, and what she
can do; and you may easily imagine there was
enough now preparing for her. He spent some
little time in painting some tribes in this neighbourhood and in Dutch Guiana, at Paramaribo, and then
we were prepared to cross the mountains, and at last

set out, after I had got pretty tired of waiting, in a
large canoe, with a family of Indians who had come
down to Georgetown to make their trade.   Our
course was up the Essequibo, and our party consisted of Mr. Catlin (or governor, as we called him) ;
the German Doctor and his servant ; an Indian half-
breed, whom the governor had hired as a guide; a
Spaniard, our interpreter ; and myself.

" We ascended this magnificent river for a hundred or two miles, to near the great falls, and then
took off to an Indian town, where we were told we
could get horses and mules to take us on to the base
of the mountains.

   *   *   *   *

" The banks of this noble river, lined with its
stately palms and other evergreen trees, are beautiful
beyond anything that can be described or imagined.
The river is alive with wild fowl and alligators, and
the shores abound in wild animals as we pass along.
The old Minié was almost constantly in my hands,
and the lead which she hove ashore was curious, I
assure you.

" The Indians in this country use no guns, and
the Indian party in our boat were constantly amused
and astonished at the distance at which I would
knock the alligators off their logs, and the manner
in which the scales would fly when I struck them.

   *   *   *   *

" The whole shore on both sides was lined with
one immense forest of palms and other trees overhanging the river, and many of these, from the

ground to their very tops, were covered with white and pink flowers. Their branches were constantly shaken by squeaking monkeys looking out at us and leaping from tree to tree, keeping opposite to us as we passed along; and parrots were chattering and scolding at us as if we had no right to be there. Peccaries, a sort of wild pig, were running on the banks in great numbers; they are fine game, and good eating.

"At night the Indians always slept in their canoe, but we stretched our hammocks and slept upon the high banks amongst the trees, lighting a strong fire, and keeping it up all night.

"There is a sort of monkey that howls in the night, making the most hideous noise that ever was heard, and they seemed to gather around us every night. As soon as it was nightfall, it was curious to see the bats come out and sail about over the shores of the river. Some of these were as large as a leather apron; and the mosquitoes, oh, horrid! they were the worst enemy we had; the old Minié couldn't touch them. There was no such thing as getting to sleep until ten or eleven o'clock at night, when they always disappeared.

"When we left the canoe and our Indian party, and took to the land, we had a hard siege of it; each one had to carry his share of the luggage, and we were all loaded down. We left in the morning, and our guide brought us to a small Indian village just before night, through swamps and quagmires, with nothing but a footpath to follow. The Indian

town, however, was upon an open plain, very beautiful, with small palms in groups standing out
upon it.

" The huts of these people were all thatched over
with palm-leaves, and there were a great number of
horses and mules grazing around them; and amongst
them some of the handsomest mules I ever saw.

" The guide led us to the chief's hut, who received
us very kindly; he was an oldish man, and was
seated on the ground. Some skins were placed for
us to sit upon, and, through the interpreter, the
governor soon commenced a conversation with him;
telling him where we were going, and what our
object was. The chief was sitting cross-legged, and
was smoking a long pipe; his head was cast down,
and he now and then gave a sort of grunt, and I saw
that the governor began to show a little concern.

" The conversation went on for some time, without much change, when the governor commenced
making some sort of masonic signs with his hands
to the chief, who raised his head a little, very suddenly, and after watching them closely for a minute
or so, he laid down his pipe, and striking both his
hands quickly together, he began making signs in
reply. The governor began to smile, and the chief,
seeing they mutually understood each other, jumped
upon his feet as nimbly as a boy. The governor
arose, and the chief embraced him in his arms, calling him his ' brother !'

" A further conversation then took place between
the two for some time, while the old chief's limbs

trembled with pleasure and excitement.   The governor then explained to him that he had come from a great many tribes of red people exactly like himself, living three or four hundred days' march to the north (in North America), who all understood the same signs, and smoked the pipe in the same manner : to which the chief replied, 'These people are our brothers, and you are their father.'

"The governor told the chief what our views were, and that we wanted to hire some horses and some of his young men to take us to the base of the mountains.   At this, the chief turned to the interpreter, who it seems had been giving him a different interpretation, and told him he was a great scoundrel to deceive the white men who had employed him, and to try to deceive him also.

"The Spaniard, seeing himself detected, was in a great rage, and demanded his pay for three months, for which time he was employed.   The governor refused to pay him a sixpence, when he advanced up suddenly in front of the governor, and placing his hand upon the handle of a large knife which he wore in his waistband, demanded his money again ; but observing the muzzle of the old Minié about that instant near his short ribs, and a click ! (a sort of a hiccup she has when she is just about to speak), he drew a little back.

"The chief then said to him, as he had acted the traitor in *his* house, it was for *him*, and not for the white man, to pay him ; that he was known to many of the young men of the tribe to be a great scoundrel, and the sooner and the more quietly he got out of the way the better. The scamp then walked off, and we never heard of him afterwards.

" All was now friendly and cheerful ; the pipe was passed round several times for us all to smoke ; the old chief holding the long stem in both hands, as he walked round and held the pipe to our mouths. The old man introduced us to his two sons, young men about my age ; they were almost entirely naked, like most of the tribe ; but I only wish that I had limbs so round and beautiful as theirs. I often thought how beautiful a racecourse of such young men would be.

" The chief told us that his house was small, and not very good, but he would do all he could to make us sleep well, and we should be welcome. We were placed, with all our things, in a small adjoining hut, and passed the night very comfortably.

" The governor commenced the conversation the next morning, by telling him he was going to show him and his people how the red-skins looked in North America, where he had come from, which the good old man could not at all comprehend, until the governor opened a large portfolio with a hundred or more portraits of Indians, buffalo hunts, etc., all in full blazing colours. Perhaps few men on earth were ever more suddenly amused and astonished than this old veteran was at that moment.

" We were seated at that time by the side of him, and all upon the ground, with the German Doctor and his man, and no other Indians in the hut. The

old man looked at them all, but very fast; and when
he was done, began to howl and sing the most droll
song I ever heard in my life, which seemed at last
to be the signal for a strange-looking being to enter,
whose visage was filled with wrinkles, his face most
curiously painted, with a fan in one hand, and a
rattle in the other, which he was shaking as he
entered.

" This, I learned, was an Indian doctor, who took
his seat by the side of the chief, and after they had
hastily looked over the pictures, the old chief got up
and took down from quite up under the roof of his
hut a little round roll of bark, like a paper scroll
some eight or nine inches long, which had several
yellow ribands tied around it, and in the middle a
string of blue beads hanging down.   He handed this
to the old doctor, who took it in his hands, and
raising it near his mouth, spirted upon it from his lips
at three or four efforts, at least a pint of some liquid
as white as milk, covering it from one end to the other.
Where on earth this was concealed, or what it was
none of us could tell.   The chief then laid it on the
fire, which he sat by, and kindled up until it was
entirely consumed, while he in silence gazed upon it.
This done, both he and the doctor got up, and
smilingly gave us their hands in a hearty shake.

" The governor never could learn what was the
meaning of all this ceremony, but supposed it was
some offering to the Great Spirit.

" The whole village was by this time assembling
out-doors, where we went, and the rest of this day

was spent in looking at the pictures, and also in
examining our guns. You know the 'old Minié,'
and the governor had always in his hand one of
Colt's six-shot rifles ; this he had nicknamed '*Sam.*'

" These people had but three or four light and
short guns in their village (and good for nothing),
their weapons being bows and arrows, and lances,
and the bolas. The governor's gun, therefore, was
the greatest of curiosities to them, as they never had
heard or thought of a revolver ; and I having given
out that the governor's gun would shoot all day
without stopping, made an exhibition of its powers
necessary.

" For this I took an old cow-skin, which was
stretched on a hoop, and had been the door of a hut,
and placing it at some sixty or eighty yards, with
a bull's-eye in the centre, the governor took his
position, and let off one ! two ! three ! four ! five !
six ! By an understanding, I at that moment touched
him on the shoulder, till we could learn from the
chief, who was standing by the side of us, whether
that was enough ; at which, on having appealed to
the crowd, they were all perfectly satisfied. While
this little parley was going on, the governor, without
their observing it, had slipped off the empty cylinder
and placed another one on, which he always carried
in his pantaloons pocket, charged and ready with six
shots more. His rifle was raised and levelled at the
target, and he was about to proceed, when the chief
advanced and said it would be wrong to expend
more powder and ball, as we might want it all on

our journey, and that his people were now all convinced that his gun would fire all day.

" The target was brought up, and the shots all in the space of the palm of one's hand : they were still more astonished, and myself a little so amongst the number.

" Next came the ' *old Minié.*' I was anxious to show them what she could do. And I carried the target and set it up at about two hundred yards, and when they saw me strike it the first shot, though it could not fire so fast, my gun was an equal curiosity, for hitting the target at such a distance. They were both considered great mysteries, and there was not a man in the tribe who was willing to touch the triggers of either of them.

" But the funniest part of this scene now took place. Some of the little boys standing near the governor having discovered in his belt a revolver pistol, which he always carried, had reported it to some of the young men, who came up to him very timidly to ask him if he hadn't a young rifle. The governor not having thought of his pistol during the excitement, began to smile, and drawing it out, said, ' Yes.' Here the squaws, who had all along been in the background, now began to come up, but very cautiously, all with their hands over their mouths as they gave a sort of a groan and a ' ya, ya.' This was really amusing.

" The governor held the pistol by the side of the rifle, and the exact resemblance, except in size, convinced them that the pistol was a ' young one ;' and if it could have said 'mamma,' it would not have created greater sympathy amongst the women than it did.

" The governor explained that it was very young, but notwithstanding, at a shorter distance, it had got so as to do pretty well. At this he levelled it at the trunk of a palm-tree, standing some six or eight rods off, and fired a couple of shots, to their great amazement. For these, the boys were cutting and digging with their knives for several days, but the report was they had not got to them before we left.

" All satisfied, the governor placed his pistol in his belt, and wrapping his capôt around him, the squaws all raised a shout of approbation, ' Keep the poor little thing warm.'

" The report of the ' *medicine gun*, that could fire all day without reloading,' went ahead of us to all the tribes we afterwards visited, and the moment we arrived, all were waiting to see it. If these poor people had had the shillings to give, I could very soon have made all the fortune I ever wanted, by exhibiting *old Sam and ' the young one.'*

" The governor having painted some portraits, and his friend the German doctor having busied himself in collecting his roots and plants, we were prepared to move on. The doctor, however, who was a feeble man, and was getting weak, and I think a little afraid of the Indians, resolved, with his man, to go back from this place, and we never heard anything further how they got on. Here our party was split, just half the number we started with gone back.

" The chief gave us one of his sons and a nephew, a fine man, and horses to ride until we reached the base of the mountains, and we had yet the faithful half-breed, who knew the route. The chief knew him well, and told the governor he was a first-rate and honest man. The governor bought a strong mule to carry our packs, and we started off.

" The country we now passed over was beautiful and delightful; most of the way rolling prairies, with here and there little patches of timber. We visited several villages of Indians, who all were much like those we had left, and the chief's son seemed to be acquainted with them all, and conversed with them, the language being pretty much the same.

" Immense herds of wild cattle were seen grazing, and of all colours—red, black, white, and striped, and as wild as deer or any other animal. In one place the governor was induced to go about thirty miles out of our way to see the 'hill of the shining stones,' that he had heard of from the Indians. We came to a little village on the bank of a small lake, and on the other bank, about a mile, were the 'shining stones.' They were glistening in the sun, and, to be sure, were very beautiful to look at; but when we got to them the governor said they were crystals of gypsum, sticking in the clay, and of no value. They were in myriads, and in a hundred different shapes, and very beautiful, perfectly transparent as water; but one could cut them with a knife, they were so soft.

" At another village much farther on, and nearer to the base of the mountains, we stopped for several days in a large town better built, on the bank of a lake some four or five miles long. The western shore of this had a broad beach of rounded pebbles, resembling exactly the sea-beach, which I should think it once had been. These pebbles were flint, and of all colours, and some of them, when broken, the most beautiful things I ever beheld. Many of them were beautifully transparent, with figures of a thousand shapes in them, some of which were exactly like the rays of the setting sun.

" We gathered and brought away some ten or fifteen pounds' weight of the most beautiful of them, difficult as it was to carry them.

" The governor was in the habit of going along this beach every morning and collecting these pebbles; and the little Indian children skulking about in the bushes and watching him at a distance, and not fully understanding what he was doing, but seeing him picking up the stones and breaking them with a little hammer which he always carried, and then wetting them with his tongue to see the colours, and when he found a right handsome one, putting it in his pocket, ran back and told their parents that here was the strangest man in the world ; declaring that ' they had seen him every morning making his break-fast on stones, and putting others into his pocket for his dinner !'   The Indians gave him the name of the ' Stone Eater.'   I forget the Indian for it.

    *   *   *   *

" Not long after we left this village, when we
halted to encamp one night in a beautiful little
valley filled with wild flowers and vines, and handsome enough for the lawn of an English gentleman's
house, after we had taken our supper, and it was
approaching nightfall, and we were preparing our
beds, I went for my saddle to make me a pillow,
having left it on the bank of the little stream a few
rods off. I took up the saddle, and reaching down
for what I took to be the girth lying on the ground,
it beginning to be a little darkish, I lifted up a huge
rattlesnake. He made a grand pass at my arm, but
just missed it as I flung him down ; and then coiling
himself up in a circle, he commenced buzzing his
rattle, and was ready for a spring ! My outcry
brought up all the party, and I must say I never
beheld so frightful a beast before in all my life. We
heard the rattle of its mate, at a few rods' distance,
which was soon looked up by the Indians, and both
were knocked on the head.

*   *   *   *

" As we were nearing the base of the mountains
we discovered ahead of us an unaccountably strange
appearance—a streak of bright red, many miles
in length, and perfectly straight. The governor
thought it must be from some mineral substance,
and we steered towards it. Our Indians knew without doubt what it was, but they had no word for it
which we could understand, and were obliged to
wait till we got to it for an explanation, when we
found it to be an immense bed of wild poppies about

as high as the stirrups of our saddles, and so thick
that no vegetables whatever grew between them;
their red heads being so thickly grouped, that in
looking over them at the distance of thirty feet from
us, the flowers formed one complete mass of red,
without another colour mixed with it.

" It took us a mile or two to go through it, and
the quantity of deer that were jumping up and
trotting off through it was really surprising. We
could only see their heads and horns above the
flowers as they were moving along, when they looked
as if they were swimming in a lake of blood !

*　　　*　　　*　　　*

" At the base of these mountains the two Indians,
with their horses, went back, and we then took to
our feet, with our mule to carry our packs; but
before we started, the governor and I sat down and
looked over our pretty little stones, and selecting a
dozen or so, left the rest ' to be called for.' "

*　　　*　　　*　　　*

CHAPTER XVI.

THESE immense mountains, which rise in a number of ridges, one after another, very rugged and barren, took us at least one hundred miles to cross, and we often wished ourselves back again; our pack-mule, poor beast, gave out about the middle of them, and we had to leave it. We left behind the heaviest of our articles, and took the rest on our own backs and got on much better than before. Horses' legs are not made for these mountains of rocks; two legs are far handier and better managed, and we can creep along almost anywhere now.

*   *   *   *

"We got at length the first glance into the great valley of the Amazon as we came out of a deep chasm we had followed for many miles.   *   *

"When we struck off into the valley, we had, I

253

do think, the most beautiful scene in the world before us—the beautiful rolling prairies, covered with grass and wild flowers, and herds of wild cattle and wild horses grazing on them ; and the deer that were springing up from the shade of every little bunch of palm-trees were tilting along for a few rods, and then standing to look at us, in fair range for a dead shot, never having heard the report of a gun. I am sure that in some places I could, with the old Minié, have easily killed some forty or fifty per day, by regular stalking. It seemed a pity to kill them, for one feels in shooting them as if he was shooting in some nobleman's park.

    *   *   *   *

" We crossed here a large stream, and followed it down some miles, the bed of which, it being nearly dry, was filled with countless numbers of round stones, some of them two feet across, which, when he broke them open, were filled with the most beautiful quartz crystals of various colours—some were purple, some were yellow, and others as pure as water : these the governor called *geodes*. There were also waggon-loads of others shaped like rams' horns ; some of these as large as two men could lift, and many of them filled with beautiful crystals.

    *   *   *   *

" We struck at last upon the Rio Trombutas, where we found some very hospitable villages of Indians ; and finding a couple of half-breeds and several Indians loading a large canoe with hides and other things for Para, we got a chance to go down with

them.   This canoe, some forty or fifty feet long and
five feet wide, was made from a solid log, dug out,
and had its sides built up a foot and a-half higher,
with ribs interwoven with palm-leaves, so as to keep
out the waves when heavily loaded, and would carry
some four or five tons with ease.

" On the head of this river we were exactly under
the equator; the sun right over our heads.   There
is no winter in this country : it is one perpetual
summer and spring-time here.   Everything out in
full blossom all the year round.   All the trees are
evergreens, and ripe fruit and fresh flowers we see
on the same trees at the same time.

"Frost never was known here, and the governor
got himself quite into disrepute in one of the small
villages, where he stopped a few days to make his
portraits, by endeavouring to explain to these people
how different the country was that he came from.
He tried to describe *hail* and *snow* to them, but
there seemed to be no words in their language for
them, and they could not understand him at all.
And when he told them of *ice*—of our rivers freez-
ing over, and becoming so hard that we could walk
and run, and even drive our horses and waggons over
them, they became entirely incredulous, and laughed
at him excessively.   And an old man (it seems, one
of their doctors), who had been strongly opposed to
the taking of the portraits, got up and began spouting
in a most violent manner against him, telling his
people it was very silly to be listening to such
stories, and they were rapidly beginning to haul off.

"The governor sent for me—I was on the boat at the time—and got me to testify to the truth of what he had stated, which I easily did; but this only made the trouble worse, and the facts no easier to be believed, for the doctor told them, '*it only made the lie stronger.*'

"We had no other means of proof to offer; and the old doctor wrapped his tiger-skin around his shoulders, and walked off in quite a huffy mood towards the village, at a few rods' distance. We were sitting under the shade of some palms on the bank of a river at the time, where the greater part of the village were assembled to witness the operation of painting the portraits.

"The greater portion of the crowd got up and followed the doctor to the village, and some of the squaws clapped their hands over their mouths, and began to howl and cry, believing that the insult given by the doctor was such as the governor would feel bound to resent, and there would soon be a fight.

"The chief, however, who was a very pleasant and dignified man, remained seated by the governor's side, and said the old doctor had behaved very foolishly; and so the affair dropped, the governor getting only a hard name—the squaws called him '*Hard Water,*' by which name he will, no doubt, be spoken of for a long time to come.   *   *

"After we had got a little recruited, the canoe loaded, and the governor had laid in a goodly number of sketches, we all set off towards the Amazon, perhaps then some three hundred miles off; and you

can well imagine that the old Minié had plenty
to do again. All the animals, and birds, and trees,
and plants seemed much the same as on the Essequibo ; but tigers and monkeys were at least three to
one.

" The tigers live chiefly along the shores of the
river, for their favourite food is the soft-shell turtles
that come out of the river to lay their eggs in the
sand in the night. The tigers watch them, and
rush upon them at that time, and turn great numbers
of them on their backs with their paws ; and after
eating as much as they want, and digging up their
eggs out of the sand as a sort of *dessert*, they just
creep up on to the top of the bank in the shade of
the timber, where they lie until they are hungry
again, when they have only to slip down and eat ;
by this means they keep so fat that their hair
glistens as if there was oil upon it.

" When they hear us talking and rowing, they
creep up to the edge of the bank, and are discovered
looking at us, showing only their heads above the
grass and weeds. We steer our canoe near enough
to the shore for a dead shot, which we never miss.
The governor counts five skins, one a beautiful black
tiger, very scarce here, and I have eight, every one
of which shows the bullet-hole as exactly between
the eyes as you could put your finger.

" There is, in fact, no *sport* in killing these fellows
in this way, for it is only like shooting at a target
at some thirty or forty paces (this you will say is
child's play). We might *find sport*, however, if we

should go ashore for these chaps ; but we had no
time nor much inclination for that, and took good
care not to go ashore where we saw fresh signs of
them. We generally know where they are by the
carcasses of turtles on the sand-beaches, and in such
cases we are all on the look out.

"We were in the habit of making a halt and
lying by a couple of hours every day at noon in the
heat of the day.   In one of theserests we had landed
by the side of a high bank, where we saw no signs,
the Indians were asleep in the canoe, and the
governor and the half-breed and myself were a-top
of the bank—the governor and I had built a large
fire, and were roasting a fat pig which I had shot
from the boat, and while the governor was sitting
down on one side and I squatting down on the other,
and he was with a wooden spoon lading some rich
gravy over the pig from a short-handled frying-pan
which I was holding underneath, I observed his
eyes staring at something over my shoulder, in the
direction of our half-breed guide, who was lying a
couple of rods from us, and fast asleep, under the
shade of some small palms.

"The governor said, 'Smyth ! be perfectly calm
and cool ; and don't spill the gravy ; and don't move
an inch ; there is a splendid tiger just behind you !'
I held on to the frying-pan, but gradually turned
my head around, when I saw the beast lying on all
fours alongside of the half-breed, who was lying on
his face, and fast asleep ! He was lifting up with
his paws one of the half-breed's feet, and playing

Plate VII.

Tiger Shooting. — *p.* 259.

with it apparently as carefully and innocently as a kitten.

"The governor who had left his hat behind him, was at this time sliding down the grass-covered bank backwards, and feet foremost, to the boat, where our rifles were left. The next moment he had one foot upon its deck and his rifle in his hand. I was in hopes he would have taken up the old Minié; but he preferred his own; and getting it to bear upon the beast (Plate No. VII.), he was obliged to stand a minute or so for it to raise its head high enough not to endanger the man's body, which was in front of the tiger, and over which he must shoot very close. Not succeeding in this, he gave a sudden whistle, which directed the attention of the animal to him, and caused it to raise its head and its eyes towards him, when he let fly.

"At the crack of the rifle the tiger gave a frightful screech, and leapt about fifteen feet into the air, falling perfectly dead. The Indian leapt nearly as far in the other direction; and at the same instant arose and darted into the thicket, the male, secreted in a bunch of weeds about fifteen feet behind the governor's back, when he had been sitting at the fire.

"After our pig was roasted, and this beautiful animal was taken on board, we pushed out a little into the stream and waited a couple of hours, in hopes the male would show himself again; but we waited in vain, and started on our course, losing our game.

* * * *

"When we had gone ashore one day, on a broad sand beach lying between the river-shore and the timber, we were startled by a loud hissing, and we discovered a huge alligator coming at full pace towards us, from the edge of the timber towards the water. We were about springing into the boat, but our daring little half-breed, better acquainted with these beasts than we were, ran, without any weapon, towards it, meeting it face to face. When they had got within ten or twelve feet of each other, the brute pulled up, and lay stock still, with its ugly mouth wide open, the upper jaw almost falling over on to its back, and commenced the most frightful hissing!

"The little half-breed kept his position, and called out for a block of wood, one of the men, running a little way up the beach, brought a log of drift-wood the size of a man's thigh, and six or eight feet long. The half-breed took this in both hands, and balancing it in a horizontal position, advanced up and threw it, broadside, into and across the creature's mouth; when, as quick as lightning, and with a terrible crash, down came upon it the upper jaw, with all its range of long and sharp teeth deeply driven into it.

"The little half-breed then stepped by the side of the animal and got astride of its back, and we all gathered round, turned the stupid creature over and over, and kicked and dragged it, but nothing would make it quit its deadly grasp upon the log of wood, and nothing ever could while it lived, for the Indians all told us it would live some eight or ten hours, but not longer.

* * * *

"The noise of a gun I don't believe was ever before heard on this river, for one has no idea of the fuss it makes when the old Minié speaks. I have sometimes fired in the middle of the day, when all was silent, and not a leaf on a tree in motion, and in one minute a thousand voices were going; and looking up and down the river, at one view you may see in the tops of the overhanging trees five hundred (not monkeys, but) little bunches of boughs and leaves shaking, where they and the parrots are peeping out to see what is going on, without your seeing hide or hair of them.

* * * *

"In one of our noonday halts, when we were taking our lunch under a grand forest of lofty trees, and not much underwood or vines, we found the monkeys assembling in vast numbers over our heads, and chattering with an unusual excitement, as they were leaping around from tree to tree. The governor and I began to get alarmed for fear they were going to attack us. They kept coming up and increasing every moment, and there was no knowing where the crowd and the bedlam were to end.

"Our little half-breed smiled at our alarm, and said they must have stolen something from the canoe to have kicked up such a rumpus. I ran down to the canoe, where all hands were asleep at the stern

end, and soon discovered that two beautiful feather
head-dresses, which the governor had that morning
purchased of some Indians we had passed, and the
governor's powder-flask, which we had left on the
deck, had been carried off; and returning, I soon
saw the proof of the theft by the hundreds of
feathers that were falling over our heads.

"These thievish little creatures had taken the
two head-dresses into the tops of the trees, and
whilst some were engaged in pulling them to pieces,
others were leaping around with bunches of the
quills in their mouths, and others with them as
regularly stuck behind their ears as the pens of
counting-house clerks are carried; and the powder-
flask we could hear knocking about amongst the
limbs of the trees, though we could not see it.

"One of the half-breeds from the boat had come
up the bank in the meantime, and became so
enraged, that he took the old Minié before I observed him, while it was leaning against a tree, and
aiming at a large monkey which he said was the
leader of the fracas, he fired and brought him down,
with his backbone shot off.

"The screams of this poor creature's distress being
understood by the throng, they were all silent in a
moment, and in less than one minute they were all
out of sight, but the powder-flask never came down.
Though it had been agreed by all parties at our
start that no one should kill a monkey, it was impossible to cure the wound of this poor brute, and
it was knocked on the head.

" The snakes on this river are very numerous, and some of them very large. The anacondas and boa constrictors, the Indians told us, had been killed here of immense size, but we were not able to see either of them. Rattlesnakes we killed several times, as we met them swimming the river.

" While passing along close to a high bank one day, where there seemed to be no timber on the top, the governor got the men to land him a moment, as he was anxious to climb the bank and see what was in the distance. The canoe came to the shore, and I held it fast by grasping to some bushes at the water's edge. The bank was fifteen feet or so in height, and covered with grass and flowers to the top.

" The governor stepped ashore, and after ascending a step or two, drew himself back a little, and with his eye fixed on something before and above him which I did not see, he said in a quick tone, as he was reaching his hand back, 'Symth! hand me my rifle!' 'Take old Minié?' said I. 'No! be quick as lightning! I prefer Sam.' I handed him his gun, which was instantly at his face, and cracked. I saw a huge snake leap from the top of the bank, much higher than his head, right towards him, and fall at his feet; the governor sprung at the same time, at one leap, quite on to the boat, with his rifle in his hand, and as pale as a ghost. This was quick work, I assure you. He said that he had fired at a rattlesnake and had missed it; that he saw the creature coiling up for a jump, and by the rattling he knew there was not an instant to lose when I handed him the gun. He said that he had missed the snake and it had struck him on the breast, but that luckily he was not bitten; and how he could have missed the snake he could not tell, unless the ball had been lost out of the cylinder. 'The snake's head was raised high up,' said he, 'and perfectly still, and looking me right in the face, and at sixty yards I could not have missed such a mark.'

"The governor wore a stout brown linen frock, tied across the throat and breast with strings, and just where he represented he had been struck I saw a spot of blood the size of a half-crown piece, and I said, 'You are bitten!' All hands gathered around him then, Indians and all. We untied and opened the frock; the blood was still more upon his shirt and also upon his flannel worn under it, which were ripped open, and on the breast a spot as large as the palm of my hand, on the skin, was covered with blood. The blood was washed off, and the faithful little half-breed was down upon his knees, and prepared to suck the poison from the wound, by which means the Indians are in the habit of extracting the poison; but looking a moment for the wound, he got up, and with a smile of exultation, he said, 'There's no harm! you'll find the snake without a head.'

"One of the Indians then stepped ashore near where the governor had stood, and pushing some weeds aside with his paddle, showed us the monster, regularly coiled up where he had fallen, and with his headless trunk erect and ready for another spring! Its head was shot regularly off, as 'Sam' had designed, and the creature, being at the instant so near the spring and so ready, with its aim made, that it leapt and struck the governor probably in the spot where it would have struck him and have made him a corpse in ten minutes, provided he had missed his mark.

"The bleeding trunk had printed its mark with blood where it struck, and driven the blood through the dress to the skin. A blow with the edge of a paddle finished the battle. The length of this brute was four feet, and its thickness about that of my arm above the elbow.

"How curious it is that if you cut off the head of a rattlesnake its body will live for hours, and jump at you if you touch it with a stick; when, if you break the spine near the tail, with even a feeble blow, it is dead in a minute! This we proved on several occasions.

"Farther down the river, one day we had a great alarm by the yelling and singing of two hundred or more Indians, men, women, and children, coming down the river in canoes behind us at a rapid rate —a party, as they proved to be, from one of the friendly villages we had passed going a little farther down the river to a famous beach, where they often go on a ' *turtle hunt.*' They invited us to join them, and we kept company with them, and encamped all together a little before night.

"These people told us the scene of their operations

was a long sand-beach just around the point, below
where we were landed; and they, knowing the
shape of the ground, were aware of the time of
night and the mode in which the attack was to be
made.   These turtles have soft shells, and are
excellent eating; and at certain seasons of the year
come out in vast numbers from the river, generally
about midnight, and creeping up the sand-banks some
five or six rods from the shore, dig holes in the
sand a foot or more deep, and lay, each one,
some fifty or sixty eggs, about the size of a
barn-fowl's egg, perfectly round, and with soft
shells; they are all yolk, and quite as good as barn-
fowls' eggs to eat.

"It seems curious that these creatures are never
seen in the day time, if you go the whole length of
the river; nor can you see them in the night before
midnight—the time that they come out to lay their
eggs to be hatched by the heat of the sun.

"The Indians, aware of this, had encamped half-a-
mile or so distant from the sand-bar above, and made
sorts of tents with mattings made of palm-leaves,
which they had rolled up in their canoes.   Their
fires were built, and a great deal of merriment passed
off, but no feasting nor dancing before the hunt,
which would take place a little before midnight.
The governor said he would not miss these scenes
for fifty pounds.   He tried to get some of the men
to give him a dance, but they said their *bellies were
too empty*, they had eaten nothing for four or five
days, neither men nor women, so that the turtle

feast might taste good; after that there would be plenty of dancing.

"During this time the women were all at work making torches, which they construct from a sort of palm-leaf that burns like pitch pine. There was a doctor, a sort of a conjuror, who was performing some sort of witchcraft to make the turtles come; he had told them he was afraid they wouldn't come up that night, and many believing him, made the party rather desponding and dull.

"However, about a quarter-past eleven, the men all started, leaving the women behind to bring up the rear with the torches; but they were all ordered not to speak a loud word from that moment.

"One of the men, who seemed to be the leader of the party, was one whose portrait the governor had painted while stopping in his village a few days before. He took the lead of the party through the point of timber we had to pass, perhaps a quarter of a mile, and had a small torch in his hand to see the way; he held a long cord for the governor and me to hold on to, that we might not lose the way; the rest of the men all followed in each other's tracks, '*Indian* file,' and without a word spoken.

"Coming up to the edge of the timber opposite to the sand-bar, and finding there was nothing on it yet, our friend and two or three others, with the governor and myself, were seated behind some palmetto bushes, which had been arranged before night for the purpose, and the rest of the men, perhaps a hundred, were all lying flat, in a row parallel to the shore of the river, but a few paces back of us.

"From behind the screen of palmettoes we had a fair view of the sand-bank, which looked white; and when the turtles appeared on the sand, the signal was given by the cord which extended from the conductor to the rear rank, who passed on the signal by touching each other. Nothing was seen for half or three-quarters of an hour; at length, when I was just falling asleep, I felt a pinch on my leg, and looking through the screen, the sands for a great distance seemed, near the water, to be black with these creatures coming up out of the water. They seemed to come up like an army of soldiers. They kept moving up farther and farther, and the Indian kept pinching my leg till I was almost ready to holloa out.

"The signal had been given to the rear-guard, and all knew what was on the beach though they couldn't see, but all lay as still as death. These creatures having got up some five or six rods from the water, went to heaving up the sand with their paws, making the holes and laying their eggs. This was very quick work, and they could not have lost much time; for in the space of half-an-hour the holes were all smoothed over, and the black mass was seen moving towards the water. The signal was then given, and as quick as the wind, the Indians were upon them and turning them upon their backs. Such a scrambling as this I never saw or thought of before! Some hundreds of them were upset in this manner, and some thousands plunged into the water, and many of these were dragged out again by the Indians, who plunged in after them.

" All this onslaught was completed in less than half-a-minute, and no noise but laughing and grunting heard. The chief then sounded a loud whistle, which was for the torch-bearers to come, and in five minutes came down the beach, at full speed, the women and children, each one carrying a blazing torch, when they joined the party with the lights, overlooking the field of battle, and counting the number of their victims lying on their backs.

" This scene, with the wild figures, the blazing torches, and the magnificent forests lighted up, the governor said was the most magnificent thing he had ever beheld. I am sure no picture could ever do it justice.

" The squaws now selected a dozen or so of the finest of the turtles for their feast, and with their torches lighted, the party went back to the encampment, leaving the prisoners on the field of battle till the next morning.

" When we got back to the encampment, where all the pots were boiling, it was equally astonishing and amusing so see how handily and how quickly these animals were cut up and cooked, and how quick the soup was made, and then how fast and how long it was devoured. The soup and the meat were delicious, and if we had had the empty bellies that these people had, we should easily, like them, have eaten ourselves into stupidity.

" The governor and I slept in our canoe that night, and got up at an early hour to see the manœuvre on the battlefield, but, to our surprise, no one moved towards it before ten or eleven o'clock, for all were asleep as if they had been in a drunken carouse. In fact they had been up all night, and then eaten so much that they could scarcely move.

" About noon, after they had all feasted again, they started in a mass and went to the sands ; here their victims lay. The women brought large baskets, and the men went around with large knives, and slicing off the under-shell and opening the carcasses of the animals, the women approached, and tearing out the yellow fat from their intestines, threw it into their baskets. After the fat was all obtained, and some more of the best animals selected for food, the women and children went in for the eggs !

" This was one of the scenes most curious of all. With the paddles brought from their canoes, they went into the *hidden treasures* like so many Irishmen into a field of potatoes ; and in much less time the surface of the ground was more completely covered than ever was seen by the heaviest crop in an Irish potato field.

" As this part of the business required no knife, nor any other weapon, it was a woman's task, and beneath the dignity of a warrior : the men sat and smoked their pipes whilst the women accomplished it.

" It was really incredible the quantity of eggs that were in the sand ; and then how they were deposited so quick ! These, however, were not only the eggs laid by the animals killed, but by the whole party, and there might have been hundreds that got back to the water to one that was taken.

"These eggs, the Indians assured us, were all laid while we were secreted and watching. This the governor didn't believe ; it was impossible that they should deposit so many in that time ; and it would be unnatural that they should all be ready to lay on the same night and at the same moment. But the Indian doctor told him it was true, and that he could always tell the very night they would come out.

"The governor, however, saw that all this thing was under the control of the doctors or mystery men, and he said it was best not to question it.

"The women and children for the most part of the afternoon were taking up the fat, the carcasses, and the eggs, and packing them in their canoes. The fat is taken to their villages and put into large troughs, where they pound out the yellow oil or grease, which is very rich and like the best of butter, and is taken to Para in earthen jars which they manufacture, and sold at a high price.

"It was too late for us to start off that day, and we stayed over night again. The governor tried again to set them dancing, but the old doctor told him that now their *bellies were too full;* and on inquiring how long before they would be ready for a dance, he said it might be several days, for they were going to remain there some days expressly to *eat,* and while they were feasting it was difficult to dance.

"So at an early hour the next morning, with three or four fine large turtles, and full a bushel of eggs laid in, we started off.

"Our turtles were a great luxury to us, and for me, the eggs more particularly so ; for I never before enjoyed any food so much ; and in the eating of them, there was a thing that bothered the governor very much—there was not a stale egg among them, but all fresh, as the Indian doctor had told us.

    *   *   *   *

"After striking out into the mighty Amazon at Obidos, we had a journey of some six or eight days from that to Santarem, which is at the head of tide-water, and a place of, may be, two hundred houses. From that we got a chance down to Para, several hundred miles nearer the coast. Para is a large and flourishing seaport town, where a great business is done.

"The governor was here a while, and left some three months since in company with a member of the Brazilian Parliament, on a steamer up the Amazon.

    *   *   *   *

"Your ever affectionate brother,

"J. S."

CHAPTER XVII.

THE above rather lengthy extracts I have ventured to make because they so graphically describe scenes and events which we witnessed together; and because, at least, such an acknowledgment is due to the talents, as well as fidelity and attachment, with which this young man volunteered to accompany and aid me through a wild and difficult country.

Smyth narrates well and correctly; but he travels fast—too fast. He has brought us to Para; Para is a great way. He has left out many things; he has forgotten my friends the Indians, and also the "story of the pigs." "Pigs?" "Yes." "What! pigs in that wild country?" "Yes, pigs: and I'll tell you more about them by-and-by."

Before leaving Demerara with my little outfit, I

273

visited the neighbouring tribes in that vicinity; the *Caribbees* and *Macouchis*, the *Accoways* and the *Warrows*, in Dutch Guiana, in the neighbourhood of Paramaribo and New Amsterdam; and the *Arowaks*, on the Rio Corontyn; and on our way, on the head-waters of the Essequibo, the *Tarumas* and *Oyaways*, which, with those on the plains of Venezuela, are, in fact, but the names of different bands or sections of the great *Caribbee* family, which occupy one-fifth at least of the Southern hemisphere.

This numerous tribe also occupied all the Lesser Antilles at the time of the discovery of those islands by Columbus, and have since been destroyed, or fled from the islands, to evade the slavery endeavoured to be fixed upon them by the Spaniards, to the coast of South and Central America, where they are living.

These people are generally rather small in stature, and inferior to the North American races, but not inferior to some that may be found there; and enough like them in features and colour; as well as in customs, to stamp them, without a doubt, as a part of the great and national American family.

These tribes in this vicinity, which show a strong resemblance to one another in complexion and customs, also speak a kindred language, showing them to be a family group. Their skin is a shade darker than that of the North American races, and their modes of dress very different; the latter of which is undoubtedly the result of the difference of climate. The weather in the tropics admits of but little clothing, and these tribes are almost naked, both women and men; yet they have and support a strict sense of decency and modesty at the same time, for which these poor creatures deserve great credit.

Their naked limbs and bodies are rubbed over with some soft and limpid grease every day, and though often reputed filthy, they are nevertheless far more cleanly and free from filth and vermin than any class of people equally poor in any part of the civilized world, where they are, from necessity, loaded with a burthen of rags that don't have a daily (and oftentimes not a weekly, nor a monthly, and sometimes not an annual) ablution.

We are now in the great and verdant valley of the Amazon! What shall I say first? The *Acary* (or Tumucumache, or Crystal) Mountains which we have passed over, forming the boundary line between British and Dutch Guiana and Brazil, are truly sublime; not unlike the Rocky Mountains in North America in some respects, and very much unlike them in some others.

The descent from these mountains, and their graceful slopes off into the valley of everlasting green, were, as my friend Smyth has said, truly grand and magnificent.

Let us sit down a few moments; we are weary— our mule died ten days ago, and our packs are now heavy. We have come out from that gorge! that awful ravine! It is frightful to look back or to think back! Why should we, when here is the blue sky, and the sun, and the ocean again before us? How warm and how cheering!

And what a curious cloud! what a straight line
it makes across the sky! Yes, it must be. And
what a boundless ocean of green and blue we are
looking over, and not a vessel to be seen! But stop!
that can't be. That can't be the ocean! we are on
our course! Give me the pocket compass. There!
that's south—there's no ocean there. We are steering into the valley of the Amazon; and here it lies
before us—we are right! And what's at our feet?
Green grass and beautiful flowers? Not at all—
yellow and blue clay, and nothing else. And what
beyond, beneath us? Clay. And what those thousand winding, twisting channels, that seem to soften
into blue in the distance, down, down, so far below
us? Clay, clay, and nothing else. Yes, *something*
else; they glisten in the sun; they have specks that
sparkle like the Bude light; they may be diamonds?
No, they are crystals of quartz, but they are very
beautiful—let's fill our pockets. But here are some
that are quite yellow, and others that are purple;
oh, how beautiful!—let's throw away those we have
got. These are topaz and amethyst, and far more
beautiful; and now and then there is one of carmine.
And still more lovely! these are smaller and more
scarce—they are rubellites. These are washed down
from the mountains? Undoubtedly. And it just
now occurs to me that some of the Spanish writers
call these the "Crystal Mountains." Gold-mines
were worked in these mountains two hundred years
ago. There is gold, then, under our feet?
Not a doubt of it; but we can't wash; there is

no water within some miles, and our tin kettle is of no use.

But we begin to see more clearly; we see streaks of light green running down between these crevices and ravines, stretching off into the ocean, as it were, they become a solid mass of green, and then of black, at last.

The first of these are the rolling prairies, and then the level valley, with its dark and boundless forests of palms. But where's the end of it? It has no end. It is infinite. Take the glass and look; it's all the same; it rises up, up, and up, until it forms that blue line we see in the clouds! It *can't* be so! It *must* be so! And that black streak we see on the left beneath us, is the timber skirting the *Rio Trombutas*, to which we have got to wend our way. Shall we reach the timber to-day? I don't think so.

We feel like boys here, don't we? Exactly so. Our shadows are all under our feet; how awkward to step on one's own head! We are now exactly under the equator. At noon; where is the south? Which is the north? No one but our little compass can tell. How droll! But this clay is not so hot? No, the rays of the sun are straight down, and there is little refraction.

Like ants, we wandered and crept along over the winding gullies of clay; and, at length, met tufts of grass and sage, and afterwards, patches and fields, and, at last, an ocean of grass, speckled, and spotted, and spangled, with all the beautiful colours of the floral world. Clumps and bunches of palms, and palmettoes, and geraniums, each little group like a peep into the glass-house at Kew, though more beautiful, and filled with gay and chattering birds and insects.

And on and over these beautiful plains, immense herds of wild cattle and horses of various colours were grazing, and flying before us as we approached.

A fine fat cow was here felled by the old Minié, and we were again happy. We had plenty of good beef, and raw hide for soling our moccasins, and a clear and running brook for bathing and for washing our shirts; what could we want more? Some three or four days' rest put us on our legs and on our route again.

The Indian trails, and at last the feeble smoke of their distant wigwams, showed us we were again in the land of the living, though we were worn almost out of it. We were kindly received and treated by all the tribes on the Trombutas, which we were now to descend. These Indians—*War-kas, Zurumatis, Zumas, Tupis,* and several others, are very different from the Caribbee races living on the other side of the mountains. They are a taller and a heavier-built race, and somewhat lighter in colour. They belong to the great family of Guarani, which may be said to occupy the whole of Eastern and Northern Brazil, and often called *Tupi,* but for what reason I cannot tell. *Tupi* is the name of a band (or section) only, of the Guarani, speaking the same language, with very little variation, and no doubt from the

same stock. It is matter of little consequence, however, whether they are all called Guarani, or all
called Tupi, for whichever they are, there never has
been, and never will be, any boundary fixed between
them.

From the early Spanish history of South America
we learn that there were somewhere in the valley of
the Amazon, a nation of *Amazons ;* and the river
and the valley seem to have taken their names from
this tradition. The Spaniards and Portuguese have
pushed their conquests and subjugations of the
Indian tribes as far as they have been able to do,
and not, as yet, having found the Amazons, their
more modern historians have placed them on the
banks of the Trombutas, where the Indians have
been successful in keeping their invaders at a
distance, and where it was natural to infer that
the Amazons resided, as they certainly were nowhere else.

At the same time, it was easy to suppose, as they
reported, that these people were cannibals, and ate
foreigners who ventured amongst them. I had all
these *frightful* reports to contend against, and it
will easily be imagined how my nerves were excited.
This required a stronger nerving up, if possible,
than the approach to the "Thunder's Nest!" But
see how many marvellous things vanish when we
come close to them !

I soon found that there were no *Amazons* on
this river, nor *Dianas,* nor *Bacchantes,* but hosts of
Gladiators, of *Apollos,* and *Fauns.* Their young

men and boys are all *Fauns*. *Castor* and *Pollux*,
and old *Silenus*, with his infant Bacchus in his arms,
may be often seen amongst them.

The nearest thing I could discover or hear of to
the Amazons, were the women in some of the tribes,
who were famous for mounting their horses, and,
with the deadly bolas, could bring down the wild
ox or the wild horse as easily as their husbands.
And on inquiring amongst the various villages for
the cannibals, I was laughed at even by the women
and children for asking so ridiculous a question ;
a thing, apparently, that they never had heard of
before.

One said they had not got to be quite so poor as to
have to eat each other yet, but they might perhaps
be reduced some time or other to the necessity of
doing it. And in the midst of this conversation, a
diffident young man stepped forward and said, "Yes,
tell the white man, there are some such persons
farther down the river. He will find some white men
living in two or three wigwams on the left bank of the
river, who eat the flesh of their own relations, and,
what was worse, they sell their skins !" This created
a great laugh amongst the Indians; and, on descending the river, some distance above Obidos, at its
mouth, we found these cannibals, several Frenchmen and Americans, killing monkeys, and sending
their skins to Paris for the manufacture of ladies'
gloves ; and living, as they told us, entirely on the
flesh of those poor brutes !

This was the nearest approach to cannibalism

that I have discovered in my travels amongst North or South American Indians. Books are full of it, but the wilderness is without it! I have travelled and lived fifteen years amongst Indians, and I have not yet found it; and I don't believe that any man has seen anything nearer to it in these countries than what I have above described.

Cannibalism may have been practised, and still may be, under certain circumstances, in some of the South Sea Islands, and in some parts of Africa. We have frequent reports of such practices from travellers, and those very respectable men; but these reports don't *prove* the fact. None of these travellers tell us they have seen it. No doubt they tell us what they have heard, and what they believe. But how do they get their information? Not from the savages; they can't speak with them. Every savage race on earth has its foreign traders amongst them. These are generally the interpreters for travellers who come, and jealous of all persons entering these tribes, to overlook their nefarious system of trade and abuse.

These traders have an object in representing the savage as ten times more cruel and murderous than he is; and amongst other things, as a cannibal, who is sure to kill and eat travellers if they penetrate farther into their country.

It is the custom with most savage tribes (and this in America as well as in Africa) to apply the term cannibal to their enemies around them as a term of reproach; but when we enter these tribes the cannibals are not there, they are in the next tribe, and then in the next, and so they fly, like a phantom, before us.

The leaders of war-parties also apply the epithet of cannibals to their enemies, in order to inflame their warriors going into battle: "You go to fight a set of cannibals ; to conquer or to be eaten !"

Some of the most recent travellers in Africa (and the most recent ought to be the most reliable) assure us that several of the tribes they were amongst were cannibals, and that they eat the very aged people, "killing them to eat them, and eating those who die of old age." Grandfathers and grandmothers I should scarcely think would be very good eating. If these people eat each other for the pleasure of eating, one would suppose that they would take the middle-aged or the young and tender.

If these travellers would merely tell us that these people eat each other, we might believe it _possible ;_ but when they qualify their statements by telling us that they only eat the very aged ones, they weaken their own evidence. They leave us as history, assertions without proof, relative to the existence of a custom both against nature and against taste ; raising presumptions formidable enough to stand against very strong positive proof.

As a ceremonial, in the celebration of victories, religious rites, etc., human flesh is sometimes eaten ; and the practice, by custom, observed as a necessary form ; but this is not cannibalism.

That savage tribes may sometimes eat their enemies whom they have slain in battle, one can easily believe. Savages always go to war on empty stomachs ; and at the end of a battle, after many days' fasting and under great exhaustion, and having no commissariat to supply them with food, it would be easy, and almost natural, to use their enemies for food.

But that any race of human beings, with humanity enough to treat unprotected strangers amongst them with " kindness and hospitality," and to " help and to protect and feed them " in travelling through their country, will kill and eat their own people for the pleasure of eating, I don't believe.

The poor Indian's remark above quoted (" We have not got to be so poor as to have to eat each other yet ; though we may some time be reduced to that necessity ") is not without its significance.

White men have in some instances been reduced to the dire necessity of eating each other, and have cast lots to decide which of the party should be first killed for food ; but this is not cannibalism. If this were cannibalism, it might with truth be predicted, that by the system of robbery and abuse practised on the American frontiers, thousands of the poor Indians will soon be compelled to become cannibals.

Some very respectable and accredited early travellers and explorers averred that they saw the Patagonians on the Atlantic coast, seven, eight, and even ten feet high ! but modern travellers who go and live amongst them find the tallest of them to be but a little over six feet. It is evident that the atmosphere, under certain circumstances, has a magnifying power, and becomes a very uncertain medium, and particularly so when persons are frightened. The first Indian I ever saw, my little readers will recollect, was a giant; but a little familiar acquaintance made him much smaller.

Some writers (who take a peep into an Indian's wigwam without knowing the meaning of things around them, see little balls of clay piled away, which every Indian stores up for cleaning his dresses, and painting his body and limbs, and of which he sometimes swallows a small pill to cure the heartburn, just as my good old mother used to make me do when I was a boy) have reported some of the tribes as " *dirt eaters,*" asserting that " when they are in a state of starvation, they live for some time upon dirt; eating a pound of clay per day." What!—a pound of clay per day on a famished stomach? what an absurdity! And what a pity the revealers of such astonishing facts should not live a while in some of these poor people's wigwams, and learn what the Indians do with these little balls of clay, before they prepare such astounding information for the world's reading.

But stop; dirt is much more digestible than stones! *I* was a " *stone eater* " a little way back—both are " giants "—and one story has just as much truth in it as the other.

———

We were near the head of the Trombutas—on its

beautiful and grassy plains ? Yes. Well, let us sit down here too, a while in the shade of these beautiful bananas—but no; these are not bananas, the pride and grace of the forest, such as we saw on the banks of the Essequibo and the Orinoco. No, but they are palms, nevertheless ; and oh, how charming and elegant, with their leaning, bending stems and pennated foliage! The graceful banana of Guiana, I think, has not yet made its way over the Tumu-cumache ; I don't see it anywhere. All the rest seem to be here.

How beautifully and gracefully these bespangled prairies wind and roll their sloping sides down to the river shore! What a beautiful lawn for a nobleman's mansion, with this very clump of trees for its centre, with these myriads of wild flowers, and all these gay and cheerful songsters in it! But look! What snake is that? That's not a rattlesnake, with a white ring around its neck? Oh, no; it's quite a harmless creature; it never bites; it's only a pilot. A pilot? I don't understand. Why, it's the rattlesnake's pilot, always with him, looking out the way. What a gentleman! Then the rattlesnake is close by us? Undoubtedly; most likely behind us : they always lie in the shade during the heat of the day. Let's move off; I can't say that I fancy the company of such gentlemen.

Our little boat rolls and glides along from day to day, and palms, and enamelled rolling prairies, and gay and chirping birds are everywhere. The river enters the deep and shady forests, and we enter with it. Who knows what we shall see when we turn that next point? and the next? and the next? Each turn is new, each is beautiful, and more and more grand.

The dense and lofty forests, into which the sun's rays can never penetrate, are before us. Twining and twisting vines, like huge serpents, are rising to their tops; some clinging to their trunks, others hanging suspended in the air like broken cordage, and on them, in clumps and bouquets, the most beautiful parasitic flowers. Crowded out from these thickets of trunks and branches, leaves and vines, so thickly grouped that neither sun nor wind can penetrate, we see the strangled palms and other trees pushing their heads out, and bending over the river for a breathing-place.

And through and above these matted forests, the tall and straight trunks of the lofty palms are seen in the distance, like the columns of vast and boundless edifices, and spreading over and above all, their pennated heads show us a *forest above a forest*, the one apparently growing out of the other. How sublime!

These, with all their grandeur, are reflected in the mirrored water; and thus we have four forests all before us at one view, the one just as distinct in form and colour as the other. How grand the mirage! The touch of the oar upon the boat comes back from these solitudes with a redoubled sound; every cough and every "whoop" is echoed back, and with them "who, who!" from the wilderness;

but we don't know from whom. Every crack of
the rifle sets a hundred squeaking and chattering
voices in motion. A hundred monkeys are shaking
the branches in the tree tops ahead of us, and taking
a peep at us, and the sleeping alligators tumble
from their logs into the water, leaving their circular
waves behind and around them.

But these solitudes are not everywhere. We turn
another bend, and before us we have, on one bank,
a vast and beautiful meadow, and on it a forest in
miniature. The grass, some six or seven feet high,
and filled with twisted and knotted vines, and dotted
with wild flowers; and above and through it, like
the stately palms in the forest, the tall and straight
shafts of the sunflowers, with their graceful yellow
and leaning heads, forming a forest of black and
gold above the green, and red, and pink, and blue
below.

What myriads of humble-bees, and humming-birds,
and butterflies are working here! But, this path!
this path? Why, it's the tigers' walk! Let's go
on; push off.

We sleep in hammocks here. Not in these prairies?
No, but always in the timber. We sling our hammocks between two trees, and build a fire on each
side of us. The fire protects us from animals and
reptiles; both are afraid of it.

We stopped our boat one day for our accustomed
mid-day rest, in the cool shade of one of these stately
forests, where there was a beautifully variegated
group of hills, with tufts of timber and gaudy prairies

sloping down to the river on the opposite shore.
Our men had fallen asleep, as usual, in the boat,
and I said to my friend Smyth, who, with myself,
was seated on the top of the bank, " How awfully
silent and doleful it seems—not the sound of a bird
or a cricket can be heard! suppose we have some
music." " Agreed," said Smyth, and raising the old
Minié, he fired it off over the water. *Sam* followed
with three cracks, as fast as they could be got off!

The party in the boat were all, of course, upon
their feet in an instant, and we sat smiling at them.
Then the concert began—a hundred monkeys could
be heard chattering and howling, treble, tenor, and
bass, with flats and sharps, and semitones, and bari-
tones, and falsettos, whilst five hundred at least were
scratching, leaping, and vaulting about amongst the
branches, and gathering over our heads, in full view,
to take a peep at us. We sat in an open place, that
they might have a full view of us, and we rose up to
show ourselves at full length, that their curiosity
might be fully gratified. With my opera-glass, which
I took from my pocket, I brought all these little
inquisitive, bright-eyed faces near enough to shake
hands, and had the most curious view of them. I
never before knew the cleanliness, the grace, and
beauty of these wonderful creatures until I saw them
in that way, in their native element and unrestrained
movements. Where on earth those creatures gathered
from in so short a time, in such numbers, it was
impossible to conceive; and they were still coming.
Like pigeons, they sat in rows upon the limbs, and

even were in some places piled on each other's backs, and all gazing at us.

To give the inquisitive multitude a fair illustration, I fired another shot, and another, and such a scampering I never saw before ! in half-a-minute every animal, and every trace and shadow of them, were out of sight ; nor did they come near us again. The woods were ringing at this time with a hundred voices— "Tso-cano ! Tso-cano ! Go on, John !" came from the tops of the highest trees ; the hideous roar of a tiger was heard, not far off, and when done, another answered on the other side of the river. The howling monkeys, who only open their throats at night, gave us a strain or two ; the white swans were piping in the distance, and the quacking ducks and geese were passing to and fro in flocks up and down the river. The gabbling parrots and parroquets and cockatoos, with their long, and red, and blue tails, were creeping out and hanging on to the outer branches to get a look at what was going on.

So far we heard but the notes of alarm, of fear, and they were soon done—there was little music in these. But then the songsters came—the joyous, merry pipers (when fear was over, and curiosity not satisfied) ; they now began to venture out from the thickets and the towering forests, and in hundreds were seen sailing over the river from their shady retreats in the copses and little groves on the hillsides, and lighting on the trees around us. Curious and inquisitive little strangers, with your red breasts and throats, your white cockades, your blue jackets, and purple tufts, and piercing eyes, and turning heads, I wish I knew your hundred names!

All yet were silent. As we sat still, gazing and ogling were the first impulses—they with their piercing little sharp eyes, and I with my opera lens; but a chirp or two opened the concert. One song brought on another, and another, as an announcement that danger was passed; and no aviary that ever was heard could produce such a concert and such a chorus of sweet sounds as was here presented.

They swelled their little throats to the highest possible key in the din of their concert; and after it gradually died away, some hangers-on gave duets, and others solos, each little warbler hopping nearer and nearer to us, and dropping his last notes with a bow of the head and a "There, there! they *can't* beat that!—mine is certainly the most beautiful!"

"But hark!" said I, "Smyth; music is contagious." The crickets and grasshoppers were singing in the grass, and at length, "P-r-r-out! p-r-r-out!" said a huge frog, whose snout and ears were raised a little above the surface of the water, amongst the water-lilies and rushes near the shore; and then, another, a smaller one, "Peut! peut!" and another, a big fellow, "El-der-gin! el-der-gin!" and then a terrible bull-frog, his mouth the size of the clasp of a lady's reticule, "Kr-r-r-ow! kr-r-r-ow!" and at least five thousand more, on both sides of the river; for, by the custom of frogs, when one sings, all must

join in, large and small, no matter what time of day
or night, as far as their voices can be heard by each
other.

All animals and birds sing in this country—it is
the land of song.   Music is the language of happiness and enjoyment—what a happy community
this!

Now for the "pigs." Pigs, in this country, are
peccaries, a species of wild hog, resembling, in colour
and in proportion, as well as in character, the wild
boar of the continent of Europe.   They are not more
than one-half the size, but have all the ferocity and
sagacity of that animal, and are equally pugnacious.
An individual one is not able to cope with the
strength of a man, but when in groups they are able
to tear a man to pieces in a little time.

Immense numbers of these animals are found
throughout the whole valley of the Amazon and the
Essequibo, living chiefly on the great quantity of
mast that falls from various trees.   They often run
in groups of several hundreds, and unite in
terrible conflicts with man or beasts for their own
protection.

We had taken our dinner one day on the bank in
a large and open forest, when Smyth took his rifle
in his hand, and said " he was going to take a walk
down the river, and see what he could murder."
His passion was for shooting; and it seemed to be
little matter with him what it was, if he could hear
the "old Minié speak" (as he called it), and see his
game fall.

He strolled off down the river bank, and after he had been gone a quarter of an hour or so, I heard the crack of his rifle; and in the half of a minute another—and in the quarter of a minute another!—and after the lapse of two or three minutes he commenced firing again! I began to fear that he had met hostile Indians or some other dangerous enemy, and seizing up my rifle, and taking one of the Indians of the boat, with his quiver of poisoned arrows slung, we started for his assistance; at this time the firing stopped, and we heard him calling out at the top of his voice for help. We then ran as fast as we could, and getting near the place, we began to advance with caution, and I at length discovered him standing on the trunk of a fallen tree, the branches of which had lodged against others, preventing it from coming quite to the ground; his rifle was in his left hand, and by the other he was holding on to a branch to balance himself, and underneath and around him a dense mass of some two or three hundred peccaries, with the bristles all standing on their backs, as they were foaming at their mouths and whetting their white tusks, and looking up at him.

Smyth saw us approaching, and called out to me to take care of my life. These sagacious little creatures knew, from the direction that he was giving to his voice, that he had help coming in that quarter; and a hundred of them at least began to turn their attention to us, and were starting to come towards us without having seen us, and without our having spoken a word to notify them of our approach.

The only shelter for us was the trunk of a large mora tree, behind which we took our positions. I stood so as to look around the tree, and getting my rifle to bear, and my position to be right for firing, and the Indian with his bow drawn behind me, we waited till the foremost of this phalanx of little warriors came advancing up slowly, and whetting their tusks, not having yet seen us. When within some seven or eight rods, I began upon the nearest— and the next—and the next—and having shot down four of the leaders, the sagacious little fellows, seeing their foremost and bravest falling so fast—and thinking perhaps, like the Indians, that this was to last *all day*, they gave a grunt and made a wheel, which seemed to be a signal understood by the whole troop, for in one instant they were all off at full speed, and were soon out of sight, leaving the four I had shot, and some eight or ten of the leaders which Smyth had killed, on the field of battle, when his powder had given out and he was obliged to call out for help.

He told me that he had discovered some parts of the group whilst they were scattered about and hunting nuts; and having no idea of their numbers, he had shot one, when the others, from all quarters, gathered around him, and that if he had not luckily found the fallen tree close by him, or that if his foot had slipped after he got on to it, he would have been torn to pieces in a very few minutes.

I had not a doubt of this fact when I saw the manner in which they had cut and marked with their tusks the log on which he had stood, and also the mangled bodies of those he had shot ; which, by their custom, they had fallen upon and torn to pieces in their fury.

CHAPTER XVIII.

South American Indians—Canoe-Indians—Nest Builders of
the Amazon—The Steamer "Marajo"—Shores of the Amazon—Upper Forest—Nature's Temple—Opera-Glass on the
Amazon—Passing Obidos—A Scene at Obidos—Indians on
the Amazon—Indian Missions—Lingua Geral—Tribes of
Upper Amazon.

ET us now for a while leave beasts, and
birds, and reptiles, for a subject of far
greater interest and importance. The
studies of my wanderings have been the looks, condition, character, and customs of *native man;* and
these their incidents or accessories merely. These
are not without their interest and importance, however, but they can be seen in the wilderness alive,
and in our museums, hundreds of years to come, as
well as now; but native man, with his modes, is
soon to disappear from the American forests,
and not even his skin will be found in our
museums.

The hand of his fellow-man is everywhere raised
against him, whilst the grizzly bears, the tigers, and
the hyenas are allowed to live—and why? because

he is unfortunately a landowner, and has the means
to *pay* for rum and whisky.

Much the same system of traffic and dissipation,
which I have before alluded to, is destroying these
poor people in this country, but without the devas-
tation which it carries with it in some parts of North
America; because there are no immigrating masses
here to push forward a frontier so rapidly, dispos-
sessing the Indians of their country.

A sort of civilization has been longer established
in this country, and more generally and more gradually infused amongst the savage races, without so
completely destroying them. By this process, a
greater mixture of races and languages has been
produced; and though there is little high civilization, and seldom extinction, there is yet an immense
extension of demi-races, and very seldom full bloods.
The true original looks and customs of the Indians
in this country are therefore, most generally, very
difficult to see.

From the warmth of the climate, the Indians in
these regions, semi-civilized or not, go almost naked.
Their character and customs are nevertheless equally
full of interest; and in this country, as in North
America, I have aimed at gathering everything per-
taining to a full and just account of them. In doing
this, the reader can imagine that I have had many
long and tedious journeys by land and by water;
some of which have been already briefly told, and
most of the others (though we may journey together
yet a little farther) must be left for a larger book.

We were at Para. Para is a large and flourishing commercial town, of forty or fifty thousand inhabitants, on the south side of the great estuary of the Amazon, and one hundred miles from the coast of the sea.

There are the remnants of several Indian tribes living around Para, who bring into its market fish and oysters, and fruits of fifty kinds, from the palms and other trees and shrubs of the forests. In the dense and lofty forests of palms on the islands and shores between Para and the ocean, we see again, as we saw at the mouth of the Orinoco, the Canoe Indians living in "nests" built in the trees. These constructions, though exceedingly rude, are nevertheless comfortable and secure for the people who live in them, and whose modes, in many other respects, are equally curious.

These are very properly called Canoe Indians, for they live exclusively on fish and oysters; and to obtain them and to travel anywhere, and on any errand whatever, they must necessarily be in their canoes. They cannot step out of their houses except into their canoes. In their canoes they dart through the dense forests of lofty palms with a swiftness which is almost incredible. They never travel in any other way, and very many of them seldom set their feet upon the dry land.

These stupendous forests of palms (called miriti) constitute one of the curiosities of the Amazon, and perhaps of the world. Hundreds, and thousands, and tens of thousands of acres around the mouths of the Amazon and the Orinoco are completely covered and shaded by these noble trees ; their trunks, almost perfectly straight and smooth, without knot or limb, rise like the columns of some lofty temple to the height of one hundred or more feet, and then throw out their graceful branches, somewhat in the form of an umbrella, which are interlaced together so thick that the sun seldom shines through them.

At low tide these trees may be said to be rising out of the mud, and at high tide they are rising out of the water. They are so far from the sea that no waves of the ocean, or even of the river, reach them ; and the water of the rising tide creeps in and around them as quietly and unruffled as if it came out of the ground, and actually has that appearance.

At low tide the Indian's canoe lies in the mud, and he is as sure to be lying, and eating, and drinking, or sleeping in his wigwam of sticks and leaves. But when the tide rises, it lifts his canoe to the steps of his wigwam, when, with his gay red feathers in his head and his vari-coloured paddle in his hand, his nets, his spears, and his black-headed little papooses in his canoe, he steps into it and darts off amidst the myriad columns of this mighty temple, echoing and re-echoing, as he glides, the happy notes of his song, and those of the thousand songsters above his head and around him.

How curious it is that a part of mankind should build their houses in the trees !—these *are*, strictly speaking, odd people. You will recollect I told you of the *Skin-builders*, the *Dirt-builders*, the *Bark-*

builders, the *Grass-builders*, and the *Timber-builders*, and here we have the *Nest-builders!* and what sort of builders shall we have next? We shall see.

In the neighbourhood of Para, on the Rios Tocantins and Zingu, I visited a dozen or more tribes, and then, on a steamer, started to see others. Lay your map of South America on the table, and see what I had before me! Look at the rivers, and realise their lengths. I took the largest first, the Amazon—rode to Tabatinga, eighteen hundred miles, the western boundary of Brazil; and from that, between Peru and Equador, to Nanta, three hundred and fifty miles, at the mouth of the Yucayali, and yet four hundred miles farther, and leaving the steamer, crossed the Andes to Lima, the most beautiful city in the world!

But this is travelling too fast again. I passed several things on the way, and we will go back and take a look at them.

From Para, I started on the steamer *Marajo*, the second or third voyage she had made, and the first steamer that ever ascended that river. There were on board several Portuguese gentlemen from Rio de Janeiro, and several others from Para, with their families, forming together a very pleasing and agreeable travelling party no doubt, if one could have spoken their language.

The first day at noon brought us into the bay of the Amazon, with its hundred islands; and the second, to Santarem, at the head of tide-water.

Above this we began to stem the current, and, for the first time, had evidence that we were ascending a river; and for the first time, also, we were fully sensible of the majesty and grandeur of its movement.

I had a few months before crept and drifted along its shores and sluices in a humble craft, from the mouth of the Trombutas, without being able to see or to understand it. But we were now lifted upon the deck of a steamer, and stemming the current and viewing it on both sides at once, which gave me some basis for its measurement.

From the middle of the river the distance was so great that the forests on either shore settled into monotony and tameness; but with my knowledge of their actual grandeur, this only served to inspire me with the real magnitude and magnificence of the sweeping current intervening. But when the vessel was running near the shore, which was generally the case, to evade the strength of the current, no pen or pencil can describe the gorgeousness and richness of the overhanging and reflected forests that changed every moment as we passed.

Every length of the boat was in itself a picture to stop and look at; but why stop? for the coming one was just as beautiful. Conversation was at an end, for exclamations and interjections took its place. A never-ending mass of green, of yellow, white, and pink, and red; and that without monotony, unless, from the never-ending changes, *change* itself became monotony !

Here the rounded tops of the lofty trees, some

white, some pink with blossoms, were crowding out their flowery heads amongst the mass of green, and extending their long branches down quite into the river, and a hundred twisting vines hung in knots and clumps, and festoons of parasitic flowers were jetting down from the tops of the highest trees—the overhanging, gorgeous, rolling, and impenetrable mass, sweeping the sides of the boat as we passed, seemed to be tumbling down upon us, while they hid from our view the lofty bank on which their stately trunks were standing.

And *there*, an opening! We see the high and sloping bank, spangled to the water's edge, and into it, with pink and purple flowers—and the graceful palmettoes, like a thousand open fans, leaning and bowing around ; and above the bank, the straight and lofty trunks of palms and other stately forest trees, like the pillars of some mighty portico, supporting their dome of branches interlocked ; and farther on, but a part of this, an "*upper forest !*" The wind has done this. Huge trees have been uprooted, and, tumbling half-way down, have lodged their branches in the crotchets of others ; falling vegetation has lodged on these until a super-soil has been formed ; descending vines have taken root in them and clambered again to their tops, and interwoven and lashed the mass to the encircled trunks and branches ; nuts and fruits have fallen on these and taken root, and trees and flowers are growing in a second forest some fifty or sixty feet above the ground !

And do these look like loathsome ruins—like a wreck—like a misfortune? No, they are rounded; they are hidden; they are looped, and festooned, and embraced with clinging and hanging vines, supporting bouquets of beautiful flowers and fig-trees bending with their blossoms and ripened fruit at the same time.

But how gloomy and desolate? Not so. This is Nature's temple; its roof is not tiles nor slates, but a bed of flowers! and man is its tenant. Blue curls of smoke are seen floating around amongst the trees, and from underneath, a hundred pair of black and sparkling eyes from behind the logs and trees, and a dozen or two of the bravest and boldest of both sexes come leaping to the brink of the bank, to salute us as we pass.

Man's abode! how splendid, how grand, how cheap, and how comfortable! Man wants but a roof in this country; the open air must be around him. How splendid a roof he has here, bespangled with flowers and dropping ambrosia! and how delicious the air that he breathes, rustling through the blossoms and spices with which he is encompassed.

We see hundreds of canoes as we pass on, gliding along the shores in different directions, filled with red heads and red shoulders, but when we get near them, they dart into the mass of overhanging branches and leaves, and disappear in an instant. Sometimes their villages stand upon the bank, and in hundreds they are yelling and saluting us as we are puffing along by them.

They have no fears; they are at a safe distance; but my little opera-glass brings them near enough to shake hands. What a beautiful sight! Men and women, wild and simple as Nature made them. It's a long time since; why have they remained so? What gleaming, laughing, happy faces! Oh, that human nature refined were half as happy.

Thanks! thanks to you, my little opera-glass! the best of all travelling companions; that reveals so much, and asks no questions. What do you show and interpret to me on such a voyage? All nature in this country will let me come within rifle-shot, but you move me near enough to shake hands! One day's seat with you upon the deck of this boat, is worth a week of nights in Her Majesty's Opera House.

The little reader who runs his eye through the pages of this book, and should at any period of his life make a tour to the Trombutas or the Amazon (and I believe there will be such), should by no means forget to take such a companion with him. It is no incumbrance in the pocket, and with it he can converse with animals at a distance; with the birds, and the fruits, and the bouquets of beautiful flowers in the tree-tops. He can scan the ugly looks of the staring tiger, or the silvery texture of the basking alligators, or the gazing multitudes of painted, streaked, and feathered Indians. He can see the bright eyes of the cunning little monkeys peeping down from the branches of the trees; he can scan the beautiful colours of the tocanos, bowing their heads from the tops of the lofty mora. He can see what he never can see in museums amongst glass eyes and *wiry* attitudes—the little humming-birds, as they are balanced on their buzzing wings, and glistening in the sun as they are drawing honey from the flowers; and all the feathered tribe of songsters, straining their little throats, giving aid and expression to their music.

With it he can explore the highest and unapproachable cliffs and rocks in the Andes, and by lying on his back, may almost imagine himself lifted in the claws of the soaring condor.

Obidos, at the mouth of the Trombutas, is where my friend Smyth and myself first launched out into the broad Amazon; a little Spanish town of one thousand five hundred or two thousand inhabitants. Our steamer was alongside and moored. Some passengers got out, and others came on board. The inhabitants were all upon the bank, and amongst them several groups of Indians, and all gazing in wonder at us. Here was work for my pencil, and groups of them were booked as I sat upon the deck. And just before the vessel was to start, as I was walking on the deck, a sudden outcry was raised amongst the squaws and then amongst the men, and all eyes were upon me, and many hands extended towards me.

It seems that amongst the crowd were a number of the Indians, men and women, whom Smyth and I had joined in the turtle-hunt six months before, who now were down in their canoes on a visit to Obidos, and who, having recognised me, were calling to me to come ashore and shake hands with them. This compliment I could not resist, nor could I deny *myself* the pleasure of shaking hands with these good creatures—these "Amazons," these "Cannibals," of the Trombutas.

I leaped ashore, to the great surprise of all the passengers, and of the captain also, and the boat delaying a little, gave me time for the interview. No one can imagine the pleasure which these poor people felt in discovering me, and then seeing me come ashore to shake hands with them. I told them I was glad to see them, and not now being quite so poor as I was when I was among them, if the captain would wait for me a few minutes I would make them some little presents.

I explained my views to the captain, and he granted me the time. I opened a box in my luggage, and supplying my pockets with a quantity of knives, fish-hooks, beads, etc., which I had laid in for such occasions, I went ashore and distributed them, when several of the men embraced me in their arms, and all, both men and women, shook me by the hand, wishing me farewell.

This scene excited the sympathies of the ladies and other passengers on board, who threw them many presents, in money and other things.

The boat was ordered to go ahead, and just as the wheels began to revolve, a little lad ran to the water's edge, and handed to the captain, who was standing on the wheel-house, a beautiful "*blow-gun*," and made signs for him to hand it to me.

Oh, how pleasing such meetings are to me! how I love to feel the gladdened souls of native men, moved by natural, human impulse, uninfluenced by *fashion* or a *mercenary motive!* Mine, I *know*, has something native remaining in it yet.

Ten days from Para brought us to *Nanta*, having passed some fifteen or twenty small Spanish towns and missions, and at least one hundred encampments and groups of Indians on the islands and shores, who seemed to have got notice in some way of our approach, and had assembled to take a look at the boat, and salute it. They stared at us with uplifted hands, and raised their voices to the highest pitch, but fired no guns, for as yet they neither have them nor know the use of them.

From the immense numbers of Indians we saw gathered on the banks, it would seem as if the country was swarming with human inhabitants, while in the whole distance these interminable forests and shores showed us not a monkey, nor a parrot, nor a tiger! The former were led to the river-shore, no doubt, in the extraordinary numbers which we saw, by feelings of curiosity; whilst the latter, from fear at the puffing and blowing of the steamer, hid themselves in the forests in silence as we passed; but no doubt a grand chorus was constantly raised behind us after we had got by.

It is estimated that there are over one hundred tribes, speaking different languages, on the shores of the Amazon, from its rise at the base of the Andes, to its mouth; and at this point we have probably passed something like three-fourths of them. I could give the names of near one hundred tribes that I have already learned of in the valley of the Amazon, but the list would be of little interest here.

If it be true that there are one hundred tribes on the banks of the Amazon, which I doubt, we may easily get five hundred different names for them, and be ignorant of their own, their real names, at last.

Bands of the same great family or tribe are often improperly called tribes, and have languages very dissimilar, and therefore the endless confusion in classification.

There is a general system of teaching by the Catholic Missions throughout all parts of South America, to which all the tribes have had more or less access, and from which they have received more or less instruction in Christianity, in agriculture, and in the Spanish and Portuguese languages.

The soothing and parental manner of the venerable *padres* who conduct these missions is calculated to curb the natural cruelties of the savage, and have had the effect in all parts of that country to cut down the angles that belong to all natural society unaided by the advances of civilization.

These missions are everywhere; and around them, in their vicinity, always more or less extensive settlements of Spanish and Portuguese, called in the Spanish language Gauchos (Gautchos), who live by a mixed industry of agriculture and the chase.

This population mixes easily with the native races, and with this amalgamation ensues a blending of languages, which is one of the most extraordinary features to be met with in the country; and particularly so on the lower half of the Amazon and its tributaries, and also throughout the whole northern and eastern portions of Brazil, where the three languages—the Spanish, the Portuguese, and Indian languages—are all about equally mixed, and in such a way as sometimes to appear the most laughably droll and ridiculous, and at others, the most absurd and inexplicable of all jargons on earth.

This language, which they call "*Lingua Geral*," is spoken by all, by Spaniards, by Portuguese, and by the Indians, much alike; and though it no doubt is a handy language for the country, it is exceedingly perplexing and embarrassing for the traveller, who may think that his Spanish and his French, which he has learnt for the occasion, are going to answer him through the country. He must employ an interpreter, or learn to speak the Lingua Geral, or be as mum as if he were in the deserts of Siberia.

At Tabatinga, eighteen hundred miles above Para, two steamers were building by Americans, who had brought the whole machinery from the United States complete and ready to be put in. These vessels were being built to run on the Amazon, and a few years will no doubt show us a fleet of these and other vessels at that place, which will be the great commercial depôt of Western Brazil and Eastern Peru and Equador.

In the vicinity of Nanta are a great many Indian
tribes, amongst which are the *Zeberos*, the *Urari-
nas*, the *Tambos*, the *Peebas*, the *Turantinis*, the
Connibos, the *Sipibos*, the *Chetibos*, the *Sensis*, the
Remos, the *Amahovacs*, the *Antis*, the *Siriniris*,
the *Tuirenis*, the *Huachipasis*, the *Pacapacuris*, and
at least a dozen others; their languages all dialectic,
and their physiological traits and colour altogether
prove them to be only bands or sections of one great
family, and that family only the fusion, perhaps, of
Ando-Peruvian and *Guarani.*

It would be next to impossible for any stranger
to trace the Amazon from its mouth to its true
source in the space of his lifetime, and it would be
ten times more difficult to trace the savage races in
South America, through all their displacements and
migrations, to their true fountain.

Of the South American tribes there are none
nearer approaching to their primitive state than
many of the tribes about the heads of the Amazon;
and amongst these I spent some time. They have
forests full of game, and rivers full of fish, and all
the varieties of palms with their various kinds of
fruit; and also the immense plains or pampas,
stocked with wild horses and wild cattle for food,
and for their skins and hair, which are articles of
commerce with them. From these combined advantages they insure an easy and independent living,
and have therefore the fewest inducements to adopt
civilized modes of life.

CHAPTER XIX.

RIDE across the *Pampa del Sacramento*, and a passage of the Yucayali in a canoe, afforded me some of the loveliest views of country I ever beheld, and some of the most interesting visits I have ever made to Indian tribes; the shores of the Yucayali are not unlike those of the Trombutas—the animals, the birds, the trees, the flowers, everything the same.

The *Connibos*, of some two or three thousand; the *Sipibos*, of three thousand; the *Chetibos*, of an equal number, and the *Sensis*, inhabit its shores. These tribes are all much alike, and their languages strongly resemble each other, yet they are constantly at war, though only the river separates them.

The Connibos live upon the borders of the pampa, but build their villages in the edge of the forest. A village generally consists of but one house, but a

310

curious house it is; it is a *shed*, and sometimes
thirty or forty rods in length, constructed of posts
set in the ground, to the tops of which are fastened
horizontal timbers supporting a roof most curiously
and even beautifully thatched with palm leaves.
Houses in this country, I have said, have no sides,
no walls, except those of the Gauchos, and the sides
and partitions in those can be perforated with the
finger, as they are but a web of palm-leaves.

The Connibo wigwam, or shed, contains sometimes several hundreds of persons, and the families
are separated only by a hanging screen or partition,
made of palm-leaves, suspended across the shed.
Like all the tribes in the valley of the Amazon, they
sleep in hammocks slung between the posts of their
sheds, when at home; and when travelling, between
trees, or stakes driven into the ground.

How curious are houses without doors, where,
instead of walking *in*, we walk *under!* I have given
an account of the *Skin-builders*, the *Dirt-builders*,
the *Bark-builders*, the *Grass-builders*, the *Timber-
builders*, the *Nest-builders*, and we now come to the
Shed-builders! And if I have room enough, I intend
to give you a brief account of the *No-builders*, the
pigmies of the *Shoshonee* race whom I found on the
heads of the Colorado in North America, who build
no houses, but creep in and sleep amongst the
crevices of the rocks.

The *Sipibos* and *Chetibos*, though only separated
from the *Connibos* by the river, have no communi-
cation with them except in warfare, and that is very

seldom; each confining themselves in their canoes
to their own shore; and their boundary line being
so definitely established, it is less often passed over
than those of tribes who have only an ideal line of
division, which is most generally the case.

The *Chetibos* and *Sipibos* may properly be said to
be Canoe Indians, their country being a dense and
impenetrable forest, throwing them, from necessity,
upon the river for subsistence and the means of
travelling; and in their narrow and light little dug-
out canoes, they are indeed one of the prodigies of the
world. When they all strike with their paddles at
once, they may almost be said to *bound* over the
waves. They ascend and descend the foaming rapids
which in some places are frightful even to look at,
and where they are at times entirely lost to the view
from the foaming spray that is rising around them.
They descend the Yucayali to Nanta, the Amazon to
Tabatinga, to the Barra, and even to Para and back
again, against a strong current for the distance of
two thousand miles, in less time and with more ease
than they could do it on horseback, provided there
were roads.

The *Chetibos* are much like the *Winnebago* and
Menomonie Indians on the shores of the great lakes
in North America, and if placed by the side of them
would scarcely be distinguished from them. Like
all the Indians in this country they wear very little
dress. The men always wear a flap or breech-cloth,
and the women wear a cotton wrapper that fastens
about the waist and extends nearly down to the

knees. The necks and wrists of the women are generally hung with a profusion of blue and white beads, which have a pleasing effect, and also, in many instances, brass and silver bands around the ankles and around the head, fastening back the hair.

Both men and women daub and streak their bodies and limbs with red and white and black paint, much in the same way as the North American tribes. In this custom I see but little difference. The *Connibos*, the *Remos*, the *Amahovacs*, and all other tribes on the Yucayali and the Upper and Lower Amazon, have the same fondness for "dress," which is paint, according to his or her freak or fancy.

The *Pacapacuris*, the *Remos*, the *Antis*, and a dozen other small tribes, and the *Connibos*, who dwell around the skirts of the Pampa del Sacramento, lead a different life from the Canoe Indians I have just mentioned, and in appearance are more like the *Sioux* and *Assinneboins* on the buffalo plains in North America.

The *Connibos* interested me very much. They are one of the most curious, and ingenious, and intelligent tribes I met with. They seemed proud of showing me their mode of manufacturing pottery, which was in itself a curiosity, and in some respects would do credit to any civilized race. They have a place somewhat like a brick-yard on the edge of the prairie near their village, where the women mix and beat the clay with a sort of mallet or paddle, and afterwards mould (or rather model) it into jars for their *turtle butter*, and also into a hundred different and most ingenious forms—into pitchers, cups, pots, and plates; and what is actually astonishing to the beholder, these are all made in the most perfect roundness and proportion without the aid of a wheel, by the rotary motion of the hand and adjustment of the fingers and mussel-shells which they use in giving form.

After these are dried in the sun sufficiently, the painting operation begins, which is a curious scene, and performed by another set of artists, and some of them, evidently, with a talent worthy of a better place.   With red and yellow, blue and black colours which they extract from vegetables, and brushes they make from a fibrous plant they get amongst the rushes at the river shore, these colours are laid on, and often blended and grouped in forms and figures that exhibit extraordinary taste.

Painted, they are then passed into the hands of old women, whose days for moulding and painting have gone by, but who are still able to gather wood and build fires on the sands at the river side where they are carried and baked; whilst the old women are tending to them, with hands clenched, they dance in a circle around them, singing and evoking the Evil Spirit not to put his fatal hand upon and break them in the fire.   Those that come out without the touch of his fingers (uncracked) are then removed to the village and glazed with a vegetable varnish or resin which they gather from some tree in the forest.

This pottery, though it answers their purpose, is

fragile and short-lived, being proof for a short time
only against cold liquids, and not proof against those
that are hot.

The sole weapons of these people, and in fact of
most of the neighbouring tribes, are bow and arrows,
and lances, and blow-guns, all of which are constructed with great ingenuity, and used with the
most deadly effect. My revolver rifle, therefore, was
a great curiosity amongst them, as with the other
numerous tribes I had passed. I fired a cylinder of
charges at a target to show them the effect, and had
the whole tribe as spectators.

After finishing my illustration, a very handsome
and diffident young man stepped up to me with a
slender rod in his hand of some nine or ten feet in
length, and smilingly said that he still believed his
gun was equal to mine; it was a beautiful "blow-
gun," and slung, not on his back, but under his arm,
with a short quiver containing about a hundred
poisoned arrows. (The reader will recollect that
just such a weapon was presented to me on the
steamer when we were about leaving Obidos.)

The young man got the interpreter to interpret
for him, as he explained the powers of his weapon,
and which, until this moment, I had thought that I
perfectly understood. He showed me that he had a
hundred arrows in his quiver, and of course so many
shots ready to make; and showed me by his motions
that with it he could throw twenty of them in a
minute, and that without the least noise, and without even being discovered by his enemy, whose

ranks he would be thinning, or without frightening the animals or birds who were falling by them; and then there was the accuracy of his aim, and the certainty of ·death to whatever living being they touched !

This tube was about the size of an ordinary man's thumb, and the orifice large enough to admit the end of the little finger. It was made of two small palms, one within the other, in order to protect it from warping. This species of palm is only procured in certain parts of that country, of the proper dimensions and straightness to form those wonderful weapons. They are manufactured most generally, and the most extensively, by the *Maycas* and *Zeberos* tribes on the Amazon, more than two hundred miles from the *Connibos*, and two hundred miles above Nanta; and they are sold to the *Connibos*, as well as the *Sipibos* and all the other tribes in those regions, and also to all the tribes of the Lower Amazon, and even taken in large quantities to Para and sold in the market-place. The prices that these blow-pipes command in the country where they are manufactured are from two to three dollars; and on the lower Amazon, at the Barra, at Santarem and Para, from three to five dollars each.

Opening his quiver, the young man showed and explained to me his deadly arrows, some eight or nine inches in length. Some of them were made of very hard wood, according to the original mode of construction; but the greater and most valuable portion of them were made of knitting-needles, with which they are now supplied by the civilized traders. These are sharpened at the end, and feathered with cotton, which just fills the orifice of the tube, and steadies the arrow's flight. The arrows are pushed in at the end held to the mouth, and blown through with such force and such precision that they will strike a man's body at sixty yards, or the body of a squirrel or a small bird on the top of the highest tree.

The ends of these arrows, for an inch or more, are dipped into a liquid poison, which seems to be known to most of the tribes in those regions, and which appears to be fatal to all that it touches. This liquid poison dries in a few moments on the point of the arrow, and there is carried for years without the least deterioration. He explained to me that a duck, or parrot, or turkey, penetrated with one of these points, would live but about two minutes; a monkey or peccary would live about ten minutes; and a tiger, a cow, or a man, not over fifteen minutes. Incredible almost as these statements were, I nevertheless am induced to believe, from what I afterwards learned from other abundant information, that they were very near the truth. One thing is certain, that death ensues almost instantaneously when the circulation of the blood conveys the poison to the heart, and it therefore results that the time, instead of being reducible to any exact measure, depends upon the blood-vessels into which the poison is injected. If the arrow enters the jugular vein, for instance, the animal, no

matter what size, would have but a moment to
live.

The interpreter assured me that neither the bodies
of birds or animals killed by these poisoned arrows
were injured for eating, and that the greater part of
the food of the Indians was procured by them; the
poison being a vegetable extract, and the quantity
at the same time so exceedingly small, that it
becomes neutralised, so as not to interfere with
digestive action.

I was anxious to witness some experiments made
with it, and observing that these people had a
number of young peccaries which they were raising
for food, I bought one of them by giving the owner
a couple of papers of Chinese vermilion, and allowing him the carcass of the pig to eat. He was
much pleased with the arrangement, and brought
the pig out. I got the young man to aim an arrow
at the neck, explaining to him that I wished him to
strike the jugular vein; but, missing that, it passed
some five or six inches into the neck. The animal
made no signs of pain, but stood still, and in two
minutes began to reel and stagger, and soon fell to
the ground upon its side, and in six minutes from
the time the arrow struck it, it was dead.

I was then informed that there was another
animal which I might like to kill. An immense
rattlesnake had been discovered a few days before
near their village, and as their superstitious fears
prevent them from killing a rattlesnake, they had
made a pen around it by driving a row of stakes,

preventing its escape, until they could get an opportunity of sending it on some canoe going down the river, to be thrown overboard, that it might land on the banks of some of their enemies.

We proceeded to the pen, and having excited the reptile to the greatest rage, when it coiled itself up and was ready for a spring, I blew the arrow myself, and striking it about the centre of its body, it writhed for a moment, twisting its body into a knot, and in three minutes, straightening itself out upon the ground, and on its back, was quite dead.

This might be considered a very fair test of the horrible fatality of this artificial poison; for I have often held the enraged rattlesnake down with a crotched stick until it has turned and bitten itself; and even then, excited to the most venomous pitch, and giving itself several blows, it will live some ten or fifteen minutes.

I bought the young man's blow-gun and his quiver of arrows, and I have also procured several others from other tribes, and several sacks of the poison, for experiments on my return, which may lead to curious and possibly important results. How awful and terrific would be the effects of an army of men with such weapons, knowing their powers, and skilled in the manner of using them!

This poison is undoubtedly a recent discovery. From the facts that I gathered in this and many other tribes, I learned that anciently the Indians went to war much oftener than they now do; that they then fought with lances, and shields, and large

bows, but since the discovery of this poison for their
arrows, they dare not come so near as to use those
weapons; and that it had almost put a stop to
warfare.

The young Connibo assured me that his tribe had
resolved not to use these arrows upon any of their
enemies, unless they began to throw poisoned arrows,
and, in that case, to be ready to kill every one of
them.   And to convince me of the cruelty and
horror of warfare waged with these weapons, he
related to me, as matter of history, much as it seems
to partake of the marvellous, that "some time
after the poison was discovered, and these blow-
guns were made, the war-parties of two neighbouring tribes met in a plain, all armed with these
weapons, and their bodies were afterwards discovered
where every man was killed on both sides.   Getting
so near to each other, every man was hit; for each
one, after he was hit, had time to strike his enemy,
or half-a-dozen of them before he was dead."

Poisoning arrows has been a very ancient custom
amongst savage tribes, and no doubt has been
practised for many centuries amongst the South
American as well as amongst the North American
races, and is too generally known and used to be
any longer a secret; but the acme of poison, which
seems to be that now used on the points of these
little darts, I believe to be very different from that
used by the same people on the blades of their
lances and arrows, and to be a modern discovery.

This poison is no doubt a vegetable extract, or a

compound of vegetable extracts; and though so extensively known and used by the Indian tribes, seems to be by them treasured as a secret so important and so profound as to have, so far, baffled all attempts to obtain it from them.   It admits of no chemical analysis which leads to anything, except that it is a vegetable extract.   That *vegetable*, and the *mode* of the extract, the analysis does not show.

Amongst the *Macouchi* and other tribes on the Essequibo, in Guiana, I obtained similar blow-guns, and, I believe, the same poison (though the colour is different).   The Indians there call it *waw-ra-li*. Many travellers, French, English, and German, have made great efforts to obtain the secret, and though some have thought themselves in possession of it, I still very much doubt the fact.

I, like many others, followed the *phantom* a long time, but in vain ; and if I had found it, what good would it do ?   I don't wish to poison anybody ; and game enough " *Sam* " and I can always kill without it—powder and ball from Sam are *rank poison*.

Amongst the *Chetibos*, the *Sensis*, and other tribes, I had painted a considerable number of portraits, which surprised them very much, and gained me many compliments and many attentions as a great *medicine man;* and of the *Connibos* I had also painted several portraits, and passed amongst them for a wonderful man ; but in the midst of all my success, my *medicine* met with a sudden reverse.

The *Great Medicine*, whom I had heard much of,

and who at that time was absent, returned from a
tour on the pampas with a party of young men who
had been out with him to visit a neighbouring tribe.
He was an ill-looking, surly, wrinkled-up old gentleman.   Of myself and my works he soon had a view,
and from his people, no doubt, a marvellous account.
He soon had his face painted black, and was
parading about with his rattle in his hand, and
singing a doleful ditty—his *death-song*, I was told ;
telling his people "this wouldn't do—that it was
very fortunate for them that he had arrived just as
he had—that here was something, to be sure, very
wonderful, but that it would do them no good."

" These things," said he, " are great mystery ; but
there you are, my friends, with your eyes open all
night—they never shut ; this is all wrong, and you
are very foolish to allow it.   You never will be
happy afterwards if you allow these things to be
always awake in the night.   My friends, this is only
a cunning way this man has to get your skins ; and
the next thing, they will have glass eyes, and be
placed amongst the skins of the wild beasts, and
birds, and snakes !   Don't hurt this man—that is my
advice ; but he is a 'bug-catcher and a monkey-
skinner !' " *

One can easily see the trouble that was here
brewing for me, and easily imagine, also, how
quickly I lost caste from the preaching of this

* A term of reproach which they apply to naturalists and
other scientific men, whom they often see making collections of
natural history.

infallible *oracle* of the tribe, and how unavoidable and irrevocable was the command when I was informed that my operations must cease, and the portraits which I had made must be destroyed.

Those whose portraits I had made all came to me, and told me they would rather have them destroyed, for if I took them away they might have some trouble. I told them we would let them remain over another night, which would give them time to think more about it (give my pictures more time to dry), and if on the next day they still continued in their resolve, I would destroy them as they desired.

I had yet another motive for this delay—the hope of being able, by a little compliment and flattery, to get the old doctor to change his views, and to take up the right side; but in this I entirely failed, almost for the first time in my life. He had been to Para, or other places, where he had seen the stuffed skins in a museum, with glass eyes, and the poor old fellow had got the idea fixed in his mind that I was gathering skins, and that by this process the skins of his people would find their way there, and soon have glass eyes!

I luckily found in the bank of a little stream some white clay; and the next morning, when the Indians came in with the doctor, I had a good quantity of clay on my palette, mixed with water and some water-colours. I then said, "There are your portraits; I am very sorry that you don't let me have them to show to my friends amongst the white people; but you have resolved to have them destroyed.

There are three ways—you may burn them! or you may drown them! or you may shoot them! You can destroy them in your own way. Your *medicine man*, who has frightened you about them, can tell you, most likely, which way will be the *least dangerous!*"

The old doctor lit his pipe, and they all sat down and smoked and talked a while, when he informed me that they were a little afraid to do either.

I then said there was another way I had, that of *unpainting* them, from which there could be no possible harm, but it required each one to sit a few minutes for the operation. This seemed to afford them a great relief, and in a few moments they were all unpainted, covered in with a thick coat of clay, which would perfectly preserve them until I wanted to see them again. All were satisfied. I took to my canoe and came off, all good friends.

From this I went west. I saw many Indians, many rivers, many rocks. I saw (and *felt*) the *Andes*, and entered Lima, on the Pacific, which I have before said is the most beautiful city in the world.

My tour was there half-finished; there will be a *time* and a *book* for the rest.

CHAPTER XX.

THE reader bears in mind that the main object
of this little work has been to convey, in a
concise way, a general and truthful knowledge of the character, condition, and customs of the
American Indian races. In order to prevent it from
being tedious, I have thus far endeavoured to weave
into it such scenes and incidents which I have witnessed as were calculated to interest the reader, and
at the same time help to illustrate the true character
of these interesting people.

Leaving scenes and scenery now for a while, we
will take a look at the Indians and learn more of
them in a different phase. Everything, to be well
understood, should be seen in different lights. We
have seen how these people look and act in their

325

own countries; we will now take a peep at them, mixing and mingling with the polished and enlightened of the world. We have seen them in the darkness of the wilderness; we will now see how they bear the light.

Whilst I was residing in London a few years since, with my whole Indian collection, and all the information which I had gathered in eight years' residence amongst them, there came to London two successive groups of Indians from North America, from two different tribes, and under the charge of two persons, their conductors, from the Indian frontiers, for the avowed object of acting out their modes before the English people.

In both instances I was applied to by the persons bringing them out to take the management of their exhibitions, which I did; which, no doubt, added much to their interest, as I was able to appreciate and explain all their modes. Their exhibitions were made both in England and France, and their mingling and mixing with all ranks and grades of society, to which I was a constant witness and interpreter, brought out points and shades in their character which I never should have learned in their own country; and I confess that until then, with all my study, I had but a partial knowledge of the character of these curious people, and that the rest of it, and even some of its most admirable parts, I learned when they were four thousand miles from their homes, and in the midst of the most enlightened society.

To give a brief account, then, of the rest of their character, as I learned it myself, I will here add a few extracts from my notes made at the time, some of which will be amusing, others will be met with surprise, and many will furnish convincing corroborations of the statements I made in the beginning of this book, that these people, in their native state, are endowed with a high degree of intelligence, of morality, of honesty, of honour, of charity, and religious sentiment. They exhibited at all times a strict adherence to decency, decorum, and social propriety of conduct, that not only excited the surprise, but gained for them the admiration and respect, of all who saw them.

No mode ever suggested itself to me while I was travelling amongst these people (nor could anything else have ever happened), so completely enabling me to learn the *whole* of their character; and there is nothing else on earth that I can communicate to the reader with so much pleasure, and with so much justice to the savage, in the remaining pages of this little book, as the following brief account of incidents which many of the civilized world witnessed, and which all the civilized world ought to know.

The first of these parties consisted of nine Ojibbeways from Canada, whom I had the honour of presenting to Her Majesty the Queen and His Royal Highness the Prince Consort, in the palace at Windsor. They gave several of their dances before the royal party in the Waterloo Gallery, and afterwards sat down to a splendid *déjeûner* in an adjoining hall.

See the remarkable speech which the old chief made, as he stood before Her Majesty and all the household, which was interpreted to Her Majesty by their own interpreter, and which I wrote down word for word:—

"*Great Mother*,—The Great Spirit has been kind to us, your children, in protecting us on our long journey here, and we are now happy that we are allowed to see your face.

"*Mother*,—We have often been told that there was a great fire in this country, that its light shone across the great water, and we think we see now where that great light arises; we believe that it shines from this great wigwam to all the world.

"*Mother*,—We have seen many strange things since we came here; we see that your wigwams are large, and the light that is in them is bright. Our wigwams are small, and our light is not strong. We are not rich, but we have plenty of food.

"*Mother*,—My friends here and myself are your children; we have used our weapons against your enemies; our hearts are glad at what we have this day seen; and when we get home our words will be listened to in the councils of our nation. This is all I have to say."

The grace, and dignity, and perfect composure with which this old man delivered the above address before Her Majesty, amid the glare and splendour that was around him, seemed to excite the surprise and admiration of all.

His Royal Highness Prince Albert replied to him in a kind and feeling response, and handsome and genuine presents were made to them by Her Majesty. They gave their dances and other amusements in various parts of the kingdom.

After their return, another party of fourteen *Ioways*, from the Upper Missouri, arrived, in charge of a Mr. Melody, and under the sanction of the United States Government. This party, from a tribe living much farther west, and more completely in their native state and native habits, were a much better illustration than the first, and probably the best that ever has crossed, or ever will cross, the ocean for such a purpose.

The names of this party were as follow :—

Jeffrey Doroway, Interpreter.

1. Mew-hu-she-kaw (the white cloud), chief, civil.
2. Neu-mon-ya (the walking rain), war-chief.
3. See-non-ti-yah (the blister feet), doctor.
4. Wash-ka-mon-ye (the fast dancer), warrior.
5. Shon-ta-y-ee-ga (the little wolf), warrior.
6. No-ho-mun-ye (the Roman nose), warrior.
7. Wa-ton-ye (the foremost man), warrior.
8. Wa-ta-wee-buck-a-nah (commanding general), boy.

Women.

9. Ruton-ye-wee-me (the strutting pigeon), wife of chief.
10. Ruton-wee-me (flying pigeon).
11. O-kee-wee-me (female bear).

12. Koon-za-ya-me (female eagle).
13. Ta-pa-ta-mee (wisdom).
14. ———— (papoose).

This party, when they arrived in London, took great pleasure in visiting my exhibition rooms and in seeing me, as I had visited that tribe some five or six years before, and had, in their own village, painted the portraits of the two chiefs of this party, and which were then hanging in my collection. I erected a strong platform in my exhibition room, on which these people gave their dances and other amusements before immense crowds of visitors assembled to see them.

On the first evening of their amusements they gave the war-dance, all dressed and painted like warriors going to war, and I stood by and explained all its features to the audience. In the war-dance, when the dance stops at intervals, it is customary for each warrior, in turn, to step forward, and, in a boasting manner, relate the exploits of his life—how he has killed and scalped his enemies in battle, etc. And in this dance, the old medicine man made a tremendous boast, brandishing his war club over the heads of his audience in a manner that caused great excitement in the crowd, and was followed by an enthusiastic applause. The old doctor was a bachelor, and had the most exalted admiration and respect for the ladies. And this compliment brought him again on to his feet at the edge of the platform, with his buffalo robe wrapped around him, and his right hand waving over the heads of the audience, when he began :—

" *My friends,*—It makes me very happy to see so many smiling faces about me ; for when people smile and laugh I know they are not angry."— (Immense applause and laughter, which lasted for some time.)

" *My friends,*—I see the ladies are pleased, and this pleases me, because I know that if the ladies are pleased they will please the men."—(Great laughter and applause.)

" *My friends,*—I believe that our dance was agreeable to you, and has given you no offence."— (Applause.)

" *My friends,*—We have come a great way, over the great Salt Lake, to see you and offer you our hands. The Great Spirit has been kind to us. We know that our lives are always in his hands, and we must thank him first for keeping us safe."— (Applause.)

" *My friends,*—We have met our old friend, *Chippehola,** here, and we see the medicine things which he has done, hanging all around us, and this makes us very happy. We have found our chiefs' faces on the walls, which the Great Spirit has allowed him to bring over safe, and we are thankful for this."— (Applause and " how, how, how," from the Indians ; meaning " yes," or " hear, hear.")

" *My friends,*—This is a large village ; it has many fine wigwams ; we rode in a large carriage

* (Red paint) the Author.

(an omnibus) the other day, and saw it all."—(A laugh, and hear.)

"*My friends*,—We came all the way from the ship on your great medicine road; it pleased us very much; and we were drawn by the *iron horse*. My friends, we think that before the trees were cut down this country was very beautiful. We think there were Indians and buffaloes in this country then."—(Applause.)

"*My friends*,—We came very fast along the medicine road (from Liverpool), and we think we saw some *quash-ee-quano*,* but we were not certain; we should like to know. This is all I have to say."—(How, how, how, and great applause.)

An omnibus with four horses was engaged to give the party a drive of a couple of hours each day, by which means they were enabled to see every part of London and its suburbs, and also its institutions, into most of which Mr. Melody and myself accompanied them, that they might see and appreciate the benefits of civilization.

These poor people were much disappointed in not being able to see the Queen, as the party of Ojibbeways, their enemies, had; but they received many friendly invitations, where they were treated with great kindness. They were invited to a *déjeûner* at the mansion of Mr. Disraeli, near Hyde Park, where they all sat at a table splendidly set out, and at

---

* A medicinal herb, the roots of which the Indians use as a cathartic medicine.

which the private friends of Mr. and Mrs. Disraeli were assembled.

The most perfect decorum and apparent *sang-froid* attended all their motions and actions, and at parting, the war-chief said :—

" *My friends,*—The Great Spirit has caused your hearts to be thus kind to us, and we hope the Great Spirit will not allow us to forget it.   We are thankful to all your friends whom we see around you also, and we hope the Great Spirit will be kind to you all.

" *My friends,*—We wish to shake hands with you all, and then we will bid you farewell."

Invited by Mrs. Lawrence, of Ealing Park, they partook of a splendid *déjeûner* on the beautiful lawn back of her mansion, at which H.R.H. the late Duke of Cambridge, the Duchess of Cambridge and the Princess Mary, the Duchess of Gloucester, and many other distinguished personages were present.   The Duke of Cambridge carved the roast beef, and the lovely little Princess Mary and the Duchess of Cambridge, and Mrs. Lawrence carried round to them their plates of plum-pudding.   After the *fête*, they gave several of their favourite dances, and taking their ball-sticks in hand, illustrated their beautiful game of ball on the lawn.

When the entertainments were over, and tne Indians were about to depart, the war-chief stepped forward and addressed the Duke of Cambridge in the following words :—

" *My great Father,*—Your face to-day has made

us all very happy. The Great Spirit has done all this for us, and we are thankful to him, first, for it. The Great Spirit inclined your heart to let us see your face and to shake your hand, and we are very happy that it has been so." (How, how, how.)

"*My Father,*—We have been told that you are the uncle of the Queen, and that your brother was the king of this rich country. We fear that we shall go home without seeing the face of your Queen, except as we saw it in her carriage; but if so, we shall be happy to say that we have seen the great chief who is next to the Queen." (How, how, how.)

"*My Father,*—We are poor and ignorant people from the wilderness, whose eyes are not yet open; and we did not think we should be treated so kindly as we have been this day. Our skins are red, and our ways are not so pleasing as those of the white people; and we therefore feel the more proud that so great a chief should come so far to see us. This, my father, we never shall forget." (How, how, how.)

"*My Father,*—We feel thankful to the lady who has this fine house, and these fine fields, and who has invited us here to-day, and to all the ladies and gentlemen who are here to see us. We shall pray for you all in our prayers to the Great Spirit; and now we shall be obliged to shake hands with you all and go home." (How, how, how.)

H.R.H. the Duke of Cambridge then took the war-chief by the hand, and replied to him—"That he and all his friends had been highly pleased with their appearance and amusements, and most of all, with the reverential manner in which he had just spoken of the Great Spirit, before whom, whether red or white, we must all soon appear. He thanked the chiefs for the efforts they had made to entertain them, and trusted that the Great Spirit would be kind to them in restoring them safe to their friends again."

Very beautiful and liberal presents were then bestowed on them by the hands of the ladies, and the party took leave in their omnibus for London.

Let us turn back for a moment to this wonderful speech of the war-chief, and read it over again—to this concise, this appropriate, this reverential, this humble and eloquent address, from the lips of a wild man from the heart of the American wilderness—that no language, that no diction, and no study could improve—translated by one of the best interpreters, sentence by sentence, and written by myself, word for word, in my note-book as it was spoken.

What a beautiful illustration have we here, and how convincing, of the truth which should be learned as the basis of all human education, that nature has endowed man, even in his most ignorant wilderness state, with a knowledge of his Creator—of an Almighty Being on whom his existence depends, and to whom his daily thanks and prayers are to ascend!

And these are not the empty pretensions drawn out of them by the society they are in, but the sentiments that are daily uttered in the forests, and over the mountains, the lakes, and the rivers of their own countries, during all the days of their lives. I have seen them there, as the reader has learned, under all circumstances. Their speeches have been made to me, and I have heard them made a hundred times to others, and they always begin by thanking the Great Spirit first.

In councils, no man speaks without inviting the Great Spirit to witness what he is going to say, and to aid him in speaking the truth. Before eating, they invariably and audibly thank the Great Spirit for the food they are going to partake of.

These people have no churches or places of worship where they congregate together as white people do; but each individual has some solitary and sacred haunt where he occasionally goes for several days and nights together, without food, lying with his face in the dirt, as he is crying to the Great Spirit, even at the risk of his life from wild beasts and his enemies.

While these people were creating a great excitement in London, two Episcopal clergymen called on me one day and desired to know if they could have an opportunity of conversing with them on the subject of religion; to which I replied that I would do all in my power to bring it about. I mentioned the subject to Mr. Melody and his party, and they all agreed, and the day and hour were appointed. Apprehending the interesting and important nature of these conversations, I resolved to attend them, and with Jeffrey, the interpreter, to preserve the most perfect report of all that was to be said on both sides; which I did; and in each case (for there were ultimately several interviews) submitted my reports to the reverend gentlemen for their approval as to their correctness.

In the interview already appointed to take place, one of the reverend gentlemen, in the kindest and most friendly manner, explained to them the objects of their visit, and with their permission, gave them an account of the life and death of our Saviour, and explained, as well as he could to their simple minds, the mode of redemption. He urged upon them the necessity of taking up this belief, and though it might be difficult for them to understand at first, yet he told them he was sure that it was the only certain way to salvation.

The war-chief, who was spokesman on most occasions, was all this time sitting and smoking his pipe, with his head cast down as he was listening; and having heard what the clergyman was anxious to explain, he handed his pipe to White Cloud, the chief, and with his arms resting on his knees, replied :—

"*My friends,*—The Great Spirit has sent you to us with kind words, and he has opened our ears to hear them; which we have done. We are glad to see you and to hear you speak. As to the white man's religion, which you have explained, we have heard it told to us in the same way in our own country, and there are white men and women there now trying to teach it to our people. We do not think your religion good, unless it be so for white people, and this we don't doubt.

"*My friends,*—The Great Spirit has made our skins red, and the forests for us to live in. He has also given us our religion, which has taken our fathers to the 'beautiful hunting-grounds,' where we wish to meet them. We don't believe that the Great Spirit made us to live together with the pale faces in this world, and we think that He has intended we shall live separate in the world to come.

"*My friends,*—We know that when white men come into our country we are unhappy. The Indians all die or are driven away before the white men. Our hope is to enjoy our hunting-grounds in the world to come, which white men cannot take from us.

"*My friends,*—You have told us that the Son of the Great Spirit was living on the earth, and that He was killed by white men, and that the Great Spirit sent Him here to get killed. Now, we don't understand this; this may have been necessary for white people, but the red men, we think, have not yet got to be so wicked as to require that. If it was necessary that the Son of the Great Spirit should be killed for white people, it may be necessary for them to believe all this, but for us, we cannot understand it.

"*My friends,*—You speak to us of the Good Book which is in your hands. We have some of these in our village. We are told that all your

words about the Great Spirit are printed in that
Book, and if we learn to read it, it will make good
people of us. I would now ask why it don't make
good people of the whites living around us ? They
can all read the Good Book, and understand all that
the *Black-coats** say, and still we find that they are
not so honest and so good a people as our own;
this we are sure of. Such is the case in the country
around us, but *here*, we have no doubt but the
white people, who have so many to preach to them,
and so many of the Good Books to read, are all
honest and good.

"*My friends,*—In our country the white people
have two faces, and their tongues branch in different
ways. We know that this displeases the Great
Spirit, and we do not wish to teach it to our
children."

One of the reverend gentlemen here asked the
chief if he thought the Indians did all to serve the
Great Spirit that they ought to do, all that the
Great Spirit required of them ; to which the war
chief replied :—

"*My friends,*—I don't know that we do all the
Great Spirit wishes us to do; there are some Indians
I know who do not. There are some bad Indians
as well as bad white people. I think it is difficult to tell how much the Great Spirit wishes
us to do."

The reverend gentleman said—"That is what
we wish to teach you; and if you can learn to

* Missionaries.

read this Good Book it will explain all that." The chief continued—

"*My friends,*—We believe that the Great Spirit requires that we should pray to him, which we do, and to thank him for everything we have which is good. We know that he requires us to speak the truth, to feed the poor, and to love our friends. We don't know of anything more that he demands. He may demand more of white people, but we don't know that."*

The reverend gentleman, and several ladies attending them, here bestowed upon the Indians several beautiful Bibles, and other appropriate presents, and took leave.

Of revealed religion the Indians in their wild state have no knowledge before it is explained to them. But of the existence of a God—a Supreme Being—whom they denominate the "*Great Spirit,*" and of a "world to come," or a spiritual existence beyond the grave, they require no teachers; for the most ignorant of them all pray to the Great Spirit when they are in danger; and, when dying, paint their faces with their finest colours, and reach for their bows and arrows as companions to supply them with food on the "long journey that is to take them to their beautiful hunting-grounds."

We have had many reports from the American

* [The reader may compare these words of the Indians in London, as recorded by Mr. Catlin, with their superstitions and practices, as seen by him, and narrated in pp. 83-98, 143, 144, 157, 168-173.]

frontiers of tribes of "heathens"—"heathen dogs," so low in the scale of human nature as to have been "*found* without the belief in a God or a future state." Don't believe one word of these, for, from ignorance or a motive, I need not say which, every one of these are false.

Every American Indian, if he be not an idiot, has an intuitive knowledge of a Creator and belief in a future pleasurable existence; and, happy people! they have no metaphysics or sophistry of their own to induce them to believe to the contrary.

In speaking of the leading characteristics of the American Indians in the beginning of this work, I stated amongst their other virtues, that they were kind and charitable to the poor, in support of which many anecdotes of this travelling party might be presented; but I will confine myself to an individual instance or two, of which I made notes.

One day whilst they were in Birmingham, a miserable-looking woman, with her little child, both in rags, and begging for the means of existence, presented herself in front of the door, where the old doctor, of whom I have before spoken, was standing, whose pity was touched by the poor woman's appearance, and who beckoned her to come in by holding out and showing her some money, but which she was afraid to take.

The doctor went for one of the men in attendance, who assured the woman there was no danger, by which she was induced to enter the Indians' apartment, where the Indians were all seated on the floor, and all sympathising with her miserable appearance. The war chief, getting Jeffrey to interpret for him, told her not to be frightened, for they were her friends; when the doctor walked up to her and put five shillings into her hand.

The war-chief then asked her some questions as to the causes of her becoming so distressed, which she explained. The Indians filled her apron with cold meat and bread, sufficient to last her and her child for several days. The kind-hearted old doctor then politely escorted her to the bottom of the stairs, and informed her by signs that, if she would come every morning at a certain hour, she would be sure to have food enough for herself and her little child as long as the party should remain in Birmingham; which was strictly performed by the doctor, and no doubt with an inexpressible satisfaction, as he found his patient every morning at the door and waiting for him.

It was thought by some friends, that if the Indians would give their exhibition for a couple of nights in the Town Hall, dividing the receipts with the two hospitals, their exhibition would be very popular, and it was agreed to. The profits of the two nights amounted to £145, 12s. And the next day I was present when the chief handed to Mr. Joseph Cadbury, president of one of the hospitals, £72, 16s.— one-half of the receipts; on which occasion Mr. Cadbury made some very feeling and friendly remarks, thanking them for the very handsome donation, and reminding them of the importance of *sobriety* and *charity*—recommending to them never to lose sight of them—which were two of the greatest virtues they could practise, and the most sure to gain them friends and happiness.

Though the war-chief, as I have said, was generally the spokesman on these occasions, it was left for the doctor to reply in this instance, and addressing himself to Mr. Cadbury, he spoke as follows:—

"*My friend,*—I rise to thank you for the words you have spoken to us. They have been kind, and we are thankful for them.

"*My friend,*—When I am at home in the wilderness, as well as when I am amongst the white people, I always pray to the Great Spirit; and I believe that the chiefs and the warriors of my tribe, and even the women also, pray every day to the Great Spirit, and he has therefore been kind to us.

"*My friend,*—We have this day been taken by the hand in friendship, and this gives us great consolation. Your friendly words have opened our ears, and your words of advice will not be forgotten.

"*My friend,*—You have advised us to be *charitable* to the poor, and we have this day handed you three hundred and sixty dollars to help the poor in your hospitals. We have not time now to see these poor people, but we know that you will make good use of the money for them; and we shall be happy if, by coming this way, we shall have made the poor comfortable.

"*My friend,*—We red men are poor, and we cannot do much charity. The Great Spirit has been kind to us though, since we came to this country, and we have given more than two hundred dollars to the poor people in the streets of London before we came here ; and this is not the first day that we have given to the poor in this city.

" *My friend,*—We admit that before we left home we were all fond of *fire-water,* but in this country we have not drunk it, nor shall we—we know that it is a sin to drink fire-water, and your words to us on that subject are good.   And if you can tell them to the white people who make the fire-water and bring it into our country to sell, then we think your words may do a great deal of good, and we believe the Great Spirit will reward you for it.

" *My friend,*—It makes us unhappy, in a country where there is so much wealth, to see so many poor and hungry, and so many as we see drunk.   We know *you* are good people, and kind to the poor ; and we give you our hands at parting, praying that the Great Spirit will assist you in taking care of the poor, and making people sober.

"I have no more to say."

Another incident relating to this subject is worthy of being recorded, and it is due to these poor people that such acts as the above, and the one to be related, should be made public.

At a subsequent time, while passing from Edinburgh to Dundee on a steamer, and when the captain was collecting his passage-money, there was a little girl in the fore-cabin, where the Indians were travelling, who could not pay her fare, as she

had no money. She was in great alarm, and told
the captain that she expected to meet her father at
Dundee, and that he would certainly pay it as soon
as she could find him. I was not on board at the
time, but my men informed me that the captain
was in a great rage, and abused the child for coming
on board without the money to pay her fare, and
said that he should not let her go ashore at Dundee,
but that he should hold her a prisoner on board,
and take her back to Edinburgh and put her in
gaol.

The poor little girl was frightened, and cried
herself almost into fits. The passengers, of whom
there were a considerable number, all seemed much
affected by her distress, and commenced raising the
money amongst them for defraying her passage,
giving a penny or two each, which, when done,
amounted to only a quarter of the sum required,
when the poor child's distress still continued.

The kind-hearted old doctor, silently observing
all this, went down below and related it to the party
of Indians, and in a few minutes came up with
eight shillings in his hand, much more than was
necessary, and offered it to the little girl, who was
frightened and ran away. The interpreter, however,
prevailed upon her to take the money, assuring her
there was no danger, when the doctor advanced and
placed the money in her hand, saying to her, through
the interpreter, and in presence of all the passengers
who were gathering around, " Now go to the cruel
captain, and pay him the money, and never be afraid

of a man again because his skin is red; but be always sure that the heart of a red man is as good as that of a white man. And when you are in Dundee, where we are all going together, if you do not find your father, as you wish, and are amongst strangers, come to us, wherever we shall be, and you shall not suffer; and if money is necessary you shall have more."

CHAPTER XXI.

War-Chief's Speech to the King and Queen—Louis Philippe
in an Indian Village.

FTER the Ioways had finished their provincial tour in England, I accompanied them to Paris, and had the honour of presenting them to His Majesty Louis Philippe and the Queen, in the Palace of the Tuileries, when most of the other members of the royal family were present.

His Majesty, in the most free and familiar manner (which showed them he had been accustomed to the modes and feelings of Indians), conversed with the chiefs, and said to Jeffrey, the interpreter, "Tell these good people that the Queen and I are glad to see them; that I have been in many of the wigwams of the Indians in America when I was a young man, and they treated me everywhere with kindness, and that I love them for it.

"Tell them I was amongst the *Senecas*, near Buffalo, and the Oneidas; that I slept in the wigwams of the chiefs; that I was amongst the Shawanos and the Delawares on the Ohio; and also amongst the Cherokees and Creeks in Georgia and Tennessee; and saw many other tribes as I descended the Ohio and Mississippi Rivers in a canoe to New Orleans, more than fifty years ago.

"Tell them also, Jeffrey, that I am glad to see their wives and little children they have with them here; and glad also to show them my families, who are now nearly all around us. Tell them, Jeffrey, that this is the Queen; this lady is the Princess Adelaide, my sister; these young men are two of my sons, with their wives; and these little lads (the Duc de Brabant and the Count de Paris) are my grandsons; this one, if he lives, will be King of the Belgians, and this one, King of the French."

The king afterwards took from his pocket two heavy gold medals, and hung them on the necks of the two chiefs, saying that silver medals of the same form and size would be sent to the others, which were received the next day, with a liberal sum in money, to be divided amongst them.

They gave the war dance at the request of the king, for the amusement of the royal family; and before taking leave, the war-chief advanced towards the king and queen, and spoke as follows:—

"*Great Father and Great Mother*,—The Great Spirit, to whom we have prayed for a long time for an interview with you, kindly listens to our words this day, and hears all that we say.

"*Great Father*,—You have made to us rich presents, and I rise to return you thanks for the chief, and his warriors and braves who are present.

But, before all, it is necessary that we should thank the Great Spirit who has inspired your heart thus to honour us this day.

"*Great Father*,—We shall carry these presents to our country, and instruct our children to pronounce the name of him who gave them.

"*Great Father*,—You know that when the Indians have anything to say to a great chief, they are in the habit of making some present before they begin. My chief has ordered me to place in your hands this pipe, and these strings of wampum" (placing them in His Majesty's hands), "as a testimony of the pleasure we have felt in being admitted this day into the presence of your Majesty.

"*My Great Father and Great Mother*,—You see us this day as we are seen in our own country—with our red skins and our coarse clothes. This day, for *you*, is like other days; for *us*, it is a *great* day; so great a day that our eyes are blinded with the lustre of it.

"*Great Father*,—We are happy to tell you that when we arrived in England, we had much joy in meeting our old friend, *Chippehola*, who has lived amongst us, and whom we are happy to have by our sides this day, to tell you who we are.

"*Great Father and Great Mother*,—We will pray to the Great Spirit to preserve your precious lives; we will pray, also, that we may return safely to our own village, that we may tell to our children, and to our young men, what we have this day seen. My parents, I have no more to say."

The king thanked the chief for his eloquent
remarks, and said, "Jeffrey, tell the chiefs that I
am happy to have this opportunity of saying to
them, that in all my travels amongst the Indian
tribes they always treated we with honesty and
kindness, and that I love them for it."

What! a king, in his palace, loves the poor,
naked savage of the wilderness! Yes; and, therefore, what a noble man is a king! And wherefore
"*love*" them? Let us see.

"Fifty-two years ago," said the King, "while
stopping in Buffalo, on Lake Erie, I went some
three or four miles out, to visit the Seneca Indians;
and being conducted to their village, and to the
chief's wigwam, I shook hands with the chief, who
came and stood by my horse's head. And while
some hundreds of men, women, and children were
gathering around, I told the chief I had come to
make him a visit of a day or two; to which he
replied, that he was very glad to see me, and that
I should be made quite welcome to the best they
had.

"He said there would be one condition, however,
which was, that he should require me to give him
everything I had; he should demand my horse,
from which I would dismount; and having dismounted and given him the bridle, he said, 'I now
want your gun, your watch, and all your money;
these are indispensable.'

"I then, for the first time in my life, began to
think that I was completely robbed and plundered.

But at the moment when he had got all, and before I had time for more than an instant thought of my awkward condition, he released me from all further apprehensions by continuing, ' If you have anything else which you wish to be sure to get again, I wish you to let me have it ; for whatever you deliver into my hands now, you will be sure to find safe when you are about to leave ; otherwise I would not be willing to vouch for their safety, for there are some of my people whom I cannot trust to.'

" From this moment I felt quite easy, and spent several days in the village very pleasantly, and with much amusement.

" When I was about to leave, my horse was brought to the chief's door and saddled, and all the property I had left in his hands safely restored. I then mounted my horse, and having taken leave, and proceeded a short distance on my route, I discovered that I had left my favourite dog, which I had been too much excited and amused to think of, and did not recollect to have seen after I entered the village.

" I turned my horse and rode back to the door of the chief's wigwam, and made inquiries for it. The chief said, ' But you did not intrust your dog to my care, did you ?' ' No, I did not think of the poor dog at the time.' ' Well then,' said he, ' I can't answer for it. If you had done as I told you, your dog would have been safe. However, I will inquire for it.'

" At this moment one of his little sons was

ordered to run and open a rude pen or cage, by the corner of the wigwam, and out leaped my dog, and sprang upon my leg as I was sitting on my horse.

"I offered the chief a reward for his honesty, but he refused to accept it, but added, that whenever I should again visit red people, he advised me to 'repose confidence in their word, and feel assured that all the property I intrusted to an Indian's care I should be sure to find safe whenever I wanted it again.'"

THE END.